Anna E. R. and

D1596786

In memory of their grandfather

Alexander Ramsey

The Psychic Mariner

Also by Tom Marshall

Poems / The Silences of Fire

The Psychic Mariner / A Reading of

the Poems of D. H. Lawrence

Tom Marshall

New York / THE VIKING PRESS

First published in 1970 by The Viking Press, Inc.
625 Madison Avenue, New York, N.Y. 10022

Published simultaneously in Canada by
The Macmillan Company of Canada Limited

SBN 670-58190-9

Library of Congress catalog card number: 74-94851
Printed in U.S.A. by Vail-Ballou Press, Inc.

Acknowledgments:

Cambridge University Press: From *The Art of D. H. Lawrence* by Keith Sagar.

Connecticut College: From *Language and Myth* by Ernst Cassirer.

Farrar, Straus & Giroux, Inc., and Faber and Faber Ltd.: From *Life Studies* by Robert Lowell, copyright © 1955, 1959 by Robert Lowell. Reprinted by permission.

Harcourt, Brace & World, Inc., and Methuen & Co. Ltd.: From *On Aggression* by Konrad Lorenz.

Harper & Row, Publishers, and Faber and Faber Ltd.: From *Wodwo* by Ted Hughes: (portion) "Still Life"—Copyright © 1964 by Ted Hughes. (portion) "Ghost Crabs"—Copyright © 1966 by Ted Hughes. Reprinted by permission.

Alfred A. Knopf, Inc. and William Heinemann Ltd.: From *The Plumed Serpent* by D. H. Lawrence. Copyright 1926 by Alfred A. Knopf, Inc., renewed 1953 by Frieda Lawrence Ravagli.

Liveright Publishing Corporation: From *Complete Poems and Selected Letters and Prose of Hart Crane.* Copyright 1933, © 1958, 1966 by Liveright Publishing Corp. Reprinted by permission.

Macmillan Co. and Gerald Duckworth & Co. Ltd.: From *The Dark Sun* by Graham G. Hough. © Graham Goulder Hough 1957. Macmillan Co. and A. P. Watt & Son: From "A Prayer for My Daughter" from *Collected Poems* by W. B. Yeats. Copyright 1924 by The Macmillan Co., renewed 1952 by Bertha Georgie Yeats. Reprinted by permission of The Macmillan Co. (New York and Canada) and Mr. M. B. Yeats.

New Directions Publishing Corp. and J. M. Dent and Sons Ltd.: From "A

Refusal to Mourn" and from "On the Marriage of a Virgin" from *The Collected Poems of Dylan Thomas.* Copyright 1943, 1946 by New Directions Publishing Corporation. New Directions Publishing Corp. and Mac-Gibbon & Kee Ltd.: From "An Elegy for D. H. Lawrence" by William Carlos Williams, from *Collected Earlier Poems.* Copyright 1938 by William Carlos Williams. New Directions Publishing Corp.: Kenneth Rexroth, "Introduction" to D. H. Lawrence's *Selected Poems.* Copyright 1947 by New Directions Publishing Corporation. All reprinted by permission.

W. W. Norton & Company, Inc., and The Hogarth Press, Ltd.: From *Duino Elegies* by Rainer Maria Rilke. Translated and with Commentary from the German text by J. B. Leishman and Stephen Spender. Copyright 1939 by W. W. Norton & Company, Inc. Copyright renewed 1967 by J. B. Leishman and Stephen Spender. Reprinted by permission.

Penguin Books Ltd.: From "Beyond the Gentility Principle" from *The New Poetry* by Alfred Alvarez.

Random House, Inc., and Faber and Faber Ltd.: From "D. H. Lawrence" from *The Dyer's Hand* by W. H. Auden. Copyright © 1962 by W. H. Auden. Reprinted by permission.

Routledge & Kegan Paul Ltd.: From *A Philosophy of Potentiality* by Leone Vivante.

Charles Scribner's Sons: From *Moments of Memory* by Herbert Asquith. Charles Scribner's Sons and Chatto & Windus Ltd.: From *The Shaping Spirit* by Alfred Alvarez.

R. G. N. Salgado: From review of *Complete Poems.* The Critical Quarterly, Winter 1965. *The Poetry of D. H. Lawrence,* Ph.D. dissertation, University of Nottingham.

The Viking Press, Inc., and William Heinemann Ltd.: From the Introduction to *The Complete Poems of D. H. Lawrence,* edited by Vivian de Sola Pinto and F. Warren Roberts. Copyright © 1964 by William Heinemann Ltd.

All writings by D. H. Lawrence quoted in this volume are published by arrangement with the Estate of D. H. Lawrence. Copyrights in the original publication of previously published material were registered in various years 1914 through 1964, and renewed in various years 1942 through 1964. They may not be reproduced without written permission from The Viking Press, Inc., or, in the case of poems from *The Plumed Serpent,* without permission from Alfred A. Knopf, Inc.

For Olwyn Hughes

Note

The Heinemann "Phoenix" edition of Lawrence's works has been used wherever possible. In most cases the Viking Press texts, available in the United States, are identical. The 1967 *Complete Poems*, edited by Warren Roberts and Vivian de Sola Pinto, and the 1970 revised edition, have been used as the basic texts for the poems, but both the original editions of the individual collections of verse and the original edition of the *Collected Poems* of 1928 have been consulted as well, in order that revisions and variations might be taken into account. Poems in periodicals and in Lawrence's manuscript notebook have also been examined.

I would like to extend my thanks to Mr. Jim Davidson of Birkbeck College, University of London, for several specific suggestions that proved very useful in the preparation of this work. I am grateful also for the criticism and practical advice of Mr. Marshall Best and Mr. Malcolm Cowley of The Viking Press. I owe a more general debt of gratitude to Warren Roberts' *A Bibliography of D. H. Lawrence* (London: Rupert Hart-Davis, 1963; New York: Oxford University Press, 1964), which greatly simplified the task of seeking out long-forgotten critical books and reviews, and to a number of those critics whose work I have examined and whose aid I have (I trust) acknowledged in my Introduction and elsewhere.

Contents

The Psychic Mariner

Introduction: Lawrence and the Critics

I

Lawrence began to write poems in 1905 or so, when he was nineteen or twenty. He told Jessie Chambers, his closest friend and earliest literary confidant, that his first attempts at composition would be in verse. In 1909 she sent several of these early poems to *The English Review*, easily the best literary journal of the time. They were accepted by the editor, Ford Madox Ford, and published in November 1909. Ford continued to publish Lawrence's poems and stories, and he also arranged for the publication of *The White Peacock*, Lawrence's first novel. In *The English Review* Lawrence's poems appeared with those of another young man, Ezra Pound, and with those of the venerable Thomas Hardy. Thereafter, he appeared in many of the best English periodicals and in Harriet Monroe's *Poetry* in America. Few young writers can have been launched so easily.

Lawrence wrote and rewrote many of his early poems in a University of Nottingham notebook; this notebook, which he called "the foundation of the poetic me," is now MS. 1479 at the University Library.[1] Here, alongside some French and other notes, is a record of Lawrence's first drafts that takes us from youth in Eastwood to schoolteaching in Croydon to the time of his mother's death. The poems of the notebook are essential to any study of Lawrence's methods of composition because they show how patiently he worked and reworked his lines and stanzas. Moreover, the version of a poem published in a periodical is usually different from that of the notebook, and the version published in one of his early collections of poems different again. Finally, in 1928, Lawrence subjected these poems to yet another thorough revision. This indicates, as subsequent chapters will show, a mind restlessly devoted to persistent and progressive engagement with certain basic themes and ideas.

Edward Marsh included Lawrence's "Snap-Dragon" in the first of his *Georgian Poetry* anthologies in 1912, but the young poet's first collection, *Love Poems and Others,* did not appear until 1913. By this time, of course, he had eloped to the Continent with Frieda Weekley and had begun to write a quite different kind of poetry. Only one poem from the later marriage sequence—"Bei Hennef"—appears in *Love Poems,* however, and most of the poems have to do with Lawrence's earlier love affairs. Those about his mother's death, like those about his union with Frieda, are withheld, but this may not have been Lawrence's decision, since the selection was made by David Garnett, at the request of his father, Edward Garnett, who had succeeded Ford Madox Ford as Lawrence's literary sponsor.

Lawrence was represented both in *Georgian Poetry 1913–15* and (at the request of Amy Lowell, who was seeking support in her quarrel with Ezra Pound) in *Some Imagist Poets* (1915). He continued thereafter to appear in both the Georgian and the imagist anthologies, and he was the only poet who did so. He did not, however, consider himself a member of either party.

His second collection, *Amores,* was published in 1916 and was dedicated to Lady Ottoline Morrell. It contains some poems ("Discord in Childhood," "The Wild Common") that are earlier than anything in *Love Poems* and also a number of the poems concerned with his mother's death. *Look! We Have Come*

Through!, which appeared in 1917, was a new departure, an attempt at something more than a mere collection of individual poems. It is a long sequence of poems, a kind of verse novel concerned with the poet's relationship with his wife in their first five years. In 1928 Lawrence added "Bei Hennef," "Everlasting Flowers," and "Coming Awake" (from *New Poems*), and a poem censored by his publishers in 1917, "Song of a Man Who Is Loved," to the sequence. Another poem that was omitted at the publisher's request, "Meeting Among the Mountains," was not restored in 1928, but the version that had appeared in *Georgian Poetry 1913–15* was later placed in *Look! We Have Come Through!* by the editors of the 1964 *Complete Poems*.

New Poems, dedicated to Amy Lowell, was published in 1918, but almost all the poems antedate those of *Look! We Have Come Through!* Many have their earlier versions in the notebook. For the American edition Lawrence added a preface, "Poetry of the Present," which, he remarked, really belonged with *Look! We Have Come Through!* This is the first important statement of his aims as a poet, and, in my opinion, it has most relevance not to *Look! We Have Come Through!* but to his achievement in *Birds, Beasts and Flowers.*

Bay, privately printed by Cyril W. Beaumont in 1919, is a small selection from Lawrence's war poems. It is dedicated to Lady Cynthia Asquith. Lawrence's thoughts and feelings about the war are probably most articulate in his letters to Lady Cynthia, and it seems probable that he hoped his ideas might, through her, reach the attention of her father-in-law. Some of the *Bay* poems are, interestingly enough, reworkings of early unpublished material from the notebook.

Lawrence's major advance as a poet may be seen in the work which began to appear in English and American periodicals after the war, and in *Tortoises*, which was published in New York in 1921. In England this sequence was included in *Birds, Beasts and Flowers*, which appeared in 1923. These are the poems written during Lawrence's travels in Italy, Ceylon, Australia, and New Mexico between 1920 and 1923. Related to them, though different in method and not nearly so impressive, are the prophetic hymns in *The Plumed Serpent* (1926) and the mainly New Mexican poems that were collected eventually (with introductions by Robinson Jeffers and Frieda Lawrence) in *Fire* (1940).

Lawrence seems to have abandoned poetry for a time after 1926. But his two-volume *Collected Poems*, which placed the early poems, now much revised, in sequence and then added to them *Look! We Have Come Through!* and *Birds, Beasts and Flowers*, appeared in 1928. The early poems were styled Rhyming Poems, though some do not rhyme, and the later ones Unrhyming Poems, though a number of those in *Look! We Have Come Through!* do, in fact, employ rhyme. These volumes were somewhat better received by the critics than most of the individual collections had been. Lawrence's Introduction is illuminating, as is the unpublished and somewhat more personal version of this Introduction.

In the winter of 1928–1929 at Bandol, France, Lawrence amused himself with a new kind of verse, his satirical *pensées* or pansies. A collection of these, *Pansies*, appeared in 1929 in two editions—a public one and a private, unexpurgated one. The police had seized the original manuscript in the mail and declared that certain poems were obscene. This and other problems with the authorities led Lawrence to publish *Nettles*, a much slighter group of satirical squibs, in 1930. Several other pansies (later collected in the "More Pansies" section of *Last Poems*) appeared in the final *Imagist Anthology* in 1930, and another one, "The Triumph of the Machine," became number 28 in Faber's series of Ariel Poems. In his last months Lawrence also contributed an esoteric commentary for each section of the new and lavish Cresset Press edition of *Birds, Beasts and Flowers*.

Lawrence died in March 1930. But in the months before his

death he had filled two notebooks with further poems. One, now called MS.B, appeared to be another collection of pansies in the making, but it also contained earlier drafts of some of the poems of MS.A. MS.A contained mythological and prophetic poems and poems about death. Edited by Richard Aldington and Giuseppe Orioli, the poems from these two notebooks were published as *Last Poems* in 1932.

Since then, there have been numerous reprints, selections, and special editions of Lawrence's poems by various publishers. The publishers have included Martin Secker, William Heinemann, Faber and Faber, Penguin Books, The Ark Press, Edward Hutton, Dent, New Directions, and The Viking Press. This is interesting, since it would seem to indicate that the poems have continued to find a wide readership, despite the manifest uncertainty of the critics about Lawrence's standing as a poet.

Probably the best of the many selections of Lawrence's poems are those of W. E. Williams for Penguin Books and Kenneth Rexroth for New Directions. The only adequate full collection is the *Complete Poems* of Vivian de Sola Pinto and Warren Roberts, which first appeared in 1964 and was then reprinted in 1967 with certain additions and corrections. This edition is not without textual errors and misprints, though these are corrected in the 1970 edition, and it contains not only the *Collected Poems, Pansies, Nettles,* and *Last Poems,* but also a number of previously uncollected poems from periodicals; unpublished early and later poems (including still more pansies); all the poems from *The Plumed Serpent;* both versions of the Introduction to the *Collected Poems* of 1928; "Poetry of the Present" (placed before *Look! We Have Come Through!*); both Introductions to *Pansies;* an intelligent selection of early drafts and variants from the Nottingham notebook and elsewhere; and a very useful set of notes. Thus it is an invaluable aid to any student of Lawrence's poems. And it enables the reader to discern for himself just how important and valuable an experience is afforded by Lawrence's poems, and consequently, just how badly, for the most part, he has been served by the great majority of his critics.

II

The reception of Lawrence's poems has always been a mixed one. But from the very beginning his was recognized as an important and original talent. Edward Thomas, one of the leading Georgians, described *Love Poems and Others* as the "book of the moment in verse," though the book of the moment obviously puzzled him. He felt that this was "as near as possible natural poetry" and that, because of Lawrence's sacrifice of lyrical smoothness to intensity and direct statement, the reader became rather a sharer in a process than the witness of a result. One has the impression that Thomas was not sure whether or not he cared to share so directly in another man's intimate experience, especially that of someone he could describe as "a sick, complex man." [2]

The response of London's most active "modernist" was equally mixed. In March 1913, the flamboyant Ezra Pound (whom Lawrence considered a poseur) wrote to Harriet Monroe, the first editor of *Poetry:*

> Lawrence has brought out a vol. He is clever; I don't know whether to send in a review or not. We seem pretty well stuffed up with matter at the moment. (D. H. Lawrence, whom I mentioned in my note on the *Georgian Anthology*.) Detestable person but needs watching. I think he learned the proper treatment of modern subjects before I did. That was in some poems in *The Eng. Rev.;* can't tell whether he has progressed or retrograded as I haven't seen the book yet. He may have published merely on his prose rep.[3]

In his review Pound makes a sharp distinction between "the middling sensual erotic verses," which he further describes as "a sort of pre-raphaelitish slush, disgusting or very nearly so," and the dialect poems, which are "great art."[4] This is hardly an adequate account of all the work in *Love Poems*, but it suggests at least some of the young poet's important strengths and weaknesses.

A third review, that of O. Shakespear in *The Egoist*, is easily the most complete and adequate, since it makes specific reference to a number of poems. Shakespear feels, like Thomas before him (and many reviewers to come), that Lawrence's poems are crude in technique yet full of vitality, and that the man who wrote them is potentially a great writer.[5] This is, roughly, the consensus of opinion that has prevailed ever since.

In the years that followed, however, Lawrence received more than his share of hostile criticism. In 1917 *The Times Literary Supplement* characterized *Look! We Have Come Through!* as "an excited morbid babble about one's own emotions which the Muse of poetry surely can only turn from with a pained distaste."[6] I have chosen to quote this remark not merely because of the quaint and rather delightful violence of its expression but because it lodges a complaint against Lawrence that is to be repeated again and again. He is too personal, too preoccupied with his own emotions to achieve a proper control of his medium.

An important statement of this point of view is that of Conrad Aiken in his essay "The Melodic Line."[7] He feels that Lawrence fails to achieve the heightened rhythmic power of great poetry precisely because he is unable to achieve detachment in the contemplation of his own feelings. Sometimes, Aiken admits, he is a very brilliant and original poet, but usually he is too urgent in the pursuit of his own feelings, so that he frequently does violence to the moods he is attempting to capture. Aiken feels that *Look! We Have Come Through!* might better have been expressed in prose, since many of the individual parts fail as poems. He does not entertain the possibility that Lawrence may be moving, in his own stumbling way, towards the creation of a new kind of poetic art.

Aiken disliked *Birds, Beasts and Flowers*, Lawrence's further development of his free-verse idiom, just as much as *Look! We Have Come Through!* [8] In fact, this volume was greeted mainly with confusion and hostility. The confusion is perhaps best exemplified in Louis Untermeyer's curious statement: "Technically, there is scarcely one satisfying poem in 'Birds, Beasts and Flowers', although there are half a dozen that almost achieve greatness." It did not, apparently, occur to Mr. Untermeyer that his conception of "technique" in poetry might be inadequate to this occasion. Like several other reviewers, he felt that Lawrence's conversion to free verse had harmed his work and that the earlier poems were very much better. Lawrence, he decided, placed his trust neither in "art nor taste." [9]

There is, similarly, a general tendency in the reviews of the *Collected Poems* of 1928 to praise the earlier poems at the expense of *Birds, Beasts and Flowers*. Most are respectful, though sometimes only grudgingly respectful, but nearly all fail to appreciate Lawrence's development of a new poetic idiom. The later Lawrence, it is felt, is a genius but not an artist: "the *shaping* imagination has been denied him"; [10] he is disturbed and in bad taste; his poems are too autobiographical to be adequate as art; [11] he is "a Victorian spasmodic in the age of Freud"; [12] the early poems are often very moving, but *Birds, Beasts and Flowers* is "a lighter harvest of travel," and closer to prose; [13] *Birds, Beasts and Flowers* is too much the product of a very special sensitivity; [14] it represents a decline from poetry to preaching;[15] Lawrence is sex-crucified, a slave to biological fact.[16] Only one notice, that of Desmond MacCarthy in *The New Statesman*, is outstandingly perceptive: he praises Lawrence's ability to attain a more intimate imaginative sympathy with animals and plants than has been achieved in literature before; he sees that Lawrence does not anthropomorphize his subjects but "feels himself into things"; and he asserts that Lawrence's poetry is of "the first importance" because it "enlarges the scope of our imaginative response to life." [17]

The reviews of *Pansies* are surprisingly favourable. Richard Church went so far as to call Lawrence's technique "unmatched": "No-one has carried free-verse so far. He has the sweep and grandeur of Whitman, but with an added grace, a susceptibility to the touch of single words, vowels, and consonants." [18] *The Times Literary Supplement* reviewer agreed that Lawrence used the sort of free rhythm popularized by translations from the Chinese with "great sensibility," and felt, moreover, that in his more serious pansies Lawrence had succeeded in giving the appearance of precision to experiences that can never *be* precise. [19] Mark Van Doren felt that, even if the "thoughts" were not poems, they were worth saying in that form, so perhaps, after all, they *were* poems. [20] It seems likely, then, that the general critical disapproval of the pansies which prevailed later was in large part the result of Richard Aldington's attack in his introduction to *Last Poems*. (See Chapter Four.)

Nettles, like *Bay*, received no serious critical attention. But the second edition of the *Collected Poems* was the subject of a number of review articles. It is a curious but interesting fact that this second round of reviews reveals a critical tendency opposite to that of the first. The reviewers tend to dismiss the early poems in order to praise *Look! We Have Come Through!* and *Birds, Beasts and Flowers*, which had formerly been slighted in favour of the early poems. One is tempted to conclude from this that the taste of the poetry-reading public had begun, finally, to accommodate itself to Lawrence's free-verse idiom and to his assumption of a greater freedom of subject matter. [21]

Last Poems was widely and, for the most part, sympathetically reviewed. Two writers, however, posed once again the formalist position. Yvonne ffrench asserted that the poems were "beautiful," but only in the way that carvings on a totem pole may be beautiful; Lawrence wasn't civilized, and his work didn't belong to any "accepted school." For he had no sense of proportion, and thus could not make poems out of his random jottings. [22] Similarly, Lord David Cecil accused Lawrence of an egotism that made it impossible for him to create "completely achieved works of art." The poems were "exclamations of joy or screams of pain"; Lawrence had not objectified his emotions as Housman had in *The Shropshire Lad*.[23] Neither critic would be impressed, one feels, by the suggestion that a contemporary poet might usefully evolve a kind of poem whose method and effect were akin to those of a totem carving or an Etruscan painting.

What *was* Lawrence attempting to do in his poems? Part of the answer may be suggested in some remarks quoted by T. S. Eliot in an unpublished lecture on "English Letter Writers" in 1933. Mr. Eliot expressed admiration, not, to be sure, for Lawrence's poems, but for his advice to Catherine Carswell that "the essence of poetry with us in this age of stark and unlovely actualities is a stark directness, without a shadow of a lie, or a shadow of deflection anywhere. Everything can go, but this stark, bare, rocky directness of statement, this alone makes poetry, today." [24] Eliot's comment is illuminating:

> This speaks to me of that at which I have long aimed, in writing poetry; to write poetry which should be essentially poetry, with nothing poetic about it, poetry standing naked in its bare bones, or poetry so transparent that we should not see the poetry, but that which we are meant to see through the poetry, poetry so transparent that in reading it we are intent on what the poem *points at,* and not on the poetry, this seems to me the thing to try for. To get *beyond poetry,* as Beethoven, in his later works, strove to get *beyond music.* We never succeed, perhaps, but Lawrence's words mean this to me, that they express to me what I think the forty or fifty original lines that I have written strive towards.[25]

As we shall see, Eliot did not feel that Lawrence himself had achieved the new poetry demanded by an age of "stark and unlovely actualities." It was left to W. H. Auden to praise the perfect transparency of the poems in *Birds, Beasts and Flowers*. In making his own experiments with language, and in developing the "transparent" kind of poetry that is perhaps best realized in the *Four Quartets*, Eliot did not appreciate or attempt to emulate the idiom that Lawrence had developed in order to pursue his own very similar technical and very different moral aims.

Perhaps it is a basic antipathy to or misunderstanding of Lawrence's moral vision that causes Eliot to write in 1937 that Lawrence was essentially "a researcher into religious emotion," not an artist at all "but a man with a sketch-book: his poetry, very interesting amateur work, is only notes for poems." [26] In this he echoes the view of I. A. Richards, who considered that Lawrence's free verse was actually scientific prose, jottings from the psychologist's notebook. Lawrence's primitivism, like Yeats's esotericism, was, he felt, a mistaken response to the modern condition of unbelief.[27] This is suggestive and illuminating, despite Richards' formal conservatism. But one suspects Richards (and perhaps Eliot) of a certain sophistry in attempting to account for the interest and effectiveness of Lawrence's work without sacrificing his own notions of acceptable form.

The question of moral bias as a determining factor in the formation of critical taste is raised again by the argument of R. P. Blackmur's essay "D. H. Lawrence and Expressive Form." [28] This is easily the most sustained and the most influential denunciation of the poems to have been written. All subsequent critics of Lawrence's verse have had to consider it.

Like Aiken and Cecil before him, Blackmur argues that because his was "a deracinated, unsupported imagination," a mind without rational structure, Lawrence failed to make effective use of the formal devices of the poet's art. Because his work was written out of a "tortured Protestant sensibility and upon the foundations of an incomplete, uncomposed mind," he was the "extreme victim" of the "plague of expressive form." The idea of expressive form leaves one with no standard of judgment, Blackmur feels, since merely to put something into words is to "express" it. Lawrence succumbed to his material, since he had no defence against it. Because he was a religious visionary without the "orderly insight" of the great mystics, disorder and hysteria prevailed in his poems.

For a number of years this was considered by many to be the last word about Lawrence's poems. Certainly, it contributed to the general decline of Lawrence's reputation in the 1930s and the early 1940s. Even Graham Hough, writing in 1956, found it impossible to disagree with Blackmur. More recently, however, Vivian de Sola Pinto, Harold Bloom, Alfred Alvarez, and Keith Sagar have effectively refuted Blackmur's argument. The crux of the matter, as a passage from Sagar's *The Art of D. H. Lawrence* will indicate, is the kind of belief in God and man that informs the work of the poet and the critic. If Lawrence's sensibility was, in some sense, a Protestant sensibility, then Blackmur's is surely a Catholic sensibility:

> Blackmur's strictures could only come from a critic who brings to the poems strong preconceptions about both art and life. Behind Blackmur's belief in the primacy of imposed form lies the assumption that life itself is chaotic or meaningless until it is transformed by art. Art is asked to provide an ordered reality as against the amorphous flux of life and experience. Such a conception of art goes with the Christian, particularly the Catholic temper: its permanent realities are states of being refined out of temporal experience—mystical, conceptual, sometimes, one suspects, merely verbal. Or it goes with cynicism, for the pose of objectivity often fails to hide disgust or indifference in the face of life. . . .
>
> The opposite kind of art is the product of a sensibility which finds life already meaningful and art a process of discovery, revelation and praise. This is also religious, but in a different sense— more often pagan or pantheistic than Christian (Hopkins being a notable exception). The prototype of the affirmative artist is Whitman, who, by divesting himself of all artificiality, transforms himself into a living probe. . . .[29]

Sagar argues further that Lawrence's best poems do not display hysteria or disordered emotions but rather "feelings so fused with and disciplined by intellect, so deeply personal in their response both to experience and to language, that they grow into uniquely fitting, almost impersonally authentic forms. . . ." [30] And Vivian de Sola Pinto is correct in denying that Lawrence believed that merely to put something into words was to give it adequate expression.[31]

Indeed, it is easy to see now that Blackmur neither understood nor appreciated Lawrence's idea of the shaping rhythm that is inherent in the felt experience itself. He was not aware of the discipline of the pure "effort of attention" that seeks to make language a transparent medium. Thus he considered the later poems to be no better than the earlier ones. Where his essay has most merit, in my opinion, is in its description of Lawrence's failure to write well in traditional forms. He cites as faults in "The Wild Common," for instance, "weakness of sound, weakness of syntactical position, lack of metrical propulsion . . . false 'poetic' language, explicit direct presentation, the vague attribute, colloquial language, and plain empty verbiage." [32] It seems to me that, aside from the suggestion that "explicit direct presentation" is necessarily a fault, this is a perfectly valid criticism of that particular poem, and it probably lent an air of authority to the whole essay (though Blackmur's remarks about the tortoise sequence are decidedly less accurate, as Harold Bloom has effectively demonstrated).[33] It is interesting that though he admitted the effectiveness of "The Wild Common," even despite its slipshod use of language, Blackmur was unable to see that the later Lawrence had developed a poetic idiom that could present his experience even more forcefully, but without the distortion of language that had marred so many of the early poems.

David Daiches, writing in 1940, was more sensitive to Lawrence's aims and methods in the early poems. He saw that Lawrence's poems were "fables designed to test a hypothesis," poems of exploration and discovery "where the imagery begins by being ambivalent and ends by dropping alternative meanings, the problem having been worked through, the hypothesis tested, the vision achieved." Thus, Lawrence's poems end at the point where most poems begin; in "Snap-Dragon," for example, Lawrence discovers in the course of the poem the effective expression of his emotions.[34] Some years later Leone Vivante, in *A Philosophy of Potentiality*, perceived the unity of Lawrence's belief and his aesthetic intention when he found that *Last Poems* argues the "inherent purposiveness" of form in art and in the natural world. And Richard Ellmann, in his essay "Barbed Wire and Coming Through," made essentially the same point in a different way when he expressed Lawrence's belief that "form and content arise together in the archetypal self, and their emergence in consort reflects that self's inner order." [35] The poem achieves coherence through this process, in which, Lawrence contends, the law comes new each time from within.

In *The Dyer's Hand* W. H. Auden takes issue with Lawrence's apparent belief that a work of art is an organic growth like a flower. This seems to me a slight misrepresentation of the theory expressed in "Poetry of the Present"; it would probably be fairer to assume (though he does not himself elaborate) that Lawrence believed that the shaping rhythm (or "law") which comes new each time from within and to which the poet ought to attend is part of a particular man's physiological and sensuous response to the world about him, and thus at least *akin* to the development of a flower. For Lawrence's ideal poet attends to his own innermost physical and mental being as it responds to the environment. Not all art, to be sure, but certainly the free verse Lawrence sought to achieve could be described as having not only its origin but also its development in such a process.

Auden recognized that Lawrence wished to present his own experience as immediately as possible, and also that he did not find a completely appropriate means of expression for this in his early poems. Only in *Birds, Beasts and Flowers* was Lawrence able to achieve his aim in "writing so transparent that one forgets him entirely and sees what he saw." In this he was aided by the example of Whitman.

Because Lawrence was more a pilgrim than a citizen, Auden wrote, he was attracted both to the manner and to the matter of Whitman's free verse. Whitman could be a beneficial influence on Lawrence's verse because the two men were, in some important respects, utterly different: Whitman had created a heroic persona in his poems while Lawrence was always, quite simply, himself; Whitman organized his small details of American experience into vast catalogues while Lawrence concentrated on single subjects. Thus Lawrence was never an imitator of Whitman but was able to develop a quite original idiom of his own.

Auden failed to accord the same approval to Lawrence's later free verse of *Pansies* (though he liked the doggerel), and he was apparently not at all interested in *Last Poems*, but he was nevertheless one of the first writers to state with any clarity or understanding just what the young poet's technical problem had been and how he had been able to resolve it. It was not the supposed disadvantage of "an incomplete, uncomposed mind" (for surely a "complete" and "composed" mind is a closed one) that led Lawrence to abandon conventional verse forms, but the longing to achieve a larger wholeness of mind and body in the honest re-creation of experience.

Thus Kenneth Rexroth, in his immensely perceptive and valuable account of Lawrence's poetic development, can speak of Lawrence's mature art as "a state of total realization." Rexroth's essay is more complete than Auden's, since it deals with each phase of the poet's development, exhibiting a very delicate and acute insight into the aims and methods of each kind of poem. Rexroth sees that the liberation of Lawrence's talent which is fully exemplified in *Birds, Beasts and Flowers* was already in process in *Look! We Have Come Through!*, and he is the first critic to include the hymns from *The Plumed Serpent* in his discussion of Lawrence's development after *Birds, Beasts and Flowers*. One may not agree with some of Rexroth's particular statements, or his more sweeping generalizations about Western culture, or even

with all of his editorial decisions (as when he prints the somewhat inferior version of "Bavarian Gentians"), but one can
hardly dissent from the spirit and imaginative intelligence of his
appreciation of the poems themselves. All students of the poems
are in his debt. With his essay came the beginnings of the Lawrence "revival" that has continued, not without active dissent, to
this day.

A most valuable book-length account of the poems is R. G. N.
Salgādo's "The Poetry of D. H. Lawrence." [36] Salgādo is very
much indebted to Rexroth, but his own approach is more purely
a critical one since he dislikes biographical and doctrinal exe-
geses of the poems. Unlike most other critics he has a considerable interest in the influence of Meredith, Browning, Blake,
Wordsworth, and Whitman on Lawrence's development. But
his finest passages are those in which he examines the structure
and method of poems from *Birds, Beasts and Flowers* and *Last
Poems.* The chief weakness of his work is that he tends to slight
Lawrence's criticism of modern society. It is not only that he dislikes most of the pansies but that he fails generally to appreciate
certain aspects of the poet's vision. And one cannot appreciate
fully the course of Lawrence's development as a poetic craftsman unless one understands what it was that motivated that
development.*

Another important study of the poems is the chapter devoted
to them in Graham Hough's *The Dark Sun* (1956). Like Auden,
Hough leans a little toward the formalist position; he feels that
Blackmur's charges are unanswerable, and that one can only de-
fend Lawrence's poetry because the whole experience it affords is
valuable and because it provides "a running commentary to the
course of development outlined in the novels." Because the work
is poetry rather than poems, Hough feels, one must be somewhat

---

* It is only fair to point out that in his review of the *Complete Poems*
of 1964 Mr. Salgādo seems to have a greater appreciation of "the wit that
is a tough unreasonableness beneath the graceless lyricism" than he displayed in his study of 1955.

more generous in dealing with it than formal criticism would allow. Hough does not, therefore, illuminate very much the formal development that may be traced in the course of Lawrence's poetic career, but his analysis of the particular faults and excellences of the poems of each period is very good. His comments about the themes and methods of the *Birds, Beasts and Flowers* poems, the pansies, and the *Last Poems* are especially valuable.

Harry T. Moore's *A D. H. Lawrence Miscellany* (1959) included no less than four essays concerned with the poems. That of Alfred Alvarez, "D. H. Lawrence: The Single State of Man," is easily the best of them, and is, indeed, one of the best things to have been written about the poems. Lawrence, writes Alvarez, was the only native poet of importance to survive the First World War. His best poems are characterized by a complete truth to feeling, since his "controlling standard" as an artist was "delicacy: a constant fluid awareness, nearer the checks of intimate talk than those of regular prosody." His was an integrity to experience rather than to traditional forms of language. Alvarez quotes "End of Another Home Holiday" in order to demonstrate how Lawrence's rhythm is controlled by the speaking voice. He argues that whereas the fashionable irony of the modern metaphysical school of poets is often merely a means of avoiding commitment, the wit displayed by Lawrence in a poem like "Red Geranium and Godly Mignonette" is one of the poetic means, "a manifestation of intelligence." Modern poetry, he feels, is badly in need of the particular Lawrentian discipline of accurate feeling.[37]

The *Complete Poems* of 1964 brought on a new wave of critical attention. Professor Pinto's introduction, "D. H. Lawrence: Poet without a Mask," which aroused a brief flurry of controversy when it first appeared in *The Critical Quarterly*, displays a sympathetic understanding of Lawrence's aims and achievements in his several phases. Professor Pinto concentrates on the finest poems but argues very persuasively that "even Lawrence's bad poems are important because they are the experiments of a major poet groping his way towards the discovery of a new kind of poetic art." Like Alvarez, he sees that Lawrence was the one poet of his time who attempted to dispense with all the poses and disguises that have been part of the traditional poet's stock-in-trade.[38]

In a long front-page article, "Lawrence the Poet: Achievement and Irrelevance," the reviewer for *The Times Literary Supplement* cast a different light on Lawrence's development. He felt that in most of the poems before *Birds, Beasts and Flowers* Lawrence had failed to make his experience sufficiently public for the reader to enter into it. He was too personal, too egotistical and self-absorbed, and thus unable to get out of the reader's way. Lawrence was inclined, the reviewer felt, to use language in a private way, giving special meanings to particular words, and he seemed to believe that his experience was significant simply because it had been *his*. In the best poems from *Birds, Beasts and Flowers, Pansies* and *Last Poems*, however, Lawrence overcame these faults.[39]

Most of the reviewer's criticism of the early poems is fair enough, but it is possible that he fails to appreciate the fact that the early Lawrence was looking, often in a very confused fashion, for a medium that would allow him to carry expressive language beyond conceptual statement. In "Snap-Dragon," for instance, which the reviewer finds obscure, he seeks to render the experience of a somewhat painful dawning of sexual awareness in terms of symbols and symbolic action, since merely to state the case would be to falsify a very delicate and subtle emotional experience. The attempt to go beyond conceptual statement, and to define a felt experience in terms of symbol and myth, is essentially the same here, though not so well developed, as in "Bavarian Gentians," where the word "darkness" takes on an enriched meaning from its rhythmic repetition in the pattern of the whole poem.

The question of Lawrence's use of language is raised again in R. G. N. Salgādo's review in *The Critical Quarterly*. Lawrence ignored metrical patterns, and sometimes even language itself, writes Salgādo, because he wished to achieve "unmediated, naked vision"; this is the condition and source of his successes and failures alike. Because language is treated as transparent, it sometimes becomes luminous. Thus Lawrence's virtues and vices as a poet both spring from his view of poetry, which was directly linked to his view of experience.

Salgādo feels that Lawrence is an important poet because he altered our notions of the possible; he offers the following formulation of Lawrence's unique qualities: "the subcutaneous awareness not only of the phenomenal world but also of emotional relationships, the wit that is a tough unreasonableness beneath the graceless lyricism, the poem, in formal terms, that is a worrying and thrashing of language till it yields up the noumenal experience."[40]

Probably, Lawrence's poems will continue to be a source of controversy. But it is difficult not to agree with D. J. Enright when he remarks that "the conception of poetry and poetic possibilities implied by the pro-Lawrence argument is considerably more congenial than the aesthetic . . . which seems to underlie the anti-Lawrence view." And, again, one is inclined to applaud when he ends his lively review on a note of brisk common-sense: "Occasional boredom and exasperation is a small price to pay for a sizeable body of major poetry. If enthusiasm for Lawrence the poet is wrong, then it is a generous misdemeanour, a sensible error." [41]

III

So far none of the essays devoted to Lawrence's poems, not even the best of them (those of Rexroth, Auden, Salgādo, Hough, Alvarez, and Pinto), has traced Lawrence's development as a poet in detail. To do so is the aim of the present work.

It is at least arguable that Lawrence continued to develop technically as a poet after he had ceased to develop as a novelist. For none of his later fiction is so original or so exploratory as *The Rainbow* and *Women in Love*, and yet there is a continuous development of the unique and quite individual free-verse idiom from the time of *Birds, Beasts and Flowers* to the end of his life. This is not to say that the poems of this period are necessarily more important than the later novels, but merely to emphasize the seriousness of his search for a completely expressive poetic idiom. The thorough revision of his earliest poems in 1928 is further evidence that he did not consider his verse to be merely an overflow from his prose.

My primary aim has been to make a study of Lawrence's growth as a poet (i.e. as a maker of poems). In doing so I have found it helpful to pay some attention both to his ideas and to his personal history as these are expressed in the poems. What many, if not most, of Lawrence's critics have not understood is the necessity for his search. This arises, as Salgādo has indicated, from the unique, almost psychic penetration of his insight into the situation of modern man as it manifested itself in his own experience. One should not, of course, underestimate the element of sheer playfulness and spirited whimsy in Lawrence's casting about for new modes of expression (in, for instance, his adoption of doggerel in *Pansies* and *Nettles*). But the best, the most striking and original of his mature poems—in *Birds, Beasts and Flowers; Pansies,* and *Last Poems*—are the results of his desire to find the form that was inherent in his own felt experience. Having diagnosed (to his own satisfaction) his own and civilization's disease, he wished his poems not only to propose but to embody the cure. The urgency of his quest for a poetic form was one with the urgency of his need to communicate his vision.

❧ One

The Blindfold Art:
Lawrence's Early Poems

I

When he collected his poems in 1928, Lawrence attempted to establish a chronological order, or, as he put it, "the order of experience." [1] * Moreover, he felt that many of the early poems had not been faithful enough to the basic nature of the experience that had inspired them. "A young man is afraid of his demon," he writes, "and puts his hand over the demon's mouth sometimes and speaks for him." [2] The mature Lawrence wanted to establish, insofar as this is possible, what really happened and how he really felt about it. Thus, Alfred Alvarez, in his excellent essay on Lawrence's poems, calls him "the foremost emotional realist of the century." [3] And Kenneth Rexroth speaks of "the uncanny 'surreal' accuracy of perception and evaluation," the "complete precision and purposiveness" of Lawrence's best poems. [4]

This is not to suggest that he conceived of poetry as pure autobiography but that his chief purpose as a poet was to find the most appropriate form for his own highly developed insight into

---

* This is not, however, the order of composition, despite what Lawrence says in his published Preface. He has arranged the poems so that they tell his story. See, for instance, my note on "Snap-Dragon," p. 62.

the ways in which the human soul may grow from confusion and fragmentation toward fulfillment and full self-realization. I am using the word "soul" in the sense in which Lawrence uses it in *Studies in Classic American Literature:*

> It's a queer thing is a man's soul. It is the whole of him. Which means it is the unknown him as well as the known. (p. 10)

The progress of the soul can be seen in terms of a personal quest for identity. How is a man to make harmony and wholeness out of the warring elements that constitute his psyche? This is the basic and universal question, but each man has his own way of approaching it. If he is David Herbert Lawrence, he will be obliged to examine the bitter conflict that dominated his early youth:

> Outside the house an ash-tree hung its terrible whips,
> And at night when the wind rose, the lash of the tree
> Shrieked and slashed the wind, as a ship's
> Weird rigging in a storm shrieks hideously.
>
> Within the house two voices arose, a slender lash
> Whistling she-delirious rage, and the dreadful sound
> Of a male thong booming and bruising, until it had drowned
> The other voice in a silence of blood, 'neath the noise of the
>   ash.
>
> ("Discord in Childhood")

Lawrence wrote to make himself whole, and he believed that this was the basic (if generally unacknowledged) motive underlying all art: ". . . one sheds one's sicknesses in books," he wrote to a friend.[5] Why not then attack the problem directly, and begin at the beginning with one's own most deeply felt experiences? The mature Lawrence saw that this self-examination had been necessary before he could address himself to the wider manifestations of the divided self in society at large. But this is to anticipate the development of Lawrence's later poetry. At the moment I want only to suggest the reasons why his early poems are concerned to such an extent with his own most personal experiences, and why he had difficulty in expressing these in the poetic forms that were fashionable when he began to write.

"The Wild Common," a poem written in rhyming quatrains, demonstrates both the conflict of organic form with imposed form and the concern for the problem of identity. It would seem at first to be a conventional celebration of the beauties of nature:

The quick sparks on the gorse-bushes are leaping
Little jets of sunlight texture imitating flame;
Above them, exultant, the peewits are sweeping:
They have triumphed again o'er the ages, their screamings
    proclaim.

Rabbits, handfuls of brown earth, lie
Low-rounded as the mournful turf they have bitten down to
    the quick.
Are they asleep?—are they living?—Now see, when I
Lift my arms, the hill bursts and heaves under their spurting
    kick!

But this is no classical Georgian landscape painting; it is too full of "quick" life and movement. The young poet sees that the world is in constant flux and attempts to give us his experience of this as immediately as possible. Thus he employs the quick, irregular rhythms of natural speech rather than a regular metrical scheme. Kenneth Rexroth has suggested that what Lawrence was doing in these early poems was to adjust the poem welling up within him "to the remembered accentual patterns, and let it go at that. I don't think he was unconscious of the new qualities which emerged, but I don't think he went about it deliberately, either." [6] And Lawrence himself wrote to Edward Marsh in 1913:

> It all depends on the *pause*—the natural *lingering* of the voice according to the feeling—it is the hidden *emotional* pattern that makes poetry, not the obvious form. . . . It is the lapse of the feeling, something as indefinite as expression in the voice carrying emotion. It doesn't depend on the ear particularly, but on the sensitive soul. And the ear gets a habit, and becomes master, when the ebbing and lifting emotion should be master, and the ear the transmitter. If your ear has got stiff and a bit mechanical, *don't* blame my poetry. . . . I always wonder if the Greeks and Romans really did scan, or if scansion wasn't a thing invented afterwards by the schoolmaster.[7]

Lawrence wants to get beyond "obvious form" (or "beyond poetry," as Eliot has it) to the "hidden *emotional* pattern," the "ebbing and lifting" rhythm of experience itself. He wants as little distance as possible between the reader and the felt experience. It is this goal of immediacy that will eventually lead him to abandon rhyming quatrains altogether.

Even as it is, the form does not really suit him. Without an exact regulating metrical pattern, some of the line-breaks and the rhymes seem arbitrary. To break the first line after "leaping," for instance, is to invite the momentary and somewhat distracting confusion as to whether the participle "leaping" is part of a compound verb "are leaping" or is an adjective modifying "jets" in the second line. Does the break come here only so that "leaping" may be rhymed with "sweeping"? It seems so. Similarly, the abrupt descent from observation to cliché in the fourth line of the first stanza is perhaps at least partly explained by the need to find a rhyme for "flame." Though the second stanza is more successful, with its swift movement and its metaphorical identification of the rabbits with the earth they inhabit (as, later, the "earth-golden" snake in "Snake" is closely associated with "the burning bowels of the earth" and even with "Etna smoking"), the necessity to rhyme "lie" with "I" makes the first and third line-endings particularly awkward. The flow of movement in the last two lines, which is intended to express and characterize the sudden movement of the rabbits, is slightly damaged by the unnatural emphasis on "I."

"The Wild Common" has as its speaker a young man or boy who is standing naked on the edge of a pond and watching his own shadow on the water. In the earlier versions of the poem the shadow was identified first with his soul and then with a passionate woman who loved him and (in the earliest notebook version) moulded him "in herself," but Lawrence later clarified this somewhat confused relationship by discarding both the soul and the mother-mistress in favour of an extended conceit in which the shadow becomes nothing but "a white dog to its master." [8] If this seems merely fanciful, and of less psychological interest than the earlier mixture of metaphors, it nevertheless allows him to place the emphasis on the importance of being "substance" rather than mere shadow:

But how splendid it is to be substance, here!
My shadow is neither here nor there; but I, I am royally here!
I am here! I am here! screams the peewit; the may-blobs burst
     out in a laugh as they hear!
Here! flick the rabbits. Here! pants the gorse. Here! say the
     insects far and near.

Over my skin in the sunshine, the warm, clinging air
Flushed with the songs of seven larks singing at once, goes
     kissing me glad.
You are here! You are here! We have found you! Everywhere
We sought you substantial, you touchstone of caresses, you
     naked lad!

Oh but the water loves me and folds me,
Plays with me, sways me, lifts me and sinks me, murmurs: Oh
     marvellous stuff!
No longer shadow!—and it holds me,
Close, and it rolls me, enfolds me, touches me, as if never it
     could touch me enough.

"All that is right, all that is good, all that is God takes substance!" declares the ecstatic poet in the final stanza. The poet's
love-affair or marriage was not with his own soul but with the
external world, the living flux. For the later Lawrence (or, more
accurately, the demon who is "timeless") places a supreme value
on being "alive in the flesh." The real meaning of the youthful
experience of nature, then, has to do with the marriage of man to
the natural world, and with that recognition of the divine "otherness" of the living universe that enables man to affirm the substantial self as an individual expression of God.

With the possible exception of "Love on the Farm," this is the
most ambitious of the earliest poems. But two others, "Virgin
Youth" and "Renascence," attempt (less successfully) to embody
Lawrentian ideas in the expression of early experience. Both have
been revised.

"Virgin Youth" is about adolescent sexual arousal. The earlier
version is a simple poem of one long stanza describing the wave
of sexual feeling that temporarily overcomes the youth, leaving
him lonely and unsatisfied. The later version is a bathetic hymn
to the penis, which is identified with the new or deeper man possessed of secret blood-knowledge. The idea is not necessarily lu-
dicrous, but the treatment is inappropriate, much too overtly didactic and preachy. The poem fails to be natural, to give the
reader the genuine experience of the youth in such a way that its
significance will be implicit. The later Lawrence is putting words
into the youth's mouth. It is not the demon but the over-insistent
preacher who is speaking. The shapeless rhythms and strained artificial diction are merely symptoms of this basic failure of imagination.

"Renascence" is less thoroughly revised. Both earlier and later
versions suffer from imprecision of statement, but the purpose of
the poem seems to be to acknowledge Lawrence's debt to the girl
he called Miriam and to express his feelings about the farm in
the valley where she lived. The title suggests that he has been

brought to new birth or to new awareness of himself by this girl
and this place. In both versions Lawrence describes the life of the
farm, his second home, and concludes that the valley is "wider
than paradise." He thanks Miriam, his Eve, for giving him this vision of a possible earthly paradise:

> She's a finer instructor than years.
> She has shown me the strands that weave
> Us all one in laughter and tears.
>
> I didn't learn it from her speech—
> Staggering words:
> I can't tell how it comes
> But I think the kisses reach
> Down where the live web hums.

That is how the earlier version ends.[9] Here is the later ending:

> She's a quicker instructress than years;
> She has quickened my pulse to receive
> Strange throbs, beyond laughter and tears.
>
> So now I know the valley
>   Fleshed all like me
> With feelings that change and quiver
> And clash, and yet seem to tally,
> Like all the clash of a river
>   Moves on to the sea.

The final emphasis is no longer on kisses but on the boy's relationship to the valley itself. The special nervous sensitivity of the
girl has brought him to an awareness of the "strange throbs" in
the living world about him. It seems probable that Lawrence
eliminated the reference to kisses as much because it was dishonest
as because it is irrelevant to his main theme. His early intimacy
with Jessie Chambers was apparently carried on in an "utterly
blanched and chaste fashion."[10] Its importance to him probably

lay in her special sensibility more than in her physical beauty. But if the altered ending serves the ideal of honesty to experience, it also expresses Lawrentian doctrine. The valley is "fleshed," and has feelings that change and quiver and clash yet somehow "tally." The word "tally" is unfortunate (though it provides a good example of Lawrence's mistake in attempting to force his demon to submit to the demands of strict rhyme), but the reference to the sea and the river suggests that what he wished to say was that the clashing, dissident life of the valley somehow achieves a unity or total pattern. The poem then exhibits a concern similar to that of "The Wild Common" (though it is not so well embodied in the poem): the idea of unity (God) underlying the diversity of living things. This is one of the basic insights for which the poet must find an appropriate or fully expressive form. But the clumsiness of "valley . . . tally" and the long shapeless lines of the earlier part of the poem defeat the poet's intention.

The other early "Miriam" poems are less complex in intention, and, at their best, they simply give the reader the experience they describe. "Dog-Tired" and "Study" are quite successful in this way. In the first the boy wishes the girl would come to him in the fields after a hard day's work; in the second he imagines her waiting for him when he must study for exams. In each case one sees the situation without being unduly conscious of the language:

> I should like to drop
> On the hay, with my head on her knee,
> And lie dead still, while she
> Breathed quiet above me; and the crop
> Of stars grew silently.
>
> ("Dog-Tired")

Here the necessity to rhyme has not done injury to the diction. The early Lawrence is usually at his best when he is most faithful to the particular event.

Sometimes he makes of a simple event a small parable, as in "Cherry Robbers":

> Under the long dark boughs, like jewels red
>> In the hair of an eastern girl
> Hang strings of crimson cherries, as if had bled
>> Blood-drops beneath each curl.
>
> Under the glistening cherries, with folded wings
>> Three dead birds lie:
> Pale-breasted throstles and a blackbird, robberlings
>> Stained with red dye.
>
> Against the haystack a girl stands laughing at me,
>> Cherries hung round her ears.
> Offers me scarlet fruit: I will see
>> If she has any tears.

There is, as Kenneth Rexroth has noted, a violence underlying the ordinary gaiety of this scene. An earlier and obviously related poem, "Song," describes a boy picking cherries in the tree, and throwing some of them at a girl below. There is no mention of the dead birds.[11] But in "Cherry Robbers" the dead robber-birds combine with the blood-drops in the hair of the eastern girl and the tears to suggest that there is another robbery and another violence in store. The speaker knows that it is inevitable that he will injure this girl.*

The early poems about the mother (and, as it proves, the father) come even closer to the heart of the young man's emotional problems. "Discord in Childhood," like "Cherry Robbers" and "Love on the Farm," develops the persistent Lawrentian analogy between disturbance in the natural world and disturbance in the psyche. The voices of the quarrelling man and woman blend with the wind that turns the branches of the ash-tree into "terri-

---

* In *Sons and Lovers* (pp. 285-86) the cherry-picking incident occurs shortly before Paul and Miriam first have sexual intercourse.

ble whips." It is interesting that the poem adopts no moral stance. It records with a shocking objectivity the conflict of "she-delirious rage" and the "male thong booming and bruising," suggesting that it is as elemental and inevitable as the wind in the ash-tree. And for the child this is so. He must carry the discord of his parents within him as a permanent part of his emotional nature. His own sexual relations will very likely be stormy ones, and he will be obliged, again and again, to strive to make some wholeness of the warring elements within him.

Lawrence's old friend and enemy, John Middleton Murry, expressed this idea well in his last book, *Love, Freedom and Society:*

> Lawrence surmised that this tension between his parents, existing previous to his own birth, was the cause of his bodily fragility. Without doubt, the strain of his inward division between love and loyalty to his mother, and his unconscious attachment to his father, vastly increased his sensitivity. He became praeternaturally aware, prematurely in love—with his mother. That particular conditioning, it may be said, was abnormal. Abnormal is always a dangerous word, difficult to use meaningfully. Lawrence's conditioning was abnormal in its intensity rather than its essence.[12]

Lawrence himself believed that his own experience could illuminate that of every man. He recognized the significance of his parents' continuing presence within himself in *Fantasia of the Unconscious:*

> . . . considering man at his best, he is at the start faced with the great problem. At the very start he has to undertake his tripartite being, the mother within him, the father within him, and the Holy Ghost, the self which he is supposed to consummate, and which mostly he doesn't.[13]

The consummation of the self—this is one of the great Lawrentian themes. It underlies and, indeed, motivates the early poems about his parents.

Lawrence tells us that "Discord in Childhood" was originally "a long poem, probably was good, but I destroyed it." But much of the success of the poem as we have it now lies in its terseness, the stark statement of the facts without further embellishment, the single metaphorical connection between the quarrelling couple and the ash-tree in the wind. The poem has the effective compactness and completeness-in-itself of some of the briefer and more successful of Lawrence's last poems. If this is discipline by accident, it is still discipline.

"The Collier's Wife," like "Discord in Childhood" and a number of other early poems, closely parallels an episode in *Sons and Lovers* (Chapter Five). Here, however, the mother is made to speak in dialect, and it is evident that Lawrence wished to depict a more typical collier's family than his own. Nevertheless, the mother's mixed emotions—anxiety at the father's accident and relief at his enforced absence from home—would seem to be Mrs. Lawrence's. And in "Monologue of a Mother" the particular situation of Mrs. Lawrence is developed. Having rejected her husband, she has turned to her sons for love, but each in turn has sought to escape such a burden. Now she waits bitterly for death as the only real release from the burden of herself, but rebels against such a fate.

Because the demands made upon him are more than he can bear, the young man feels alienated from his environment. Thus, his attachment to Miriam's family and their farm life is an escape from his own home. Eventually, he will find the relationship with Miriam as difficult as that with his mother, but he will continue to find relief in the impersonal life of the natural world. This will always be his "Eden."

It is mingled love and resentment of his mother that motivates the poem "The Little Town at Evening," in which the grey shadow of the church covers the houses of the town but excludes the speaker. The meaning of this remains undeveloped, however, so that the poem seems stillborn. In an earlier version the church is quaintly described as a great brooding hen with mist wings that cover her chickens. The speaker feels excluded from the peaceful unity of the town that is centred on the maternal church.[14] In both versions the poem seems rather trivial—the overindulgence of a melancholy mood. In the later poem "Weeknight Service," Lawrence is openly hostile to the church, but not till "End of Another Home Holiday" does he see what it is that is troubling him. Here, the poet has not truly discovered his subject.

In fact, none of the early mother or Miriam poems do more than hint at the emotional conflict that aroused them. It is, interestingly enough, a "fictional" poem, "Love on the Farm," that most forcefully and completely expresses the young man's dilemma.

The man in the poem is related to the George Saxton of *The White Peacock* (based on Jessie Chambers' brother, Alan, a close friend of Lawrence), but he resembles Lawrence's father as well, as R. G. N. Salgādo has aptly noted.[15] It is possible that Alan Chambers, who was a few years older than Lawrence, served for a time as a kind of positive father-substitute for the boy, who was obliged, on the conscious level, to take his mother's side in the family quarrel. In any case, the male figure in the poem resembles the two men who were most important in the young Lawrence's emotional life.*

The woman of the poem is similarly a composite figure. She resembles Miriam in her shrinking from the necessary brutalities of farm life and in her fear of her lover, but she seems also to be, like the Lettie of *The White Peacock*, a projection of the feminine side of Lawrence's nature. To the extent that he identifies himself with his mother and her grievances, he must identify

---

* Alan's temporary importance to Lawrence may be seen in Cyril's attachment to George in the "Poem of Friendship" chapter of *The White Peacock*. It is also evident in the notebook version of the poem "Study." The speaker is studying for exams; he imagines not only the girl waiting for him, but also his friend who is falling asleep and "Dreaming; doubtless, of me." The girl and the friend are given about equal weight in his thoughts. But in the later version of the poem the role of the friend is lessened.

with this woman who suffers from the knowledge of male cruelty. It becomes evident that though Alan and Jessie and his parents have given him insights into the problem, it is really the division in his own soul that he has dramatized in this poem. In "Love on the Farm" the man and the woman in Lawrence confront one another, and their conflict is resolved by the woman's submission to her deepest self.

This is, in fact, a piece of considerable dramatic and psychological interest. Despite the melodramatic woman's-magazine quality of some of the writing ("he flashes bare / His strong teeth in a smile") and the awkward insistence of the rhymes, the poem has a definite emotional impact. Its effect is probably partly due to the fact that it is a dramatic monologue spoken by an over-wrought woman—i.e., there are certain dramatic excuses for the language she employs, if not for the rhymes. Again, her identification with trapped and hunted animals is made highly credible. One is inclined to conclude that Lawrence has considerable dramatic skill but is, at this stage in his career, extremely uncertain about how he might best deploy this within the idiom of traditional lyric poetry. In "Love on the Farm" the rhyme-scheme is constantly changing throughout the poem, and the rhythm is largely irregular, but to no useful purpose, since there seems no consistent principle of form in the poem.

In the first stanzas the anxious woman watches at her window. Already she sees the leaves as "large dark hands" and the sunset as "the wound of love," and she then thinks of a moth hovering over the woodbine in terms of sexual yielding. She sees the terror of a swallow and a water-hen as the man comes on the scene. The terror of a rabbit caught in a snare becomes an image of her own terror:

The rabbit presses back her ears,
Turns back her liquid, anguished eyes
And crouches low; then with wild spring
Spurts from the terror of *his* oncoming;

To be choked back, the wire ring
Her frantic effort throttling . . .

The man kills the rabbit, then enters the house and flings it on
the table:

                              With his hand he turns my face to him
And caresses me with his fingers that still smell grim
Of the rabbit's fur! God, I am caught in a snare!
I know not what fine wire is round my throat;
I only know I let him finger there
My pulse of life, and let him nose like a stoat
Who sniffs with joy before he drinks the blood.

And down his mouth comes to my mouth! and down
His bright dark eyes come over me, like a hood
Upon my mind! his lips meet mine, and a flood
Of sweet fire sweeps across me, so I drown
Against him, die, and find death good.

Only with the last four words is a resolution effected. The
woman must die, and find death good. This sexual surrender is
related to the death that occurs in the natural world, since it involves an acceptance of man's nature as a hunter.* At a level
deeper than the personal there is satisfaction in accepting life as it
is. Such death involves rebirth as well, and the possible restoration
of harmony both to the Edenic valley of the lovers and to Lawrence's divided self.

II

Lawrence's removal to Croydon in 1908 provided him with
new surroundings and new experience. Probably, it enabled him

---

* In the story "Second Best" the Miriam-like Frances, having been jilted
by her educated lover, must overcome her repugnance at the killing of
moles (like rabbits, a threat to the farm) in order to prove herself to her
new love.

to see his friends and family in Nottinghamshire with greater objectivity. In "Last Hours" he regrets that he must soon go southward, leaving behind the simple, undemanding life of the country where he can be like "an insect in the grass / Letting life pass," but in other poems he sees his emotional entanglements with his mother and Miriam in a steadily more critical light.

The best of the new poems are simple descriptions; the worst are marred by a forced moralizing and a straining after significance. In "Morning Work," for example, the young poet, who is inclined to be romantic about working men (whether he finds them on the farm, in the mines, or on the railroad), sees a gang of labourers as "trolls at the cave of ringing cerulean mining"; and in "Transformations" the same men remind him of rainbows, rockets, yachts, rhododendrons, sweating and fighting beasts, beech-leaves, kittens, a swarm of bees, and rotting bean-pods in turn. This apotheosis of the working man is probably influenced by Whitman, but the riot of confused simile suggests that Lawrence has not really found out what it is that fascinates him about the men. Early and late Lawrence admired simple working men like his father, but it is doubtful whether the young man allowed himself to know that they were like his father. Having consciously rejected the man his mother had rejected, he seems, unconsciously at least, to be seeking for some similar male figure as a viable substitute.* There is some accurate observation in "Morning Work," but because he has not understood his own motives deeply enough, the two poems lack any very compelling force or direction.

By contrast, the two poems about his landlady's baby are unpretentious and charming. Lawrence simply observes the baby

---

* In *The White Peacock* Annable the gamekeeper becomes for a time a kind of father and teacher for Cyril, whose real father has died in disgrace. Also noteworthy is Cyril's admiration of George's physical rhythm as he works in the fields. *The White Peacock* concludes and *The Rainbow* opens with a passage celebrating men at work on the land. Cf. *Letters* (p. 251) and "Prologue" to *Women in Love* (*Phoenix II*, pp. 103–107), in which Lawrence speaks of a homosexual tendency and the need to deny it.

and delights in its small but active life. When he declares that the baby's feet are "firm and silken as young peony flowers," the simile does not distract the reader but enhances his impression of the delicate, young life of the baby.

The school poems present about equal parts of accurate observation and what Ezra Pound called "a sort of pre-raphaelitish slush, disgusting or very nearly so." The schoolmaster passes through a variety of moods, ranging from pleasure in his influence on the boys to frustration and anger at their resistance and indifference. Like Ursula Brangwen in *The Rainbow*, he concludes that only a strict discipline will make it possible for him to give them anything, and he suffers considerable disillusionment. This process is registered quite sharply, and the physical presence of the school is successfully presented in a poem such as "School on the Outskirts." By contrast, virtually the whole of the "Old" part of "Dreams Old and Nascent," a poem favoured by Miriam, may be taken as a prime example of "pre-raphaelitish slush."

Several poems record the young man's response to the city's glamour. Sometimes Lawrence's own concerns get between him and his ostensible subject, as when he describes marching men in terms of blood undergoing "a crisis, a meeting, a spasm and throb of delight," but at other times he is sharply observant. And at times his exotic imagery does capture the garish quality of London's night life, as in "Clerks." But the best of these poems are those which rely least on such language. In "Charity" Lawrence makes us feel acutely his pain and embarrassment in giving a coin to a woman crouched on a bench, and in "Outcasts" he presents a vivid picture of the huddled sleepers under the bridge at Charing Cross. "After the Opera," a slighter poem, is similarly vivid, and completely convincing:

> Down the stone stairs
> Girls with their large eyes wide with tragedy
> Lift looks of shocked and momentous emotion up at me.
> And I smile.

Ladies
Stepping like birds with their bright and pointed feet
Peer anxiously forth as if for a boat to carry them out of the
    wreckage;
And among the wreck of the theatre crowd
I stand and smile.
They take tragedy so becomingly;
Which pleases me.

But when I meet the weary eyes,
The reddened, aching eyes of the bar-man with thin arms,
I am glad to go back to where I came from.

Such a poem is, I suppose, imagist. It aims at a perfect transparency, a technique so unobtrusive that one is not aware of technique. The diction is clean and exact, the rhythm perfectly natural, the whole expression so precise and direct that the experience is immediately shared by the reader.

The Miriam poems of the Croydon years show Lawrence slowly growing away from his closest friend in Nottinghamshire. In the two "Letter from Town" poems, however, he longs for her and for the country, and in "Lightning" he is aroused to a sexual passion:

I felt the lurch and halt of her heart
    Next my breast, where my own heart was beating:
And I laughed to feel it plunge and bound,
And strange in my blood-swept ears was the sound
    Of the words I kept repeating,
Repeating with tightened arms, and the hot blood's blindfold
    art.

But his passion becomes rage when he discovers her sexual fear and her willingness to sacrifice herself to him though she feels no real desire:

I leaned in the darkness to find her lips
    And claim her utterly in a kiss,
When the lightning flew across her face
And I saw her for the flaring space
    Of a second, like snow that slips
From a roof, inert with death, weeping "Not this! Not this!"

A moment there, like snow in the dark
    Her face lay pale against my breast,
Pale love lost in a thaw of fear
And melted in an icy tear,
    And open lips, distressed;
A moment; then darkness shut the lid of the sacred ark.

And I heard the thunder, and felt the rain,
    And my arms fell loose, and I was dumb.
Almost I hated her, sacrificed;
Hated myself and the place, and the iced
    Rain that burnt on my rage; saying: Come
Home, come home, the lightning has made it too plain!

The force of this passage is only slightly marred by the distracting reference to the sacred ark. There is no other such lapse: on
the contrary the snow imagery is highly appropriate to the situation of the frightened virgin, as the iced rain and the thunder are
appropriate to the man's anger and frustration. The immediacy of
the natural world, the participation of the elements in this out-
door love affair, somehow makes acceptable to the reader what
might otherwise seem mere melodrama. Throughout the poem
Lawrence employs an unusual ABCCBA (and, once only, an
ABCCAB) rhyme-scheme that rescues him from his usual heavy-
handed way with rhyme, and he makes each stanza conform approximately to a basic balance of longer and shorter lines.*

* Incidentally, in the earlier version of the poem printed on p. 918
Roberts and Pinto have left out the final stanza. Someone forgot to turn
p. 19 of *Love Poems*. (This has been corrected in the Viking Compass
edition and in the 1970 Heinemann reprint of the *Complete Poems*.)

The later Miriam poems are anticlimactic. "Sigh No More," a Pre-Raphaelitish lyric about a deceived woman, ends with a "decent short regret for that which once was very good." "Aware" and "A Pang of Reminiscence" express moods of regret and guilt, and "A White Blossom" seems to sum up his feelings:

> A tiny moon as small and white as a single jasmine flower
> Leans all alone above my window, on night's wintry bower,
> Liquid as lime-tree blossom, soft as brilliant water or rain
> She shines, the first white love of my youth, passionless and
>   in vain.

All three poems are short lyrics that present the moon as an image of the beautiful lost love. It is interesting that in the earlier version of "A White Blossom" Lawrence wrote not "passionless and in vain" but "which all sin cannot stain." [16] The later Lawrence goes to the heart of the problem, even in an exquisite lyric.

"A White Blossom" expresses feelings similar to those expressed in the conclusion of Yeats's "Adam's Curse":

> We sat grown quiet at the name of love;
> We saw the last embers of daylight die,
> And in the trembling blue-green of the sky
> A moon, worn as if it had been a shell
> Washed by time's waters as they rose and fell
> About the stars and broke in days and years.
>
> I had a thought for no one's but your ears:
> That you were beautiful, and that I strove
> To love you in the old high way of love;
> That it had all seemed happy, and yet we'd grown
> As weary-hearted as that hollow moon.

In each case the poet feels the pathetic futility of an "ideal" love. It is probably significant that in their later work Lawrence and Yeats developed similar concerns and mythologies. Each felt profoundly the unhappy effects of mind dissociated from body. But here Yeats has developed his insights in a much more dramatic way than Lawrence, through the conversation of his three characters about the effort that must be expended in order to create art, love, and beauty, as well as through the striking imagery of the final stanzas. Again, he handles traditional forms with an apparent ease that seems beyond Lawrence's reach.

We know that Yeats went to great pains (as he says himself in the poem) to achieve such smoothness and unity of effect. Was Lawrence simply temperamentally incapable of the same sustained effort? Certainly his mercurial temperament has some bearing on the matter, but this is surely not in itself an adequate explanation for his failure to use traditional forms with complete success. An examination of his college notebook and of the various versions of his early poems shows that, like Yeats, he revised a great deal in order to come closer and closer to the particular effect he desired. The problem, then, is not, I think, one of insufficient determination or industry. More likely, it is that the young Lawrence had an instinctive, not yet fully understood need to express in some appropriate form the irregular but ultimately patterned and meaningful rhythm of the felt experience itself as it developed within him. His subject is the self in its immediate encounter with the external world, and his chief concern is to capture the whole physical and mental engagement of the self with that world. Thus the exquisite lyrics to the lost Miriam are possible only because the poet is, for once, retrospective in his "effort of attention." Usually, the formal verse pattern is an inappropriate means of expressing the self's immediate physical and mental apprehensions, as in "The Wild Common," but it is highly appropriate when the speaker wishes to lay stress on the distance in time or emotional intensity of an experience that is contemplated rather than relived. The problem arises because such distancing is not usually part of this poet's aim.

Nevertheless, Lawrence's removal to Croydon almost certainly helped him to achieve a more objective view of his relations with friends and family at home. In "End of Another Home Holiday," which concerns a visit to Eastwood, Lawrence is able at last to examine his painfully close relationship with his mother. In the poem he contrasts her demanding, possessive love with the magnificent impersonality of the natural universe:

> Love is the great Asker.
> The sun and the rain do not ask the secret
> Of the time when the grain struggles down in the dark.
> The moon walks her lonely way without anguish,
> Because no one grieves over her departure.

> Forever, ever by my shoulder pitiful love will linger,
> Crouching as little houses crouch under the mist when I turn.
> Forever, out of the mist, the church lifts up a reproachful
>   finger,
> Pointing my eyes in wretched defiance where love hides her
>   face to mourn.

> Oh! but the rain creeps down to wet the grain
> That struggles alone in the dark,
> And asking nothing, patiently steals back again!
> The Moon sets forth o' nights
> To walk the lonely, dusky heights
> Serenely, with steps unswerving;
> Pursued by no sigh of bereavement,
> No tears of love unnerving
> Her constant tread:
> While ever at my side,
> Frail and sad, with grey, bowed head,
> The beggar-woman, the yearning eyed
> Inexorable love goes lagging.

As in "The Little Town at Evening" and "Weeknight Service," the church appears to be reproachful, arousing the boy's guilt.

But this is the first poem to confront the problem directly. Lawrence is able to express his experience with astonishing vividness and directness in a dramatic monologue of this kind in which the irregular rhythms and stanzaic divisions follow in a perfectly natural way the course of his thought. In the modified repetition of the images the poet discovers his own feelings. This is "expressive form" at its most effective.

The poem moves from the particular to the general situation in a very natural way. In the first of the three sections the speaker dwells upon those particular things—a "black sycamore," "the dim white phlox," "the midnight bell," the "sharp clean trot of a pony down the road," and the sound of a train across the valley —that seem to focus as they arouse his painfully ambivalent feelings about "home." In the second section of the poem he recognizes that the true centre and cause of this complex of feelings is his mother, and also that her world of possessive, demanding love is but a small island in the larger and more splendid world of natural process. In a sense, the poem has come into existence so that the speaker may bring to conscious articulation this discovery. Thus his attempt to imagine the sun, the rain, the grain, and the moon in terms of human motive and action goes beyond the conventional use of "pathetic fallacy" in its stress on the gulf between the concerns of men and those of natural things. As with the ironic suggestions of human motivation in the animals of certain of the *Birds, Beasts and Flowers* poems, these passages tend to underline man's alienation from his natural environment.

There is an element of fantasy in the later part of the poem, perhaps because Lawrence found it too painful at this early stage to deal with his personal problem any more directly than this. Thus his mother becomes "Love" personified, "the great Asker" whose demands are endless and piteous. Finally, in the brief third part of the poem, the poet appears to succumb to the conventional and to abandon the ironic use of the pathetic fallacy in his assertion that the corncrake that calls and calls monotonously from across the valley is, like his mother, asking "yet more" of him. He appears to admit defeat; this world is still his mother's world, and he is still hopelessly involved in it. The process of discovery that is generated in the poem has proceeded so far, but no resolution of the personal (and the formal) problem that is here revealed seems possible to the young poet. Both the method and the emotional flow come to a temporary dead end.

Two fictional poems, both in dialect, are concerned to launch an attack on the superficiality and meanness of the ideal of purity upheld by mother and Miriam. In "Violets" the speaker concludes that his dead brother will be "gladder of" the warm violets from a strange girl's bosom than of his disapproving sister's pure lilies; and in "Whether or Not" a young policeman sleeps with his middle-aged landlady because his self-righteous fiancée arouses him without satisfying him. When the widowed landlady becomes pregnant, and the fiancée discovers the affair, the policeman rejects both women. His girl is too sure of her own rightness, "too much i' th' right," and with the widow "somehow it isn't right," so he will marry neither of them.

It is tempting to consider this short story in verse a disguised expression of Lawrence's feelings about his relations with Miriam and with Alice Dax (the woman who provided much of the inspiration for the Clara Dawes of *Sons and Lovers*). But even if more were known about the affair with Alice (for example, just when it began and when it ended), it would not make any difference to one's reading of the poem. In "Love on the Farm" Lawrence was primarily concerned to dramatize his own inner conflict. Here he is primarily concerned to tell a story and (in 1928, anyhow, when he added the section that allows his passionate policeman to escape both women) to point a moral. Love that is to be fulfilling must be so generous and so deeply committed as to transcend mere possessive egotism.

III

You, Helen, who see the stars
As mistletoe berries burning in a black tree,
You surely, seeing I am a bowl of kisses
Should put your mouth to mine and drink of me.
("The Appeal")

The "Helen" poems have their origin in Lawrence's interest in
Helen Corke, a fellow teacher, but the story they tell is complicated by the fact that Lawrence is exploring not only his and
Helen's friendship but also her troubled relations with a married
man who later committed suicide. Since Lawrence identified himself to some extent with the other man, it is possible that some of
the poems are re-creations of events in the earlier story. Others
may well be fictional, or else, as Harry T. Moore suggests, concerned with another woman whose identity Lawrence was concerned to conceal.[17]

As Kenneth Rexroth has noted, the character "Helen" is more
than an ordinary woman:

> Probably the girl's name was not Helen. Lawrence thought of
> her as dim, larger than life, a demi-goddess, moving through the
> smoke of a burning city. For certain Gnostics Helen was the name
> of the incarnate "female principle", the power of the will, the
> sheath of the sword, the sacred whore who taught men love.
> Helen seems to have been the midwife of Lawrence's manhood.[18]

These remarks are true to the spirit of some of the Helen poems.
Helen is variously described as "Night's bacchante," a mystic
priestess, the "Most High," and even "the earth I hover over." At
least, this is the way the man of the poems wishes, at first, to see
her. In fact, she proves to be a priestess of sublimated ideal love
rather than love fulfilled in physical passion. The lover pleads for
sexual communion and seems at least once to have aroused the de-

sired response (see "Release"), but most of the poems tell a tale of frustration at the beautiful and mysterious woman's frigidity and anger at her seemingly malicious teasing of the male.

This woman's manner and appearance arouse the man's sense of the sacred mystery underlying the ordinary, but he finds that her responses are superficial. In "Under the Oak" he senses an elemental druidic terror in the beautiful night, but she feels only the sentimental thrill of the voyeur; in "These Clever Women" he condemns the intellectuality that prevents her from experiencing anything deeply.

It is possible that the Helen of the poems is largely an invention of Lawrence's. At times she seems to be no more than a variant of Miriam, a Miriam hardened by bitter experience. Certainly the "moral" of these poems is fairly close to that of the Miriam poems. But a feeling of unreality pervades them, so that they fail to be wholly convincing. We know what Lawrence thinks and feels about Helen, but we have very little sense of her as a substantial being. The real Helen Corke probably presented a more complex problem than he allows. It seems likely that Lawrence was finally more interested in projecting his own problem than in illuminating hers. "Coldness in Love," the best of the Helen poems, takes Helen's account of a sudden anxiety and makes of it a statement of *his* inner conflict. She merely provided the occasion. In Miriam and in Helen Lawrence recognized an aspect of himself. He came gradually to realize that it was a different kind of woman he needed.

The importance of Woman to him he never doubts. Not only a priestess, she is the mysterious Other itself, the rich life of the instincts with which the intellect must somehow establish a living relationship. This is evident in "Red Moon-Rise," in which he sees the moon as a portent out of the womb of the universe. "Glad as the Magi," he rejoices at this evidence of the other world. The poem goes on to relate all human creativity and growth to the image of the womb, the dark world within the world we see, a world whose discovery is as important as that of the Magi. The mating that Lawrence so ardently desires is for him a passage into this world, a basic way to life and growth. Thus his marriage is meant to be an image and focus of the larger marriage with the world.

IV

The illness and death of Lawrence's mother in the autumn of 1910 aroused a sequence of poems that are remarkable for the intensity of their expression of grief. Only Lawrence's own words can adequately convey the emptiness and desolation of the speaker of these poems:

> The church clock struck two. Far away he could hear the sharp clinking of the trucks on the railway. No, it was not that they were far away. They were there in their places. But where was he himself? [19]

> From his breast, from his mouth, sprang the endless space, and it was there behind him, everywhere. The people hurrying along the streets offered no obstruction to the void in which he found himself. They were small shadows whose footsteps and voices could be heard, but in each of them the same night, the same silence.[20]

Many of the incidents of the poems are closely paralleled in the closing chapter of *Sons and Lovers*. Both the poems and the novel make it evident that the sickness of grief and despair was the most intense emotional experience of Lawrence's youth. He came to see that his mother had mattered to him far more than any other person and that he had lived for her as much as she had lived for him. It is because he loved her like a lover that he could not love Miriam or Helen enough to overcome their fears.

The mother's death brought home to her son the cruel fact that she did not achieve the fulfilment in marriage that he desired for himself. And her failure seems to be his failure. In "The Virgin Mother" he suggests that in her death he must be as faithful to her as he was in her life. She has issued him not only from her womb but from her soul, so that he is "free of all hearts." It is possible he will never be able to love another woman in a whole way.

Now that she is dead the mother has her only consummation of self:

My love looks like a girl tonight,
    But she is old.
The plaits that lie along her pillow
    Are not gold,
But threaded with filigree silver
    And uncanny cold.

She looks like a young maiden, since her brow
    Is smooth and fair;
Her cheeks are very smooth, her eyes are closed,
    She sleeps a rare,
Still, winsome sleep, so still and so composed.

Nay, but she sleeps like a bride, and dreams her dreams
    Of perfect things.
She lies at last, the darling, in the shape of her dream,
    And her dead mouth sings
By its shape, like thrushes in clear evenings.

This poem, "The Bride," is the best of the three poems about his mother's death. As in "A White Blossom," Lawrence wishes to achieve an effect of distance, this time as a temporary strategy against the overwhelming knowledge of the intensity of his grief. Again, the lyric form seems the best means to the desired end. Without in any way minimizing the event Lawrence places it at a certain distance and sees it in its proper perspective, the knowledge of "perfect things." The poem develops the exquisite irony of the appearance of felicity in the fact of ultimate defeat. Underlying the irony is the contemplation of perfection and the consolation offered by such exercise of the imagination. The image of the bride's mouth shaped for song in the last lines gives expression to this need in a very delicate and poignant fashion. There is here none of the awkwardness that plagues Lawrence in "Love on the Farm" and "The Wild Common." It would seem, then, that the traditional lyric is highly suited to the elegiac and to the nostalgic, but not to that rendering of one's immediate experience that Lawrence called "poetry of the present." It is more suited to a detached observation (as in Philip Larkin's best poems), or to emotion recollected in tranquillity, than to the highly engaged observation that Lawrence attempts in most of his love poems, and in much of *Look! We Have Come Through!*, *Birds, Beasts and Flowers*, *Pansies*, and *Last Poems*. Fine lyrics occur among Lawrence's mature poems, but they usually constitute moments of pause or rest from the struggle, as in "History," which views the early marital battle in retrospect and from the vantage of achieved calm.

Subsequent poems explore the nature of his grief in a much more immediate way. "Sorrow" registers the shock of recognition with a precision that is marred only by somewhat affected "soft-foot malady":

Why does the thin grey strand
Floating up from the forgotten
Cigarette between my fingers,
Why does it trouble me?

Ah, you will understand;
When I carried my mother downstairs,
A few times only, at the beginning
Of her soft-foot malady,

I should find for a reprimand
To my gaiety, a few long grey hairs
On the breast of my coat; and one by one
I watched them float up the dark chimney.

Another such moment is described in "Brooding Grief":

A yellow leaf, from the darkness
Hops like a frog before me;
Why should I start and stand still?

I was watching the woman that bore me
Stretched in the brindled darkness
Of the sick-room, rigid with will
To die: and the quick leaf tore me
Back to this rainy swill
Of leaves and lamps and the city street mingled before me.

These poems have the sharpness and immediacy of Lawrence's best poems of the city. But their effect is intensified by the cumulative movement of the sequence.

In fact, the poems of grief seem like parts of one long poem. It is not impossible to consider them separately, but it is probably unfair. For, taken altogether, they achieve an effect that one cannot deny or demonstrate by reference to the individual poem. Certain images of silence and darkness recur, expressing a sense Lawrence will never lose. Surrounding the little area of our daytime consciousness is the vast womb or sea of silence and darkness. Upon this mysterious flood sails the ship of our ordinary world:

The earth again like a dark ship steams out of the dark sea over
The edge of the blue, and the sun stands up to see us glide
Slowly into another day . . .

Compare this passage from "The Shadow of Death" to a passage from the late poem "The Ship of Death":

Now launch the small ship, now as the body dies
and life departs, launch out, the fragile soul
in the fragile ship of courage, the ark of faith
with its store of food and little cooking pans
and change of clothes,

upon the flood's black waste
upon the waters of the end
upon the sea of death, where still we sail
darkly, for we cannot steer, and have no port.

The first ship is the ship of earth that the young Lawrence sails upon, and the second the ship of his death. But even the ship of earth is very much *his* ship, the ship of his dark presence in the visible world of day: he speaks in the poem of holding his own in the midst of winds, lifting his "shadow" for sail on the breeze. The emphasis is on his awareness of death—i.e., on building a ship of death for the "dark sea." The "Shadow of Death" will eventually become the "Ship of Death." It is interesting that the myth of the ark and the flood that is central to the late poem should have its first very tentative expression in this early one.

There are other parallels between the late and the early poems about death. In "Bavarian Gentians" Lawrence sees the gentians as "black lamps from the halls of Dis, burning dark blue, / giving off darkness, blue darkness . . . ," and in an early poem he thinks of death as a blue shadow he carries within him:

Many years have I still to burn, detained
Like a candle-flame on this body; but I enclose
Blue shadow within me, a presence which lives contained
In my flame of living, the invisible heart of the rose.
                                        ("At a Loose End")

The vast darkness is, then, inside us as well as outside us.

Like the Persephone of "Bavarian Gentians," the mother is now the bride of darkness. If the female speaker of so many of Lawrence's poems is, finally, his own soul (whatever disguise she takes on herself), then her ultimate consummation is reached in "Bavarian Gentians." But Persephone is not merely an image of Lawrence's soul; she is the mother within, the mother whose frustration and despair he felt so deeply in himself and was una-

ble to escape. Lawrence was always to be acutely aware that his
mother was one of the "unhappy dead" of his late poems. For
himself, and for her spirit in him, he wishes the nobler fate that is
so magnificently expressed in his re-creation of the myth of Persephone.

In the war years he wrote of the persistence of the dead in the
living:

> Those that die return to the most beloved, enter in, and at last
> live in peace, gladly, at one with the most beloved. So that the liv-
> ing are always living. . . . It is inexplicable *how* they are present
> in us, but is a physical fact that they are. . . . Souls that find in
> death itself a passionate consummation return to us appeased, and
> add the beauty and richness of their presence to us. But what of
> the souls that are caught out of life unliberated and
> unappeased? . . . They enter into us angrily and fill us with their
> destructive presence. There is no peace in death to those who die
> in the terrible deadlock of frustration. And if there is no peace
> for them, there is none for us. They return home to us. They are
> the angry, unappeased shades that come darkly home to us, throng-
> ing home to us from over the seas, entering our souls and filling us
> with madness, ever more and more madness, unless we, by our ac-
> tive living, shall give them the life that they demand, the living
> motions that were frustrated in them now liberated and made
> free. . . . What is the use of a mother's sacrificing herself for her
> children if after death her unappeased soul shall perforce return
> upon the child and exact from it all the fulfilment that should have
> been attained in the living flesh, and was not? [21]

For his mother and for himself Lawrence desired a "passionate
consummation" in life and in death.

The stories of the ark and of Persephone are controlling myths
in the late poems. In the poems of grief we have only the basic
insights that his mother's death revealed to Lawrence. The
sources of his images are immediate and poignant. He is haunted
by the blueness of his mother's eyes, and it is this, somehow, that
has brought the endless blue sky so near. Lawrence has come to
believe that the bright world we know is only a film on the sur-

face of the larger darkness. Death is the final passage into this darkness, which is also the great womb of renewed life. In "Blueness" Lawrence attempts to state his new idea of the dependence of what we know on the vast surrounding silence, the dependence of light on darkness:

> Out of the darkness, fretted sometimes in its sleeping,
> Jets of sparks in fountains of blue come leaping
> To sight, revealing a secret, numberless secrets keeping.
>
> Sometimes the darkness trapped within a wheel
> Runs into speed like a dream, the blue of the steel
> Showing the rocking darkness now a-reel.
>
> And out of the invisible, streams of bright blue drops
> Rain from the showery heavens, and bright blue crops
> Of flowers surge from below to their ladder-tops.
>
> And all the manifold blue, amazing eyes,
> The rainbow arching over in the skies,
> New sparks of wonder opening in surprise:
>
> All these pure things come foam and spray of the sea
> Of darkness abundant, which shaken mysteriously
> Breaks into dazzle of living, as dolphins leap from the sea
> Of midnight and shake it to fire, till the flame of the shadow
>   we see.

The visible rises from the invisible only to return to the invisible again. In order to express a similar idea of the ultimate union of life and death Rainer Maria Rilke developed the organizing myth of the angel, "the creature in whom that transformation of the visible into the invisible we are performing already appears complete." [22] * The young Lawrence is able to give only a series of

---

* Rilke wrote to his Polish translator: "Death is our reverted, our unilluminated, SIDE OF LIFE: we must try to achieve the greatest possible consciousness of our existence, which is at home in BOTH OF THESE UNLIMITED

loosely linked images. Twenty years later the sea of darkness, the dolphins, and the blue flowers find their place in poems of very much greater coherence and power.

"Piano" is a different case. Since it is primarily a poem of memory rather than grief, and one, moreover, in which Lawrence has conscientiously worked to achieve a certain detachment from his materials, it could be considered elsewhere. But if it is not a part of the sequence of poems concerned with the mother's death and the son's grief, it is certainly related to it. More than an expression of Lawrence's sense of loss, it demonstrates the "presentness" of past experience that he speaks of in his unpublished foreword to the *Collected Poems* of 1928.[23]

As in many later Lawrence poems (especially in *Birds, Beasts and Flowers*) a particular object or event—in this case a woman singing—contains intimations of some "other" world or "other" mode of consciousness. One becomes aware of the mysterious underworld, an extra dimension to experience—one that was there all the time but beneath the level of our normal daytime consciousness. In the later poems this special sense is most frequently expressed in images of darkness—a sea of darkness or an underground world (in "Snake," for instance, or "Bavarian Gentians," to choose the most obvious and famous examples). Here the "other" world arises from the darkness within. It is the living past or "flood of remembrance" that overwhelms the psychic mariner.

To speak of the poem in these terms is, of course, to anticipate the development of a "myth" or informing pattern of imagery and symbol in Lawrence's later poetry. But it is evident that such a pattern begins to emerge in the poems that follow the mother's death, and this movement towards a greater coherence and a more unified vision seems to me one of the two significant devel-

PROVINCES, which is INEXHAUSTIBLY NOURISHED OUT OF BOTH. . . . The true form of life extends through BOTH regions, the blood of the mightiest circulation pulses through BOTH: THERE IS NEITHER A HERE NOR A BEYOND, BUT ONLY THE GREAT UNITY, in which the 'Angels', those beings that surpass us, are at home." (*Duino Elegies*, p. 93)

opments in Lawrence's early poetry. The other is, as we have seen, the gradual achievement of a greater clarity and particularity in the honest treatment of experience.

"Piano" is a good example of this second development, as the discussion of it in I. A. Richards' *Practical Criticism* demonstrates. In rewriting the poem Lawrence eliminated a sentimental passage about his sister's first love. More important, he strongly qualified his own nostalgia by his description of the song's effect as an "insidious mastery" that "betrays" him and causes him to lose his manhood.[24] The poet stands aside from his experience in order to see it more clearly. As Vivian de Sola Pinto has remarked, "Piano" is an early example of Lawrence's use of "controlled imagination." [25] But, as we have seen, many of the early poems demonstrate an equal objectivity.

V

My love lies underground
With her face upturned to mine,
And her mouth unclosed in the last long kiss
That ended her life and mine.

She fares in the stark immortal
Fields of death;
I in these goodly, frozen
Fields beneath.

Something in me remembers
And will not forget.
The stream of my life in the darkness
Deathward set!

And something in me has forgotten,
Has ceased to care.
Desire comes up, and contentment
Is debonair.

("Hymn to Priapus")

This passage from *Look! We Have Come Through!* strikes the proper balance between Lawrence's permanent sense of death and his renewed commitment to life in the flesh. In "The Enkindled Spring" he sees spring as a "conflagration / Of green fires" and thinks of himself as the gap in it all. But he continues to seek out the woman he will marry.

At the time of his mother's illness Lawrence became engaged to Louise Burrows, an Ilkeston girl he had known since his college days. Several poems—"Snap-Dragon," "Kisses in the Train," and "The Hands of the Betrothed" among them—are concerned with this relationship. Lawrence felt that his "Louie" was a healthy, sensuous creature and not burdened with fears and inhibitions like Miriam. Since he wished to find fulfilment in marriage, he decided (on the spur of the moment after a chance meeting on a train) that he ought to marry her. Yet he continued to think about Miriam and to see her occasionally. He had once told Miriam that he was not physically attracted to her, but that he could marry Louie "from a purely physical standpoint." [26]

"Last Words to Miriam" is an attempt to explain the nature of Lawrence's and Miriam's love and the reasons for its failure. As before, he gives her credit for waking his spirit and bringing him to fuller consciousness. In revising the poem Lawrence places increasing emphasis on his own failure to bring Miriam to full womanhood, to make her alive in the flesh.[27] This honesty is commendable, but the poem suffers from the artificiality of its language. It lacks the dramatic immediacy of "Lightning."

"Ballad of Another Ophelia," a poem much admired by several of Lawrence's critics, is a fantasy which seems to be based upon Miriam's situation as Lawrence imagines it.* The speaker is a

* Usually, these critics hold the opinion that this poem is one of the few worth reading; ". . . there remains the task of explaining how the poet who wrote the *Ballad of Another Ophelia* and *Aware* and, above all, *The White Peacock*, should have wandered through his own zeal misdirected, so far from the paths which once appeared to be his alone to open" (I. A. Richards, *Science and Poetry*, pp. 75–76). "(He did indeed write verse, but not much of it is poetry, though it is very interesting in various ways: he rarely

mad farm girl whose lover has seduced and deserted her. Now
she sees the life of the farm in terms of her own situation:

> What then is there hidden in the skirts of all the blossom?
> What is peeping from your skirts, O mother hen?
> 'Tis the sun that asks the question in a lovely haste for wisdom;
> What a lovely haste for wisdom is in men!

> Yea, but it is cruel when undressed is all the blossom
> And her shift is lying white upon the floor,
> That a grey one, like a shadow, like a rat, a thief, a rainstorm
> Creeps upon her then and ravishes her store!

This is, with "Snap-Dragon," the only early Lawrence poem that
might be considered *symboliste*. In the mind of Lawrence's farm
girl the distinction between subject and object has broken down
so that all objects in the external world become fully symbolic
features of her psychic landscape. At a level deeper than the personal, one's instincts and emotions are analogous to natural processes. In "Discord in Childhood" and "Love on the Farm" Lawrence merely drew the analogy. Here he shows the nature of our
deepest consciousness by imagining an individual whose instinc-
tual life has overwhelmed her ordinary self and broken down the
bounds of her normal social ego. In other words, there is method
in this madness. It exemplifies Lawrence's famous remarks about

attained the level of the *Ballad of Another Ophelia*)" (F. R. Leavis, *D. H.
Lawrence*, p. 6). "Lawrence had all the elements of a great poet as one
can see from such early poems as the 'Ballad of Another Ophelia', but he
had too little respect for his art" (R. P., "Dragging in Mr. Pound," *The
Christian Science Monitor*, March 25, 1933, p. 8). "In the early derivative
wallow of the *Rhymed Poems*, which are nearer Shelley or Yeats than
Whitman, Lawrence does at times tear away his hand from his mouth;
suddenly, for example, in *Wedding Morn, Guards, Scent of Irises, Kisses
in the Train*, and supremely in his least impeded speech of the *Ballad of
Another Ophelia* . . ." (Geoffrey Grigson, *The London Magazine*, May
1958, p. 68). It would seem that for those who do not greatly care for
Lawrence's poems the "Ballad" has special qualities. Perhaps my remarks
about its uniqueness in Lawrence's early work can provide some of the explanation.

"another *ego*, according to whose action the individual is unrecognizable, and passes through, as it were, allotropic states which it needs a deeper sense than any we've been used to exercise to discover are states of the same single radically unchanged element." [28] Some weeks after he wrote this to Edward Garnett, Lawrence was writing to Harriet Monroe, the editor of *Poetry:*

> Don't you see the poor thing is cracked, and she used all those verses—apples and chickens and rat—according to true instinctive or *dream* symbolism? This poem—I am very proud of it—has got the quality of a troublesome dream that seems incoherent but is selected by another sort of consciousness. The latter part is the waking up part, yet never really awake, because she is mad.[29]

As a dramatic device the madness of Lawrence's Ophelia is not any more remarkable than the madness of Shakespeare's Ophelia; it is in *The Rainbow* that he attempts to express his ideas of the "other ego" in terms of outwardly quite normal people. If we compare the "Ballad" to, say, Dylan Thomas's "In the White Giant's Thigh," we can see that while Thomas writes with complete directness of the chalk hill as a giant, Lawrence needs the dramatic device of the mad farm girl before he can allow himself to write in this way. He is always a literalist of the imagination, and not truly a *symboliste*.

In "Ballad of Another Ophelia," as in "Love on the Farm," there is a dramatic context which contains the melodramatic utterance of the speaker and makes it somewhat more acceptable than it might otherwise be. Moreover, the imagery in this poem is startling and vivid, and the rhythm still irregular but somewhat more patterned, in that the first and third and the second and fourth lines of each quatrain are usually at least approximately equal in length. Again, the rhymes seem less forced than in "The Wild Common" or "Love on the Farm," and most of the line breaks make syntactical sense so that each line becomes a unit and seems to fall naturally into place. The imagery of the opening lines has an almost hallucinatory quality; this is, of course, highly appropriate to the speaker and suggestive of her mental and emotional state. The poem is close to folk song both in its subject matter—love and madness—and in its simple use of natural imagery to express basic human experiences and emotions. The fifth stanza is especially easy to imagine as part of an old song.

The poem as a whole has more sophisticated designs on the reader, of course, as Lawrence's letter to Harriet Monroe indicates. In the latter stanzas of the poem (what Lawrence called "the waking up part") the simple sexual symbolism is made more explicit in the passage about man's lovely haste for wisdom and for ravishment. This explicitly Freudian intrusion tends to qualify somewhat the dreamlike atmosphere that had prevailed earlier in the poem. Nevertheless, the attempt to get beyond the limitations of the character's normal social ego is at least a partial success.

There is a somewhat similar attempt in "Snap-Dragon," one of Lawrence's earliest poems. In this, perhaps the most intensely erotic of all the love poems, there is a similar use of natural objects as symbols of emotional states. The speaker of the poem falls into a kind of trance as he observes a girl and a flower:

> She laughed, she reached her hand out to the flower,
> Closing its crimson throat. My own throat in her power
> Strangled, my heart swelled up so full
> As if it would burst its wine-skin in my throat,
> Choke me in my own crimson. I watched her pull
> The gorge of the gaping flower, till the blood did float
>
> >Over my eyes, and I was blind—
> >Her large brown hands stretched over
> >The windows of my mind;
> >And there in the dark I did discover
> >Things I was out to find . . .

"The essential quality of poetry," wrote Lawrence twenty years later, "is that it makes a new effort of attention and 'discovers' a

new world within the known world." [30] Here, the world within
the world, the world of vision, is expressed in the symbolism of
the cup (or grail) of the man's heart and the bird that descends
upon it:

Again I saw a brown bird hover
Over the flowers at my feet;
I felt a brown bird hover
Over my heart, and sweet
Its shadow lay on my heart.
I thought I saw on the clover
A brown bee pulling apart
The closed flesh of the clover
And burrowing in its heart.

She moved her hand, and again
I felt the brown bird cover
My heart; and then
The bird came down on my heart,
As on a nest the rover
Cuckoo comes, and shoves over
The brim each careful part
Of love, takes possession, and settles her down,
With her wings and her feathers to drown
The nest in a heat of love.

The bird is the girl who accepts the man's love. This acceptance
is wordless and takes place in the darkness, at a level deeper than
the personal where the "old stable *ego*" of character does not
exist.[31]

Then I laughed in the dark of my heart, I did exult
Like a sudden chuckling of music. I bade her eyes
Meet mine, I opened her helpless eyes to consult
Their fear, their shame, their joy that underlies
Defeat in such a battle. In the dark of her eyes
My heart was fierce to make her laughter rise.

Till her dark deeps shook with convulsive thrills, and the
    dark
Of her spirit wavered like water thrilled with light;
And my heart leaped up in longing to plunge its stark
Fervour within the pool of her twilight,
Within her spacious soul, to find delight.

Here, as in *Birds, Beasts and Flowers*, the underground or dark
world within the world is the substantial world of sense-percep-
tion when it is experienced in depth. "They call all experience of
the senses *mystic*, when the experience is considered," writes the
Lawrence of *Last Poems*. Here he sees the dawning awareness of
sexual desire between a man and a woman as a mystical communion.*

In the last stanza of the poem the man decides he will have passion, even if he will be punished for it:

And I do not care, though the large hands of revenge
Shall get my throat at last, shall get it soon,
If the joy that they are lifted to avenge
Have risen red on my night as a harvest moon,
Which even death can only put out for me;
And death, I know, is better than not-to-be.

* The symbolic method of this poem seems all the more remarkable when
we know that it was written in 1907, and was substantially the same as it
is now. In revising it for publication in *The English Review* (June 1912)
Lawrence shortened it and altered the rather diffuse ending. But the method
does not change.

According to Jessie Chambers (p. 142), Lawrence went to tea at Louie's
house one day in the summer of 1907 in order to see if his feeling for her
"was what he thought it was." Some days later he showed Jessie the poem
that had resulted, yet he made no attempt to establish a special tie with
Louie for three years. In 1928, however, he placed this poem just before
two poems dealing with his engagement to Louie (1910–1911) and just
after a poem, "After Many Days," whose occasion was a visit to Jessie in
February 1912. This is not a literal but an emotional rendering of the
"order of experience." And it shows that Lawrence abandoned the attempt
to keep his poems strictly to the "order in which they were written."

This rather desperate conclusion completes the pattern of the imagery, reminding us once again that there is a relationship between love and cruelty. Such an ending is also a reminder of Lawrence's problems with Miriam, Helen, and the morality his mother attempted to instill in him. But he is willing to pay the price in guilt and conflict, if only he can sometimes be fully alive.

"Come Spring, Come Sorrow" and "The Hands of the Betrothed" are poems that oppose a "natural" morality to the conventional sexual morality of his mother's and Louie's social world. The latter poem provides a sardonic glimpse of the passionate but prudish fiancée. In the last quatrain Lawrence's detachment and his sense of humour are evident. He was fond of his Louie, and he admired her warmth and spontaneity, but in the end he did not marry her, perhaps because she lacked the intelligence and imagination that Miriam possessed in abundance. Frieda Lawrence felt that Louie had been largely "an escape from Miriam." [32] Lawrence needed a woman both sensual and imaginative, a woman generous and yet independent, and he could not wholly commit himself until he found one.

His continuing concern for Miriam is evident in "Two Wives." This is a longer poem in seven parts, but only the first five appeared in *New Poems*.[33] In I the scene is set: a man has just died in his bed. In II his wife enters, and sinks to the floor in her grief. She does not hear the other woman enter, but in III the stranger begins to speak. She says that she died first and that now "in the after life" she is the man's true wife. In IV she reveals herself as his first love, who grew up with him and "for one strange year was as a bride" to him. But he set her aside, and she grieves that she was not able to defeat his "baser stuff." In V she claims him, now that he is dead. Their spiritual union is eternal.*

* *Cf. A Personal Record* (p. 147): "There were moments, too, in our desperate struggle, when we seemed to touch another sphere of existence, and it flashed upon me that never here in this life, but somewhere beyond the human bourne lay the unity we were striving for. He perhaps at times

Here the *New Poems* version ends, with the ghostly or spiritual bride triumphant. But, as with "Whether or Not," Lawrence
had second thoughts in 1928. In VI the living wife replies that
the other woman's "ideal" love was nothing but a dream of self,
and never a genuine homage to the Other. She "only roused /
His mind until it burnt his heart away!" He never loved her with
desire. Therefore, continues the earthly wife in VII, the sacred
love must stand away from the body. It has nothing to do with
her.*

Lawrence told Jessie Chambers that he needed her for his art
but that he must marry a different woman for his physical need.
In 1916, commenting on Philip Heseltine's problems, he remarked
that there are some men who can only be happy with two
wives.[34] This idea is expressed again in *The Boy in the Bush*. He
himself seems to have needed the close friendship of such women
as Ottoline Morrell, Mabel Luhan, and Dorothy Brett. In *Women
in Love* Ursula berates Birkin for clinging perversely to his
"spiritual brides." [35] It is evident that "Two Wives" is similarly
related to the "split" that Lawrence detected in himself. But
while it shows his continuing fascination with the Miriam figure,
it also shows his disapproval of her. This is, in effect, a rejection
of the possessive and egotistical way of loving (disguised as purity) that his mother taught him. The young man is consciously

felt something similar, because he once exclaimed: 'You push me beyond
the very bounds of human consciousness.' "
  This was written, of course, after Jessie Chambers had had a vision of
Lawrence on the day of his death (*The Intelligent Heart*, p. 439). "Two
Wives" indicates that Lawrence understood Jessie's mystical tendency. He
told her once that she was like Emily Brontë, though he forbade her to
read *Wuthering Heights* (*A Personal Record*, pp. 102, 310). By the time
she came to write about her friendship with Lawrence she undoubtedly had
read it.
  * Cf. Frieda Lawrence's *Memoirs and Correspondence* (p. 293): "L.
talked to me by the hour about Jessie Chambers. He owed her a lot, considering L's home, but the human relation between them did not work, she
was a blue stocking and he had more warmth for her than she for him.
She sort of wanted to run him too much in that humble bullying way. She
would have wanted him to be a nice tame English little poet." (*Cf.* p. 300.)

mother-dominated, but the demon within struggles to free himself.

This analysis is not, of course, intended to denigrate the very real contribution to Lawrence's development that was made by Jessie Chambers. She was, clearly, an extraordinary woman, and the early poetry is very largely a testament to her intelligence and spirit. As Vivian de Sola Pinto has noted, Lawrence was very lucky in his women:

> In Jessie Chambers, this girl "whose eyes were usually dark . . . but could flame with light like a conflagration", Lawrence for the first time came into contact with a mind comparable with his own. Her collaboration with him in the formative years of his life is one of the great partnerships of literature, comparable with the collaboration of Dorothy Wordsworth and her famous brother.[36]

"All my poetry belongs to you," he once told her.[37] The irony of their situation was that he had to free himself from her before he could achieve his maturity.

The struggle for wholeness has a significance wider than the personal. In "The North Country" Lawrence addresses himself for the first time in a poem to what Jessie termed "the leprosy of industrialism." [38] This poem expresses Lawrence's vision of the man-made nightmare of the dominance of the machine:

In another country, black poplars shake themselves over a
    pond,
And rooks and the rising smoke-waves scatter and wheel from
    the works beyond:
The air is dark with north and with sulphur, the grass is a
    darker green,
And people darkly invested with purple move palpable
    through the scene.

Soundlessly down across the counties, out of the resonant
    gloom

That wraps the north in stupor and purple travels the deep,
    slow boom
Of the man-life north imprisoned, shut in the hum of the pur-
    pled steel
As it spins to sleep on its motion, drugged dense in the sleep
    of the wheel.

Out of the sleep, from the gloom of motion, soundlessly,
    somnambule
Moans and booms the soul of a people imprisoned, asleep in
    the rule
Of the strong machine that runs mesmeric, booming the spell
    of its word
Upon them and moving them helpless, mechanic, their will to
    its will deferred.

Yet all the while comes the droning inaudible, out of the
    violet air,
The moaning of sleep-bound beings that toil and are will-less
    there
In the spell bound north, convulsive now with a dream near
    morning, strong
With violent achings, heaving to burst the sleep that is now
    not long.

Lawrence came to believe that the mechanical existence imposed
by the machine was related to mechanical behaviour in human relations. In each case what he dislikes is the imposition of a rigid
pattern on the spontaneous life that wells up from within. Genuine individuality, Lawrence feels, arises from one's impersonal elemental being. "Personality" is a superficial thing imposed by the
social mechanism.

None of this, of course, is explicit in "The North Country."
But such reflections are aroused by the fact that this is the only
early poem that directly anticipates the late poems of social
prophecy. And it will be important to the consideration of these

later poems to understand the connection between Lawrence's own problems and the sickness he discovered in the civilization that produced his parents, his lovers, and himself.

VI

It is evident that the young Lawrence was a poet of very great promise attempting to deal with important problems. "Reading Lawrence's early poems," observes W. H. Auden, "one is continually struck by the originality of the sensibility and the conventionality of the expressive means." [39] Or, as Lawrence himself put it, the poems are "struggling to say something which it takes a man twenty years to be able to say." [40] If they do not always succeed, even in their revised versions, it is because the manner is not really appropriate to the matter. The poet has not found his own idiom, his way of happening."

The young poet's need, whether he understood it or not, was to present his own experience with such honesty and immediacy and precision that it would reveal its meaning to him and enable him to heal his inner divisions. But rhymed, metrical verse imposes a regularity on the expression of experience, placing it at a certain distance from the reader. This may, of course, be a good thing; in "Giorno Dei Morti," for instance, the stately rhyme and rhythm are highly appropriate to the event—a funeral procession. But Lawrence was not the kind of artist who wishes to make such patterns for their own sake. He wished always to find the pattern that was inherent in the immediate experience. For the most part, this meant that he worked best with the shaping rhythms of free verse, since he was determined to express his own most intimate and intense experience—he did not seek for distance but for a certain impersonality. And he sought to justify what might otherwise have seemed merely a monstrous self-indulgence by asserting that his experience was a microcosmic part of the psychic experience of a whole civilization.

When he understood what it was he had to do, Lawrence spoke of the "poetry of the present," "poetry whose very permanency lies in its wind-like transit." [41] Traditional forms were too final, too perfect to express one's experience of the present moment. The great Victorians—Tennyson, Swinburne, Meredith, Hardy, Browning—had worked in forms that were largely irrelevant to Lawrence's needs. Of all the poets he admired as a youth, only Whitman offered him a means of expression appropriate to his need.

> Whitman pruned away his clichés—perhaps his clichés of rhythm as well as of phrase. And this is about all we can do, deliberately, with free verse. We can get rid of the stereotyped movements and the old hackneyed associations of sound or sense. We can break down those artificial conduits and canals through which we do so love to force our utterance. We can break the stiff neck of habit. We can be in ourselves spontaneous and flexible as flame, we can see that utterance rushes out without artificial form or artificial smoothness. But we cannot positively prescribe any motion, any rhythm. All the laws we invent or discover—it amounts to pretty much the same—will fail to apply to free verse. They will apply to some form of restricted, limited unfree verse.[42]

Free verse, for Lawrence, is verse that finds the appropriate rhythmic and verbal expression for the immediate experience. It will then seem "instantaneous like plasm." And each poem will have its own order. "The law," says Lawrence, "must come new each time from within."

Lawrence wrote this piece in 1919. He felt that it could serve as an introduction to *Look! We Have Come Through!* But it took him some time to prune away his own clichés. Not until *Birds, Beasts and Flowers* did his practice really overtake his theory. Though he attempts free verse at times in *Look! We Have Come Through!*, most of these poems lack the definitive shape and compelling authority of the best poems of the later collection. Before 1920 Lawrence was an apprentice poet, albeit one who wrote a number of memorable poems.

The best early poems are highly readable. One is inclined to ignore the formal defects of poems so immediate and moving as "Discord in Childhood," "Lightning," or "End of Another Home Holiday." The lyricism of "A White Blossom" and "The Bride" is perhaps just a trifle *fin de siècle* and precious in nature, but it has its own pleasures. And the charming transparency of "After the Opera," which resembles some of the early Pound and Eliot poems set in London, suggests that this is indeed a poet who may develop a new kind of poetic art.

Far from being a limited poet, the young Lawrence seems to have been aware of too many possible kinds of poem—traditional lyric, dramatic monologue, ballad, imagist description, free verse. What he needed was a poetic idiom that would enable him to fuse his various but related impulses—lyric, dramatic, prophetic, analytic, descriptive—in single poems of commanding quality.

❧ Two

Sufficiency of Death:

Look! We Have Come Through!

and the War Poems

I

In *Look! We Have Come Through!* Lawrence attempted to make a book of poems that would have the effect of an important long poem. His most sympathetic critics have honoured him for his good intentions. In her long review Amy Lowell declared:

> "Look! We Have Come Through!" is an amazing book. It is to my mind a greater novel even than "Sons and Lovers", for all that it is written in a rather disconnected series of poems.[1]

And Kenneth Rexroth has written that in the Rhine Journey poems poetry becomes "vision, the pure act of sensual communion and contemplation," for here "everything stands out lit by a light not of this earth and at the same time completely of this earth, the light of the Holy Sacrament of Marriage, whose source is the wedded body of the bride." [2] Harry T. Moore makes the same point somewhat less rhapsodically, when he says that the *Look!* poems "are essentially a prothalamion—a great marriage poem, a celebration of conjugality, a festival of love." [3] But, unfortunately, Lawrence's performance does not equal his conception. *Look! We Have Come Through!* may well be more impressive than any of the other collections of poems Lawrence published before 1920, but it is just as uneven. As Rexroth has noted, there are several kinds of poem in the sequence, and some are much more successful than others.

The great subject of the sequence is marriage, or, as Lawrence puts it, the "conflict of love and hate . . . between the man and the woman," a conflict which is finally transcended in "some condition of blessedness." [4] The first poem, "Moonrise," suggests the kind of blessedness in which Lawrence believes:

> And who has seen the moon, who has not seen
> Her rise from out of the chamber of the deep,
> Flushed and grand and naked, as from the chamber
> Of finished bridegroom, seen her rise and throw
> Confession of delight upon the wave,
> Littering the waves with her own superscription
> Of bliss, till all her lambent beauty shakes towards us
> Spread out and known at last, and we are sure
> That beauty is a thing beyond the grave,
> That perfect, bright experience never falls
> To nothingness, and time will dim the moon
> Sooner than our full consummation here
> In this odd life will tarnish or pass away.

This poem, consciously somewhat bardic in tone, asserts that there is a kind of permanence (or eternity) residing in the perfection of the present moment. This is not the intersection of the timeless with time, as in Eliot's *Four Quartets*, but a quality of timelessness that is inherent in every moment that is experienced to the full. The beauty of the rising moon is like that of a bride emerging from her marriage chamber to confess her delight in love. The moon shaken out on the waters is "known at last." The speaker is somehow assured by the spectacle of the moon spread out in bright flux that the full beauty of his own consummation is perfect and can never be lost. It would seem, then, that the notion of the moon and her bridegroom in their cosmic chamber is meant as a mythic expression of the union of the lovers in their own sphere. More important than the myth itself, however, is the suggestion that it seems to convey. Does the consummation of the man and woman have its chief significance as a part of some larger consummation? In *Birds, Beasts and Flowers* this question is answered.

In "Moonrise" Lawrence anticipates the conclusion to the story that *Look! We Have Come Through!* is intended to tell. Later poems restore to us the grief-stricken mother's boy of Eastwood. But even in his grief Lawrence is able to see that such meaning as the artist or any man makes in his life must proceed from his knowledge of the impersonal sea of darkness. In "Hymn to Priapus," one of his finest poems, he commits himself to life *because* he is consciously committed to death:

> My love lies underground
> With her face upturned to mine,
> And her mouth unclosed in the last long kiss
> That ended her life and mine.
>
> She fares in the stark immortal
> Fields of death;
> I in these goodly, frozen
> Fields beneath.
>
> Something in me remembers
> And will not forget.
> The stream of my life in the darkness
> Deathward set!
>
> And something in me has forgotten,
> Has ceased to care.
> Desire comes up, and contentment
> Is debonair.
>
> I, who am worn and careful,
> How much do I care?

How is it I grin then, and chuckle
Over despair?

Grief, grief, I suppose and sufficient
Grief makes us free
To be faithless and faithful together
As we have to be.

It is sufficiency of grief, the sufficient reliving of the experience
of loss, that makes it possible for Lawrence to go on to a new
life. The occasion for this reflection is his initiation of a "big, soft
country lass," one for whom he feels as he felt for the girl in
"Snap-Dragon." It is significant that in this later poem Lawrence
seems to have overcome his own feelings of guilt, and the manner
in which he does so is instructive:

Now I am going home
Fulfilled and alone,
I see the great Orion standing
Looking down.

He's the star of my first beloved
Love-making.
The witness of all that bitter-sweet
Heart-aching.

Now he sees this as well,
This last commission.
Nor do I get any look
Of admonition.

He can add the reckoning up
I suppose, between now and then,
Having walked himself in the thorny difficult
Ways of men.

He has done as I have done
No doubt:

Remembered and forgotten
Turn and about.

Here, Lawrence appeals to a cosmic male figure for authority
(reminding us, as he does so, of his unsatisfying relations with
Miriam), and asserts that Orion, who has been a man, must have
done as he has done. In this he seems, consciously or unconsciously, to identify himself with his father. In this complex poem
the hopeless love for the mother recedes a little, and the worship
of Priapus is brought to the fore.

In fact, this poem marks a new phase in the protagonist's
psychic growth. "Ballad of a Wilful Woman" develops, in
mythic terms, the story of his mating with a woman who is already married. This woman, like Ursula Brangwen in *The Rainbow*, needs a visionary or demon lover. She leaves her child and
her husband, significantly called Joseph, for a mysterious wandering beggar who distills curious liquors and attempts to sell them
in the market place. He takes her to Patmos, supposedly the
dwelling-place of the author of the Book of Revelation, at one
point in the poem. Lawrence would seem here to be depicting
himself as one of those "sons of God" who take the daughters of
men for brides. He, the visionary artist, is a revelation to the wife
of Joseph, the annunciation of a new and sometimes difficult way
of life. The new way apparently requires a rejection, or, at the
least, a considerable revision of the Christian myth, but the inten-
tional blasphemy is not fully developed in this poem. What is
chiefly noteworthy is that Lawrence sees his elopement and
struggle with Frieda Weekley not as an ordinary love story but
as the intense religious experience of a prophet or (as John Middleton Murry eventually saw it) a "daemonic" man.[5] His marriage is intended to have a religious significance beyond the personal fulfilment it will bring.*

* *Cf. Letters* (p. 237): "Don't put my 'Ballad of a Wayward Woman'
lightly aside. It is woman trying the various ideals—Aphrodite, Apostle
John etc." This comment raises the possibility that the several lovers of

This is clear even in the intensely personal poems that follow. The poems from "Moonrise" to "Ballad of a Wilful Woman" are introductory poems in traditional modes. Those that follow are looser, more organic in structure and more immediate in expression:

In front of the sombre mountains, a faint, lost ribbon of rain-
     bow;
And between us and it, the thunder;
And down below in the green wheat, the labourers
Stand like dark stumps, still in the green wheat.

("On the Balcony")

As always, one is made aware of Lawrence's intense appreciation of the visible world. But there is also the knowledge of darkness and of the lovers' immediate problems.

"She Looks Back" combines the prophetic and the personal themes. The controlling metaphor here is Frieda as "Lot's wife" looking back to England and her children. To the degree that she looks back she is as a pillar of salt to him, "devastating the vision." In her yearning for her children she becomes an image of *his* mother, one that summons up the anguished past instead of the visionary consummated present. Frieda is Lot's wife because she will not completely abandon her past for his vision. For Lawrence now sees the England they have fled as Sodom, a place where human relations are perverted by a wicked mechanical civilization.*

the poem are meant to be distinct. I am inclined, however, to see them as aspects of Lawrence. The naked man in the foam of the first and second parts and the prophet of the third and fourth parts are combined in the artist of the fifth and sixth parts.

* Cf. the conclusion of "The Lemon Gardens" in *Twilight in Italy* (p. 53): "I thought of England, the great mass of London, and the black, fuming, laborious Midlands and north-country. . . . There was London and the industrial counties spreading like a blackness over all the world, horrible, in the end destructive. And the Garda was so lovely under the sky of sunshine, it was intolerable. Far away, beyond, beyond all the snowy

In several poems the woman retaliates by accusing the man of
attempting to imprison her and destroy her with his own perverse morbidity and gloom. She confesses that she is afraid of his
"darkness" and finds it painful to love him. In "Mutilation" he acknowledges, for his part, that his life would be meaningless if she
left him. This poem ends with the first of Lawrence's poetic in-
vocations to the dark gods:

> She too suffers.
> But who could compel her if she chose me against them all?
> She has not chosen me finally, she suspends her choice.
> Night folk, Tuatha De Danaan, dark gods, govern her sleep,
> Magnificent ghosts of the darkness, carry off her decision in
>   sleep,
> Leave her no choice, make her lapse me-ward, make her,
> Oh Gods of the living Darkness, powers of Night.

The Tuatha De Danaan are dark gods of ancient Ireland; Lawrence probably discovered them in the early work of Yeats. In all
these poems he insists on the importance of his awareness of the
dark, "other" half of life, and hopes that the unacknowledged
powers deep within her will make Frieda want to stay with him.*

His prayer seems to have been answered in "Green," a tiny imagist lyric that nevertheless conveys intimations of Eden and of
communion with the moon and the sky:

> The dawn was apple-green,
>   The sky was green wine held up in the sun,
> The moon was a golden petal between.

Alps, with the iridescence of eternal ice above them, was this England,
black and foul and dry, with her soul worn down, almost worn away. And
England was conquering the world with her machines and her horrible
destruction of natural life."
  * Cf. D. H. Lawrence: A Composite Biography (Vol. III, p. 467): "I must
just tell you how Lawrence died, so splendidly that I am filled with admiration—you do understand, he gave me most of my life and now he gave
me death—that great other that I knew nothing about." (Letter from Frieda
Lawrence to Brewster Ghiselin, March 31, 1930)

She opened her eyes, and green
  They shone, clear like flowers undone
For the first time, now for the first time seen.

The lady has eyes that open like a flower for the first time. She reveals herself, unfolds herself to her lover as a flower unfolds itself.

The symbol of the rose dominates the next few poems. In "River Roses" a reconciliation between light and darkness, night and day, is suggested:

By the Isar, in the twilight
We were wandering and singing,
By the Isar, in the evening
We climbed the huntsman's ladder and sat swinging
In the fir-tree overlooking the marshes,
While river met with river, and the ringing
Of their pale-green glacier water filled the evening.

By the Isar, in the twilight
We found the dark wild roses
Hanging red at the river; and simmering
Frogs were singing, and over the river closes
Was savour of ice and of roses; and glimmering
Fear was abroad. We whispered: "No one knows us.
Let it be as the snake disposes
Here in this simmering marsh."

At this place, where two rivers meet in a kind of mysterious deepening twilight, love is balanced by fear. The two seem inextricably mingled. Dark and light, ice and roses, fear and love are not only contrasted but joined in the final surrender to the simmering marsh. That this surrender is expressed in the image of the snake suggests that there is something necessarily predatory in love, and that this must be accepted as a natural part of it. Such a statement is reminiscent of "Love on the Farm" and looks forward to "Snake." But this is altogether a more subtle and ambivalent poem. It retains an air of mystery not found in the others.

Some of its meaning may be suggested in passages from *Twilight in Italy:*

> In the rosy snow that shone in heaven over darkened earth was the ecstasy of consummation. Night and day are one, light and dark are one, both the same in the origin and in the issue, both the same in the moment of ecstasy, light fused in darkness and darkness fused in light, as in the rosy snow above the twilight.[6]
>
> Where then is the meeting-point: where in mankind is the ecstasy of light and dark together, the supreme transcendence of the afterglow, day hovering in the embrace of the coming night like two angels embracing in the heavens, like Eurydice in the arms of Orpheus, or Persephone embraced by Pluto?
>
> Where is the supreme ecstasy in mankind, which makes day a delight and night a delight, purpose an ecstasy and a concourse in ecstasy, and single abandon of the single body and soul also an ecstasy under the moon? Where is the transcendent knowledge in our hearts uniting sun and darkness, day and night, spirit and senses? Why do we not know that the two in consummation are one; that each is only part; partial and alone for ever; but that the two in consummation are perfect, beyond the range of loneliness or solitude? [7]

Here, as always, Lawrence is concerned about integrity of being through the union of the spirit and the senses. It is significant that, in searching for a mythic statement of this idea, he refers not only to the marriage of Pluto and Persephone and that of Orpheus and Eurydice, but to "two angels embracing in the heavens." Again, he is close to Rilke, and even to Rilke's myth (though Lawrence's angels are rather different from Rilke's, as we shall see), in his attempt to integrate light and darkness in one transcendent whole.

The rose itself, as Lawrence well knew, can symbolize such perfect wholeness. In the superb "Gloire de Dijon" the bride is seen in terms of the rose: the woman reveals herself to the man as a flower reveals itself, opening to its full glory. The beautiful woman somehow belongs to the same order of being as the most beautiful of roses.

In the following, less intense poems the symbolism of the rose becomes more explicit. In "Roses on the Breakfast Table" the roses are images of the man's disclosed self. A natural analogy is used to express the transfiguring power of a love whose goal is the growth and perfect unfolding of the individual self of each lover. Lawrence should probably have left well enough alone, and ended this small sequence here. "I am like a rose" is merely a banal restatement of the obvious, and "Rose of all the World" an unnecessarily didactic extension of it:

> Is that it, woman? Does it strike you so?
> The Great Breath blowing a tiny seed of fire
> Fans out your petals for excess of flame,
> Till all your being smokes with fine desire?

Here, as in "Virgin Youth," Lawrence achieves an unintended comedy. In this poem, however, he does manage to express his belief that it is flowering and not fecundity that matters. The flowering of love exists not primarily for the children it may bring to birth but for its own sake in "fiery transiency." This is heaven and perfection enough, the cosmic or alchemical rose.*

* The earlier version of the rose-sequence, called "All of Roses," was briefer and was more purely a celebration of Frieda. "River Roses" was wholly idyllic; there was no snake. Lawrence made it more powerfully suggestive in revision. On the other hand, the later poems of the sequence were less sententious in their earlier versions. (*Complete Poems*, pp. 948–49.) Probably, Lawrence's revisions have to do with feelings expressed in the wartime essay "The Reality of Peace": "This is when I am like a rose, when I balance for a space in pure adjustment and pure understanding. The timeless quality of *being* is understanding; when I understand fully, flesh and blood and bone, and mind and soul and spirit one rose of unison, then I *am*. Then I am unrelated and perfect. In true understanding I am always perfect and timeless. In my utterance of that which I have understood I am timeless as a jewel." (*Phoenix*, p. 680.) The rose is a symbol of wholeness, perfected single being. Love is only part of the means to this individual goal.

The following poems are, with some exceptions, less coherent and less well-shaped, but they serve to advance the "story." Once again the conflict of love and hate between the man and the woman is brought to the fore. The man demands that the woman be serious about their relationship and not treat it as just another romantic adventure. The prophet needs a woman's support if he is to struggle with his vision. She must therefore commit herself wholly to him, accepting as she does so that she will hate as well as love him. For the limitation imposed by a genuine relationship is hateful to human beings. Eventually, the woman undergoes a new birth in her acceptance of the man. "Paradise Re-entered" celebrates the achievement of an elemental being beyond conventional conceptions of good and evil. The lovers are burned "clean by remorseless hate." They fuse their pain and their joy, and return through "the strait gate of passion" to Eden, the "primal loam." Unfortunately, this triumph is expressed in heavy-handed rhymes, peculiar inversions and language of excruciating banality:

> The Lord of Hosts and the Devil
> Are left on Eternity's level
> Field, and as victors we travel
> To Eden home.
>
> Back beyond good and evil
> Return we. Even dishevel
> Your hair for the bliss-drenched revel
> On our primal loam.

"Even" was a misprint that persisted even to 1967; the original *Look! We Have Come Through!* had "Eve," [8] and the *Collected Poems* of 1928 also had "Eve." [9] "Even" appears only in the Phoenix *Complete Poems* of 1957.[10] But even when this is corrected, in the 1970 edition, the poem may serve as a good indication of how bad a poet Lawrence can be when he does not find a concrete embodiment or objective correlative for his ideas. It is, paradoxically, his urgent intellectual passion that causes him sometimes to mistreat the language in this way.

A number of the *Look!* poems are, though in varying degrees, quite successful in themselves. In "A Doe at Evening," for instance, there is a complete clarity of statement and purpose:

As I went through the marshes
a doe sprang out of the corn
and flashed up the hill-side
leaving her fawn.

On the sky-line
she moved round to watch,
she pricked a fine black blotch
on the sky.

I looked at her
and felt her watching;
I became a strange being.
Still, I had my right to be there with her.

Her nimble shadow trotting
along the sky-line, she
put back her fine, level-balanced head.
And I knew her.

Ah yes, being male, is not my head hard-balanced, antlered?
Are not my haunches light?
Has she not fled on the same wind with me?
Does not my fear cover her fear?

In this magical and delicate poem Lawrence perceives the doe so truly and completely that he becomes a stag. She is a living creature like himself, and she is female to his male. As in the best poems of *Birds, Beasts and Flowers*, Lawrence puts himself, insofar as this is possible, inside the skin of an animal. He is able to do this because he senses the flowing life in the beast that is akin to his own life. This perception of the final unity of separate and distinct living things is surely part of the meaning of all those fables in which men become stags or other animals. Wordsworth's ability to see into "the life of things" is shared by Lawrence to a very high degree.

"Meeting Among the Mountains" is a far more ambitious poem. In it Lawrence attempts to relate his own guilt in taking a woman from another man to the general guilt imposed on western man by Christianity. In fact, the spirit of this poem is that of Swinburne's famous attack on Christ:

> Thou hast conquered, O pale Galilean; the world has grown
>   grey from thy breath;
> We have drunken of things Lethean, and fed on the fulness of
>   death.
>
> ("Hymn to Proserpine")

This much is clear from the poem itself. What is not made clear is the nature of the wrong that fills the speaker with guilt and causes him to identify not only a wooden Christ but a passing bullock-driver with the wronged man. If the reader is lenient, he will allow that the reason for guilt is given in earlier poems of the *Look! We Have Come Through!* sequence. But how is the bullock-driver like Frieda's husband? And in what sense is the husband's misery and hate appropriately expressed in the image of Christ? These relationships are not developed fully enough for the poem to be wholly successful.* But the poem retains a haunting power.

---

* But *cf. Twilight in Italy* (p. 10) and *Women in Love* (p. 465), where similar incidents occur. Gerald is somehow destroyed by Christ, and the peasant in *Twilight in Italy* fears and respects Christ the Deadly One. Obviously, Lawrence feels that Christ has come to be the appropriate symbol for the most life-denying and repressive forces in Christian cultures.

"History" examines the process by which the lovers "come through":

The listless beauty of the hour
When snow fell on the apple-trees,
And the wood-ash gathered in the fire
And we faced our first miseries.

Then the sweeping sunshine of noon
When the mountains like chariot cars
Were ranked to blue battle—and you and I
Counted our scars.

And then in a strange, grey hour
We lay mouth to mouth, with your face
Under mine like a star on the lake,
And I covered the earth, and all space.

The silent drifting hours
Of morn after morn
And night drifting up to the night
Yet no pathway worn.

Your life, and mine, my love
Passing on and on, the hate
Fusing closer and closer with love
Till at length they mate.

This is one of the more effective lyrics, since it begins with sharp images—snow, wood-ash, blue mountains—and then relates the conquest of "all space" to the act of love. Only the last two stanzas are a slight disappointment in their reversion to an abstract statement.

"The Song of a Man Who Has Come Through" is one of the

best and the most revealing of all Lawrence's poems. It is a statement both of his way of life and of his aesthetic:

> Not I, not I, but the wind that blows through me!
> A fine wind is blowing the new direction of Time.
> If only I let it bear me, carry me, if only it carry me!
> If only I am sensitive, subtle, oh, delicate, a winged gift!
> If only, most lovely of all, I yield myself and am borrowed
> By the fine, fine wind that takes its course through the chaos
>   of the world
> Like a fine, an exquisite chisel, a wedge-blade inserted;
> If only I am keen and hard like the sheer tip of a wedge
> Driven by invisible blows,
> The rock will split, we shall come at the wonder, we shall find
>   the Hesperides.
>
> Oh, for the wonder that bubbles into my soul,
> I would be a good fountain, a good well-head,
> Would blur no whisper, spoil no expression.
>
> What is the knocking?
> What is the knocking at the door in the night?
> It is somebody wants to do us harm.
>
> No, no, it is the three strange angels.
> Admit them, admit them.

The "three strange angels" are those who appeared to Abraham
in Genesis 18. In this chapter the Lord confides to Abraham his
plans to destroy Sodom. Abraham himself is to have a son, and is
to bear the seed of the future.[11] * Lawrence wrote years later to
his friend Earl Brewster: "Let us go from this Sodom of angels
like Lot and Abraham before the fire falls." [12] His feeling of the

---

* As evidence of Lawrence's interest in these angels, *cf. The Rainbow:*
"Once three angels stood in Abraham's doorway, and greeted him, and
stayed and ate with him, leaving his household enriched for ever when they
went" (p. 290). The emphasis is on the positive message, as in "Song."

impending doom of a corrupt civilization had, of course, been greatly intensified by the war. As a man of vision, Lawrence felt that he must prophesy the ending of the old order and the coming of the new.

This, then, is the meaning of the myth of Sodom in *Look! We Have Come Through!* Insofar as Frieda is not with him, she is Lot's wife, but when she is wholeheartedly with him, then he is able to be, not powerless in the wind of change, but its chosen instrument. "I believe," wrote Lawrence,

> there is no getting of a vision, as you call it, before we get our souls fertilized by the *female*. I don't mean the feminine: I mean the female. Because life tends to take two streams, male and female, and only some female influence (not necessarily woman, but most obviously woman) can fertilize the soul of man to vision of being. Then the vision we're after, I don't know what it is—but it is something that contains awe and dread and submission, not pride or sensuous egotism and assertion. I went to the British Museum—and I know, from the Egyptian and Assyrian sculpture—what we are after. We want to realize the tremendous *non-human* quality of life—it is wonderful. It is not the emotions nor the personal feelings and attachments, that matter. These are all only expressive, and expression has become mechanical. Behind in all are the tremendous unknown forces of life, coming unseen and unperceived as out of the desert to the Egyptians, and driving us, forcing us, destroying us if we do not submit to be swept away.[13]

In art and in life one must respond to the "tremendous unknown forces" that underlie those conventions and expressions that have become mechanical. For this, a new expression must be found. Thus Lawrence welcomes the warning angels. And his concern for the new order that will arise from the destruction of the old explains the presence of angels and of the "Luminous Ghost" in the war poems "Ruination" and "The Attack," of which more later.

The myth of Sodom is combined in "Song" with that of the Hesperides, a variant of the return to Eden. To achieve this end,

Lawrence must yield himself up, surrender himself consciously to the elemental impulses welling up within. "If only I am sensitive, subtle, oh, delicate, a winged gift!" This is not only a way to personal happiness and social regeneration. It is the way to write a good poem. If only he can yield himself with subtlety and delicacy to his emotions, Lawrence believes, and make the required "new effort of attention," these emotions will suggest their own proper form. It is just this patience and discipline that he must learn in order to be able to write poems like "Snake," poems that "blur no whisper, spoil no expression." "I have always tried to get an emotion out in its own course without altering it," he wrote to Edward Marsh. "It needs the finest instinct imaginable, much finer than the skill of the craftsmen." [14] And here, in "The Song of a Man Who Has Come Through," the joyful urgency of the emotion is perfectly embodied in the urgency of the rhythm; the shape of such a free-verse poem is created by the rhythm of the emotion itself when it first expresses itself as sound. The poet must attend to this original shaping rhythm just as carefully as he attends to the visible world in developing his imagery.

"One Woman to All Women," the following poem, is a celebration of the star-equilibrium achieved by the lovers. It expresses Lawrence's idea of polarity, the proper balanced relationship between the sexes. Such a relationship is both "human" (involving particular individuals) and "inhuman" (in tune with the elemental energies of the cosmos). Lawrence's own nature, his fear of possessive mother-love, demands a cosmic extension (or projection) of his love for Frieda. The lovers must hold each other in their places as the stars do.

This is given a more dramatic expression in " 'She Said As Well to Me.' " The woman proclaims her joy in the man's body, which she describes as the perfect instrument of God, but the man is not flattered by such appreciation and instead rebukes her. One must, he argues, acknowledge the unique "otherness" of the loved one as one respects the strangeness of animals. In this poem, as later in

Birds, Beasts and Flowers, Lawrence asserts that the best and most natural relationship is not "merging" or the attempt of one person to possess and know another absolutely. It is the commitment of two free individuals who respect each other's strangeness. Lawrence's ideal star-lovers are like Rilke's two solitudes that protect one another's aloneness.

It is the "otherness" of the beloved that is sacred. In "New Heaven and Earth" Lawrence discovers a whole new world of objective reality. As the poem develops it becomes clear that the new world has its source in the body of the beloved. The speaker becomes, in the words of Horace Gregory, a type of Adam, "the new man waking at his wife's side, her breasts the new world's mountains and the hollows of her body its valleys, and its orifices the deep mystery of oblivion and resurrection." [15]

The poem begins with the announcement of a new world:

> And so I cross into another world
> shyly and in homage linger for an invitation
> from this unknown that I would trespass on.
>
> I am very glad, and all alone in the world,
> all alone, and very glad, in a new world
> where I am disembarked at last.

In Parts II and III Lawrence says that he was weary of the old world because "it was all tainted with myself," perfectly self-enclosed and self-referring, and thus "a maniacal horror in the end." So poisonous was his self-consciousness that it became necessary to die in order to rise and view the world with innocent eyes.

> True, it is strange to inhabit the earth no longer,
> to use no longer customs scarcely acquired,
> not to interpret roses, and other things
> that promise so much, in terms of a human future;
> to be no longer all that one used to be

in endlessly anxious hands, and to lay aside
even one's proper name like a broken toy.
Strange, not to go on wishing one's wishes. Strange,
to see all that was once relation so loosely fluttering
hither and thither in space. And it's hard, being dead,
and full of retrieving before one begins to espy
a trace of eternity.—Yes, but all of the living,
make the mistake of drawing too sharp distinctions.
Angels (they say) are often unable to tell
whether they move among living or dead. The eternal
torrent whirls all the ages through either realm
for ever, and sounds above their voices in both.

This passage is not from Lawrence's poem, of course, though the
first ten lines or so could probably be incorporated fairly easily in
it, but from the first of Rilke's *Duino Elegies* (translated by
J. B. Leishman and Stephen Spender). In it the poet advises himself to adopt the point of view of the youthfully dead. For it is in
the full awareness of the mystery of death that one can experience the eternity of the present moment most purely. With a
very similar intent, Lawrence proceeds to discuss the war as a
necessary process of death for the old self. His expression is characteristically more violent and less economical than Rilke's. But
each is concerned with the rediscovery of the world about him.

In Part V of "New Heaven and Earth" the protagonist experiences a strange resurrection, and in VI this is seen to be accomplished by the touching of the unknown. In VII the discovery of
this sacred "other" is declared to be so overwhelming that it
leaves him "a madman in rapture." In VIII, finally, the new country is described:

Green streams that flow from the innermost continent of the
    new world,
what are they?
Green and illumined and travelling for ever,

dissolved with the mystery of the innermost heart of the continent,
mystery, beyond knowledge or endurance, so sumptuous
out of the well-heads of the new world.—
The other, she too has strange green eyes!
White sands and fruits unknown and perfumes that never
can blow across the dark seas to our usual world!
And land that beats with a pulse!
And valleys that draw close in love!
And strange ways where I fall into oblivion of uttermost living!—
Also she who is the other has strange-mounded breasts and
strange sheer slopes, and white levels.

Here, the significance of marriage for Lawrence is revealed more clearly than ever before. Woman is the great unknown, the other country, a constant reminder of the sacred mystery of potentiality in all living things. True marriage is a marriage with the whole universe of life, not a merging with it, but a recognition of related, individual expressions of the creative mystery. As Kenneth Rexroth has noted, the poems of *Birds, Beasts and Flowers* are direct results of such an apprehension:

> Beyond Holy Matrimony lies the newly valued world of birds, beasts and flowers—a sacramentalized, objective world. "Look, we have come through"—to a transformed world, with a glory around it everywhere like ground lightning. The poems of *Birds, Beasts and Flowers* have the same supernatural luster that shines through the figures of men and animals and things, busy being part of a new redeemed world, as they are found carved around the mandala of the Blessed Virgin above some cathedral door or on some rose window.[16]

In this respect "New Heaven and Earth" is the most important (though certainly not the best) poem of the *Look!* sequence. It is, as Anaïs Nin has written, "an allegory of Lawrence's cycle of experience." [17]

"Manifesto" extends the statement of "New Heaven and Earth." The speaker begins by admitting his debt to the woman, and then proceeds to speak of different kinds of hunger, concluding that the one deep and ravenous hunger he has known is the hunger for woman. Many women could not satisfy it, but one woman could. And this is the only real heaven he can imagine:

> Let them praise desire who will,
> but only fulfilment will do,
> real fulfilment, nothing short.
> It is our ratification,
> our heaven, as a matter of fact.
> Immortality, the heaven, is only a projection of this strange
> but actual fulfilment,
> here in the flesh.

For this he is grateful to the woman.

But she has yet to know him as he has known her. She thinks still that they are "all one piece," but this is "painfully untrue." She must perish through "being pressed up against the *other*," as he has done. "Then we shall be free, freer than angels, ah, perfect. . . . It is in pure, unalterable resolvedness, distinction of being, that one is free," contends Lawrence. This is the whole being possessed by his (as by Rilke's) angels and gods. It might, of course, be argued that the angels who are perfect in single being do not seem to be the same angels (or dark gods or life-impulses) that knock on the door in the night, but, in fact, they are. For these impulses from within, each in its turn, provide the "resolvedness" and "distinction of being" that makes man an angel— i.e., he is momentarily possessed by the angel (or demon) within, and thus becomes fully himself. This, for Lawrence, is genuine individuality as opposed to mere personality.

Characteristically, Lawrence will not be content with his and his woman's achievement of wholeness. In his vision of the future every man must be free:

Every man himself, and therefore, a surpassing singleness of
    mankind.
The blazing tiger will spring upon the deer, undimmed,
the hen will nestle over her chickens,
we shall love, we shall hate,
but it will be like music, sheer utterance,
issuing straight out of the unknown,
the lightning and the rainbow appearing in us, unbidden, un-
    checked,
like ambassadors.

We shall not look before and after.
We shall *be, now.*
We shall know in full.
We, the mystic NOW.

In the new dispensation both the tiger and the deer in us will
have, each in its turn, their full expression. We shall live in the
present moment, the present wonder. Each impulse of hatred or
love will be allowed full sway in a universe in which spontaneity
is the supreme virtue. A balance of hatred (or selfhood) and love
(or union) may thus be attained.*

One might be forgiven for thinking that the inevitable result of
such a program must be violent chaos. But a fairer expression of
Lawrence's doctrine will take into account the good sense of his
plea, here and elsewhere, for honesty in human relations. In a
very real sense our emotional impulses are "ambassadors," ambassadors come to tell us about our real feelings as opposed to our
conventionalized or imaginary ones. And our emotional health
depends to a considerable degree on the ability to release such

* *Cf.* "The Reality of Peace" (*Phoenix,* p. 693): "It is not of love that
we are fulfilled, but of love in such intimate equipoise with hate that the
transcendence takes place. It is not in pride that we are free, but in pride
so perfectly matched by meekness that we are liberated as into blossom.
There is a transfiguration, a rose with glimmering petals, upon a bush that
knew no more than the dusk of green leaves heretofore. There is a new
heaven and new earth, the heaven and earth of the perfect rose."

pent-up emotional energies. Lawrence believed, as we shall see, that it was the failure of the intellect to keep in touch with deep physical instincts that caused the war. In some way the ambassadors, or angels knocking at the door, had to be admitted so that they might achieve their momentary fulfilment.

Lawrence's insistence on the supremacy of the present moment is repeated in "Poetry of the Present." In the essay, as in the poem, he refers to Shelley's "To a Skylark," rejecting the point of view expressed in the line "We look before and after." His concern is the "incarnate carnal" present:

> The bird is on the wing in the winds, flexible to every breath, a living spark in the storm, its very flickering depending upon its supreme mutability and power of change. Whence such a bird came: whither it goes: from what solid earth it rose up, and upon what solid earth it will close its wings and settle, this is not the question. This is a question of before and after. Now, *now*, the bird is on the wing in the winds.
>
> Such is the rare new poetry. One realm we have never conquered: the pure present. One great mystery of time is terra incognita to us: the instant. The most superb mystery we have hardly recognized: the immediate instant self. The quick of all time is the instant. The quick of all the universe, of all creation, is the incarnate carnal self. Poetry gave us the clue: free verse: Whitman. Now we know.[18]

This, then, is the goal of Lawrence's free verse. Unfortunately, both "Manifesto" and "New Heaven and Earth" fail to achieve the kind of immediacy that is achieved in Lawrence's best poems. Poems as repetitive, abstract, and didactic as these can hardly give the reader much sense of the immediate experience. In "A Doe at Evening" and "Snake" Lawrence gives us the present. Here, he gives us occasional patches of impressive poetry surrounded by much abstract theorizing loosely arranged as verse. The rhythm is frequently rather limp, though it achieves a kind of urgency in the conclusion of "Manifesto," and the imagery is not sustained enough to be really effective. If, in "New Heaven and Earth," there were the vivid sense of a physical voyage that there is in "The Ship of Death," the poem would be much more impressive. Lawrence fails to dramatize or objectify his ideas sufficiently. He is content merely to assert them.

Any survey of *Look! We Have Come Through!* must conclude, I think, that it lacks stylistic unity. Moreover, a few poems —"Hymn to Priapus," "Bei Hennef," "On the Balcony," "River Roses," "Gloire de Dijon," "A Doe at Evening," "History," and "The Song of a Man Who Has Come Through"—are very much better than the rest. Nevertheless, one feels that somehow the whole is greater than the sum of its parts. There *is* a new world, however awkwardly it is presented, in these poems, the world of Lawrence's growing vision. The flight from England in 1912 and the union with Frieda have given the poet new insights into his own nature and experience. He has found brighter and more congenial landscapes than the industrial Midlands, and these are somehow symbolic of the new country of sexual fulfilment that he has come to occupy. The result is a poetry of absorbing interest. One feels that Lawrence has truly entered a new country, and that the process of exploration will continue, the vision achieve greater coherence and clarity

Conrad Aiken felt that Lawrence would have been better advised to tell his story in a novel than to experiment with verse forms. His whole argument is a very sophisticated one, but it reflects, nevertheless, the sort of commonsensical conservatism adopted by most of Lawrence's early reviewers—an eminent good sense that would have made the poet's coming breakthrough into a highly individual and effective idiom impossible. Lawrence's later poems surely demonstrate that he was correct in seeking his own way of expression. Such a flawed poem as "New Heaven and Earth" is still a voyage of discovery. The *Look!* poems are important because they mark Lawrence's liberation from old conceptions and clear the ground for his mature achievement as a poet.

II

This conflict is no invention of mine. It is acknowledged and exhibited, with a terrifying veracity, by Lawrence himself, in such a document as *Look we have come through*. It is a conflict in his most intimate being, in his relation with his wife, wherein the struggle between the light and the darkness, between love and hate, reaches an intensity far beyond any known to common experience. We need not doubt that, as Lawrence proclaimed, he (or rather they) had emerged from this conflict, with his personality intact, but deepened. But, on top of this, and at a moment when he may be fairly described as convalescent rather than completely re- covered, came the disaster of the war. An apocalypse in the macro- cosm followed hard upon an apocalypse in the microcosm. It was the same organic sensibility which had to endure both.[19]

These remarks of John Middleton Murry may help to suggest the way in which Lawrence felt personally involved in the war. His discomfort in the jingoistic climate of the war years may be seen in the "Nightmare" chapter of *Kangaroo*. More important than this is the vision of a sick and suicidal civilization that is ex- pressed here as well:

In Sicily, a sudden fear, in the night of some single murderer, some single thing hovering as it were out of the violent past, with the intent of murder. Out of the old Greek past, that had been so vivid, sometimes an unappeased spirit of murderous-hate against the usurping moderns. A sudden presence of murder in the air, be- cause of something which the modern psyche has excluded, some old and vital thing which Christianity has cut out. An old spirit, waiting for vengeance.[20]

In Cornwall, too, in the war years Lawrence felt the continuing presence of druidic blood-sacrifice in the atmosphere. He be- lieved that it was because these ancient human impulses were ex- cluded from its scheme that the Christian civilization had ex- ploded in violence.

John Middleton Murry, who lived for a while with the Lawrences in Cornwall, tells us that Lawrence "made the communion of physical love into a kind of sacrament by which he participated in the horror and destruction of the war." [21] Murry was then repelled by such a process, but it would seem that Lawrence hoped that by openly expressing in his relationship with Frieda the closeness of love and hate, he might free himself from the polarization of human energy created by Christianity. Murry has expressed the personal application of this notion fairly well:

> . . . according to him [Lawrence], it is the exclusion of this dark, demonic encounter at the level where love and hate are not differentiated, from the modern experience of sexual love which has made it so shallow and nervous a thing, in which, beneath the outward appearance and profession of love, there is a vast accumulation of suppressed and unsatisfied hate.[22]

The important thing in any consideration of Lawrence's war poems is that he extends this theory to social and political relationships as well. It is, in Lawrence's view, the repressed hatred (or perhaps, more accurately, the aggressive instinct) underlying the Christian profession of ideal love, that has caused the war. Somehow, as in the wartime essay, "The Crown," the lion of power through the fulfilment of the senses must achieve a proper balance with the unicorn of love through the fulfilment of the spirit.

In 1915 Lawrence wrote to Lady Cynthia Asquith:

> If I love, then, I am in direct opposition to the principle of war. If war prevails, I do not love. If love prevails, there is no war. War is a great and necessary disintegrating autumnal process, like spring, the making of an integral unity out of many disintegrated factors. We have had enough of the disintegrating process. If it goes on any further, we shall so thoroughly have destroyed the unifying force from among us, we shall have become each one of us so completely a separate entity, that the whole will be an amor-

phous heap, like sand, sterile, hopeless, useless, like a dead tree. This is true, and it is so great a danger, that one almost goes mad facing it.[23]

And again, a week later:

When I drive across this country, with autumn falling and rustling to pieces, I am so sad, for my country, for this great wave of civilisation, 2000 years, which is now collapsing, that it is hard to live. . . . It has been 2000 years, the spring and summer of our era. What then, will the winter be? [24]

He saw the war as the death agony of the old order, but he came to hope that it might also be the birth pangs of the new.

In "Noise of Battle," the first war poem in the selection that he included in his *Collected Poems*, Lawrence depicts the war as a great eruption of the mysterious sea of darkness:

An invisible woe unseals
    The flood, so it passes beyond
        All bounds: the great old city
Recumbent roars as it feels
    The foamy paw of the pond
        Reach from immensity.

But all that it can do
    Now, as the tide rises,
        Is to listen and hear the grim
Waves crash like thunder through
    The splintered streets, hear noises
        Roll hollow in the interim.

The suggestion here would seem to be that one must attend to this phenomenon of war in order to learn its meaning. In a sense, the war is an ambassador from the unknown. One must discover the "invisible woe."

Another poem, "Ruination," reminds us once again of Lawrence's angels:

The sun is bleeding its fires upon the mist
That huddles in grey heaps coiling and holding back.
Like cliffs abutting in shadow a dead grey sea
Some street-ends thrust forward their stack.

On the misty waste lands, away from the flushing grey
Of the morning, the elms are loftily dimmed, and tall
As if moving in air towards us, tall angels,
Of darkness advancing steadily over us all.

These angels of darkness advancing on Christian Europe are mes-
sengers of doom, but perhaps also of renewal. In "The Attack"
the light from the assault is seen as a religious revelation:

In front of the terrible rage, the death,
This wonder stood glistening!
All shapes of wonder, with suspended breath
Arrested listening

In ecstatic reverie;
The whole, white Night!—
With wonder, every black tree
Blossomed outright.

I saw the transfiguration
And the present Host.
Transubstantiation
Of the luminous Ghost.

Here, the black trees of "Ruination" break into strange blossom.
It is evident that Lawrence hopes the war may in the end prepare
the ground for a new world. Thus, he describes a Zeppelin as a
"new world in the heavens" in a letter to Lady Ottoline Morrell:

So it seems our cosmos has burst, burst at last, the stars and
moon blown away, the envelope of the day burst out, and a new
cosmos appeared; with a long-ovate, gleaming central luminary,

calm and drifting in a glow of light, like a new moon, with its
light bursting in flashes on the earth, to burst away the earth also.
So it is the end—our world is gone and we are like dust in the air.

But there must be a new heaven and a new earth, a clearer eternal moon above, and a clean world below. So it will be.[25]

Lawrence, then, sees the war as the inevitable explosive clearing of
the rotten old order. Thus, the explosion in "The Attack" may
be likened to the Host. For there *is* a kind of transfiguration
going on, a transformation of values that will ultimately create a
new civilization. The "Luminous Ghost" or Mystery is to have a
new incarnation. As in "New Heaven and Earth," a sufficiency of
death will bring new life.

Something of this view may be detected in "Bombardment," a
brief imagist treatment of the bombing of London:

> The Town has opened to the sun.
> Like a flat red lily with a million petals
> She unfolds, she comes undone.
>
> A sharp sky brushes upon
> The myriad glistening chimney-tips
> As she gently exhales to the sun.
>
> Hurrying creatures run
> Down the labyrinth of the sinister flower.
> What is it they shun?
>
> A dark bird falls from the sun.
> It curves in a rush to the heart of the vast
> Flower: the day has begun.

In its sexual imagery this poem resembles "Green." Here, such
imagery seems designed to suggest the possibility of new birth in
this deathly consummation. A new day has begun. The sharpness
of image and the absence of overt theorizing make this probably
the most finished and satisfying of Lawrence's war poems.

"Town in 1917" suggests the character of the new London that is born of war:

London
Original, wolf-wrapped
In pelts of wolves, all her luminous
Garments gone.

London, with hair
Like a forest darkness, like a marsh
Of rushes, ere the Romans
Broke in her lair.

It is well
That London, lair of sudden
Male and female darknesses,
Has broken her spell.

The primitive force that existed under the conventions of the old order is now revealed. Lawrence thinks this is for the best.*

But he does not forget the cost in human misery. In a number of poems he attempts to imagine the feelings and experiences of men at the front. In "Winter-Lull," for example, he imagines soldiers lost in a world of silent snow, "folded . . . into nullity" and "disastrously silence bound," and in "Going Back" he depicts a soldier who thinks of the front as "Pure relief" because there he can exist in the "perfected / Presence of men," the significant hour of intense activity that is a point of balance, an "axis" or "pivot." This man has surrendered himself mindlessly to the impersonal process of war in order to be able to bear the agony of dissolution.

---

* By contrast, his view of London in 1915 was more like T. S. Eliot's vision of the early twenties. Lawrence wrote: "London seems to me like some hoary massive underworld, a hoary ponderous inferno. The traffic flows through the rigid grey streets like the rivers of hell through their banks of dry, rocky ash." (*Letters*, p. 339)

Lawrence's own attitude is expressed in "The Reality of Peace, 1916." He wrote to Lady Cynthia Asquith in this year:

> Peace and war lie in the heart, in the *desire*, of the people—say what you will. Germany, nations—are external facts. The reality of peace, the reality of war, lies in the hearts of the people: you, me, all the rest.[26]

And Herbert Asquith, Lady Cynthia's husband and son to the Prime Minister, has left this account of Lawrence's views in 1915:

> He seemed to assume—almost as a matter of course—that the cause of the evil was the "will to destroy", existing in the nature of each individual fighter, and that the cause of the war was the sum of all these separate desires demanding their satisfaction.[27]

In the poem Lawrence presents the war as a process of seeds being scattered. Each seed is a "knot of life" to be unravelled. What, he asks himself, "is it internecine that is locked" within the "storm of corrosion" in the autumn? We cannot know, he concludes, but must wait attentively for "new florescence." One must endure, but one cannot know the exact nature of the new world that is to come. "The blue grain" or spark of creative life must somehow be preserved (in the hearts of the people where the reality of war and the reality of peace lie) for its next flowering. This is the burden of Lawrence's meaning, but unfortunately the poem is expressed so obscurely that one needs to turn to the letters and other evidences of Lawrence's wartime attitudes to be able to decipher it. It is perhaps worth noting here that Lawrence will use images of falling leaves and fruit to much better effect in his late poems.

In "Erinnyes" Lawrence writes of the angry dead who possess the living, spreading an atmosphere of terror and hysteria. Somehow, these spirits of vengeance must be appeased and accommodated if there is to be an end to the vicious cycle of death and murder. As he sought fulfilment in the flesh to appease the spirit of his mother within him, Lawrence now longs for a general effort to appease and exorcise the masses of unconsenting dead. "Eloi, Eloi, Lama Sabachthani," a related poem, expresses the agony of a soldier whose self-loathing has become so great that its only release and consummation is in murder. The enemy becomes the bride, "planted and fertilized" by the bayonet in a foul travesty of the cosmic marriage Lawrence believed in.

In "The Crown" Lawrence enlarges upon the notion of the passion for death:

> And still, as far as there is any passion in the war, it is a passion for the embrace with death. The desire to deal death and to take death. The enemy is the bride, whose body we will reduce with rapture of agony and wounds. We are the bridegroom, engaged with him in the long, voluptuous embrace, the giving of agony, the rising and rising of the slow unwilling transport of misery, the soaking in of day after day of wet mud, in penetration of the heavy, sordid, unendurable cold, on and on to the climax, the laceration of the blade, like a frost through the tissue, blasting it.
>
> This is the desire and the consummation, this is the war. But at length, we shall be satisfied, at length we shall have consummation. Then the war will end. And what then?
>
> It is not really a question of victories or defeats. It is a question of fulfilment, and release from the old prison-house of a dead form. The war is one bout in the terrific, horrible labour, our civilization labouring in child-birth, and unable to bring forth.[28]

For civilization, as for the individual, it is a question of fulfilment and of release from the prison-house of a dead form.

Insofar as they reveal his ideas about war and the health of society, Lawrence's poems of this time are very interesting. But they are seldom shaped or finished enough to be really satisfying as poems. Only "The Attack," "Bombardment," "Winter-Lull," and "Town in 1917" have the force that war poems surely should have, and this is because they are clear in statement and definite in shape. In "Bombardment," for example, Lawrence's myth of death and renewal is inherent in the structure and imagery of the

poem itself. In most of the war poems it is, too often, merely asserted, and sometimes so obscurely as to bewilder the reader.

One reason for this is that Lawrence probably was unable
really to imagine the feelings of men at the front. He knew a
good deal about loneliness and despair, and he was far from indif-
ferent to the sufferings of the men in uniform, but he was not,
after all, in their situation of immediate, physical danger. As a
noncombatant Lawrence found it difficult to find an immediate
embodiment or objective correlative for his prophetic feelings
about the war. His true poetry of the present had to wait for the
war's end.

III

It is useful, perhaps, at this point, to consider some of the poetic influences that may be detected in the poems Lawrence wrote
before 1920. These are many and various, but even a superficial
review of nineteenth-century poetry in English reveals several
quite obvious stylistic and thematic influences—Hardy, Meredith,
Swinburne, and Browning being only the most prominent. More
important than this, however, is Lawrence's intellectual and psychological affinity with the great Romantics, particularly Blake
and Wordsworth in England and Walt Whitman in America. Finally, one might consider Lawrence's association with the Georgian and imagist schools of the prewar and war years.

Hardy's poems are full of situations and characters that might
have influenced Lawrence's poems of the country. "She at His
Funeral," for example, offers the contrast of a dead man's "grief-
less" kindred and his sweetheart whose "regret consumes like
fire." As in Lawrence's "Violets," the girl is either unrecognized
or disapproved of by the family, since she follows the procession
"at a stranger's space." Hardy's poem is brief, beautifully economical, almost epigrammatical. Lawrence's dialect poems develop such situations further.

Other such analogues suggest themselves readily enough. "The Well-Beloved" might be compared with "Two Wives." "The Revisitation" has "the peewits plaining round" on the "rugged ridge" where the speaker's love once left him. The peewits are mentioned again later in the poem, suggesting a continuity in nature that does not seem to prevail in the history of love. This may have contributed something to the first stanza of "The Wild Common."

"Hymn to Priapus" resembles Hardy's "Night of the Dance," as Kenneth Rexroth suggests. The speaker of Hardy's poem feels the moon and the stars looking at him. But it is before the dance, and the lover is only expectant. There is no counterpoise of death, and no strong sexuality. It is possible that another poem, "After the Club Dance," contributed something to "Hymn to Priapus." The speaker is a girl who has apparently given herself. She notes that the birds have done the same.

Hardy has many poems about lovers' meetings, lovers' letters, separations, the town, and the city. His interest in the common folk is more concrete, detailed, and sensible than that of Wordsworth, but it no doubt owes something to Wordsworth, and thus provides a link between Wordsworth and Lawrence. For all his fatalism, Hardy has not the mystical tendency of Wordsworth and Lawrence. On the other hand, he has a much stronger sense of humour, as a poem such as "The Ruined Maid" indicates. Lawrence could not allow himself to be so flippant as this in any of his dialect poems.

It has been suggested (by Conrad Aiken, among others) that *Look! We Have Come Through!* is related to Meredith's "Modern Love." There may well be an influence. Consider the following passage:

What are we first? First, animals; and next
Intelligences at a leap; on whom
Pale lies the distant shadow of the tomb,

And all that draweth on the tomb for text.
Into which state comes Love, the crowning sun:
Beneath whose light the shadow loses form.
We are the lords of life, and life is warm.
Intelligence and instinct now are one.
But nature says: "My children most they seem
When they least know me: therefore I decree
That they shall suffer." Swift doth young Love flee,
And we stand wakened, shivering from our dream.
Then if we study Nature we are wise.
Thus do the few who live but with the day:
The scientific animals are they.—
Lady, this is my sonnet to your eyes.

This may be a source for the later Lawrence's much-overworked phrase "lords of life." And the problem outlined so deftly in the above stanza, the difficulty of relating and joining the intellectual ideal and the instinctive desire, is precisely the problem that disturbed Lawrence.

Swinburne is another distinct influence. We know that Lawrence admired him extravagantly even into the war years. And it is obvious that "Hymn to Proserpine" made a strong impression on him. The title "Hymn to Priapus," given to a poem not directly concerned with Priapus, was probably suggested by Swinburne's title. And Proserpine remains a prominent character throughout Lawrence's whole body of work. More important, Swinburne's attitude to Christianity directly anticipates Lawrence's own theories, as my remarks about "Meeting Among the Mountains" should have indicated. Swinburne defies Christ in the cause of a fully sensuous life, though he admits Christ's power. But Christ is doomed, like other gods before him; "Time and the Gods are at strife" in Swinburne's poem, as in Shelley's *Prometheus Unbound*. Gods come and go, are born and die, for "there is no God found stronger than death; and death is a sleep." Proserpine reigns in the end:

Thou art more than the Gods who number the days of our
    temporal breath;
For these give labour and slumber; but thou, Proserpina,
    death.

Also of interest is Swinburne's "To Walt Whitman in America,"
in which the English poet admires the American's freedom from
the injustice and bigotry of the old world. Swinburne may have
been associated with Whitman in Lawrence's mind, since both
were pioneers in the treatment of erotic experience in literature.

Less easily pinpointed is Swinburne's stylistic influence, but it
would seem to be apparent in most of the poems that deserve
Pound's condemnation as "pre-raphaelitish slush." "In a Boat" and
"Sigh No More" are good examples. To overcome such preciosity Lawrence had to learn the toughness, particularity and dramatic skill of Hardy and Browning. For, like Pound and Eliot, he
is almost certainly influenced by the great dramatic monologues
of Browning. And the exploration of the relationship of the artist
and his woman in "Andrea Del Sarto," a poem mentioned by Jessie Chambers, may have provided an intellectual stimulus as well.
It is suggested in this poem that the woman Lucrezia prevents the
artist from achieving the spirit of Leonardo, Rafael, and Michelangelo. Lawrence, who depended so much on the support of
women, may well have been interested in this. When he was
young, Jessie tells us, Browning was "a great favourite."

Another favourite of Lawrence's was Robert Burns. But it
would seem to be Burns's general attitude more than particular
poems which influenced him. Possibly Burns pointed him in the
direction of the dialect poems. "Mary Morison" and other lyrics
were favourites of Lawrence and Jessie, but probably it was
Burns's free, happy spirit that Lawrence most admired—perhaps
because he was himself relatively sombre and inclined to the didactic.

In this last quality he is closer, temperamentally and intellectually, to Blake.* It is not difficult to find "Lawrentian" passages in Blake:

> The pride of the peacock is the glory of God.
> The lust of the goat is the bounty of God.
> The wrath of the lion is the wisdom of God.

> The tygers of wrath are wiser than the horses of instruction.
> ("The Marriage of Heaven and Hell")

The conclusion of "Manifesto" echoes Blake's insistence on the wisdom of the tiger. Less significantly, Lawrence's "Michelangelo" echoes the structure of the poem "The Tyger."

Blake's belief in the holiness of living things, as expressed in "America," is shared by Lawrence:

> For everything that lives is holy, life delights in life;
> Because the soul of sweet delight can never be defil'd.
> Fires inwrap the earthly globe, yet man is not consumed;
> Amid the lustful fires he walks; his feet become like brass,
> His knees and thighs like silver, and his breast and head like
>   gold.

It is possible that Lawrence might have felt that this has too much of the spirit of a Whitmanesque "merging" with the cosmos, but he could accept it as an expression of the idea of God gleaming in individual living things.

Blake has notions of the demon (or angel) within. But he condemns Wordsworth's "natural man," declaring that "The Natural Man is at Enmity with God." He was not inclined to pantheism but believed that nature (or the vegetable world) was fallen— there was no such thing as "natural piety." Lawrence is closer to the Wordsworth of the "Great Decade" in his faith in the value

---

* Cf. *A Personal Record:* ". . . he talked to me in his rapt way about Blake, telling me what a wonderful man he was. . . . For a little time we lived with Blake and his wife." (pp. 62–63)

inherent in living things. His "effort of attention" is akin to Wordsworth's desire to see into "the life of things."

"Tintern Abbey" speaks of the process by which "we are laid asleep in body and become a living soul" through the proper use of the senses and the imagination. This is close to Lawrence's idea of a "considered" or mystic sensuous apprehension of living things. And Wordsworth's "eye made quiet" is like Lawrence's insistence on darkness and invisibility, the experience of physical reality that goes deeper than mere appearances, farther than the artificial limitations we "normally" impose on our senses. Wordsworth's "power of harmony" is akin to the perception of the sacred spark of life in all living things that corresponds to our own deepest instinct.

Wordsworth describes his imaginative possession of daffodils and primroses. Lawrence does more with his flowers. In *Birds, Beasts and Flowers* he seeks to express *their* living spark, the thing that is akin to deepest human instinct and potential. In the essay ". . . Love Was Once a Little Boy" he writes:

> One understands Wordsworth and the primrose and the yokel. The yokel had no relation at all—or next to none—with the primrose. Wordsworth gathered it into his own bosom and made it part of his own nature. "I, William, am also a yellow primrose blossoming on a bank." This, we must assert, is an impertinence on William's part. He ousts the primrose from its own individuality. He doesn't allow it to call its soul its own. It must be identical with *his* soul. Because, of course, by begging the question, there is but One Soul in the universe.
>
> This is bunk. A primrose has its own peculiar primrosy identity, and all the oversouling in the world won't melt it into a Williamish oneness. . . . The primrose will neither be assimilated nor annihilated, and Boundless Love breaks on the rock of one more flower. It has its own individuality, which it opens with lovely naïveté to sky and wind and William and yokel, bee and beetle alike. It *is* itself. But its very floweriness is a kind of communion with all things: the love unison. . .
>
> Ah William! The "something more" that the primrose was to

you, was yourself in the mirror. And if the yokel actually got as far as beholding a "yellow primrose" he got far enough.[29] *

Here, Lawrence accuses Wordsworth of the same process of assimilation that infuriates him in Whitman; in another (and later) reference to Wordsworth, however, he praises him for revealing a gleam of creative chaos. "The joy men had when Wordsworth, for example, made a slit [in the umbrella of conventional response] and saw a primrose! Till then, men had only seen a primrose dimly, in the shadow of the umbrella. They saw it through Wordsworth in the full gleam of chaos." [30] It would seem, then, that Lawrence admired Wordsworth's ability to give the reader the thing itself, but disliked his further procedure of assimilating it into his own self-conscious ego. Lawrence's own aim was to find and express the creative spark in a thing, the "floweriness" that is a "kind of communion with all things: the love unison."

Two other passages, one from "Hymns in a Man's Life" and one from *The Rainbow*, further illuminate Lawrence's kind of natural piety:

> Plant consciousness, insect consciousness, fish consciousness, animal consciousness, all are related by one permanent element, which we may call the religious element, inherent in all life, even in a flea: the sense of wonder. That is our sixth sense. And it is the *natural* religious sense.[31]

> For what purpose were the incalculable physical and chemical activities nodalised in this shadowy, moving speck under her microscope? What was the will which nodalised them and created the one thing she saw? What was its intention? To be itself? Was its purpose just mechanical and limited to itself?
>
> It intended to be itself. But what self? Suddenly in her mind the world gleamed strangely, with an intense light, like the nucleus of the creature under the microscope. Suddenly she had passed away into an intensely-gleaming light of knowledge. She could not understand what it all was. She only knew that it was not limited

* Lawrence is referring to a passage in Wordsworth's "Peter Bell."

mechanical energy, nor mere purpose of self-preservation and self-assertion. It was a consummation, a being infinite. Self was a one-ness with the infinite. To be oneself was a supreme, gleaming triumph of infinity.[32]

For Lawrence, the "wonder" is inherent in the thing itself.

Leone Vivante, in *A Philosophy of Potentiality*, argues that such passages express a belief in "the intrinsic purposiveness of form." He writes:

> We must understand "potentiality" (or "potency"), not as that which is in fact unreal, in opposition to actuality, but as a power which is not entirely predetermined—and not fortuitous. This potentiality implies gradations of shade in the vital unity of the mental act, and therefore, as I maintain, it makes possible or accounts for that amplitude or profundity, or breadth, which is the proper characteristic of mental life. It is a formless—though not absolutely formless—craving for form. It is perpetually at war with form insofar as formed, and it cannot be reduced to a multiplicity of objective existents. Is it an illusion, or is it at the core of being (subjective being), to be accepted in the full dignity of logical thought? If it is an illusion, are we wrong in asking why this non-reality should play such an important part in Lawrence's searching language? For in fact the words "potential", "potentiality" and "potency" (as implying something indeterminate and creative) occur most frequently in his writings. I do not know another author who employs them so often and with so pregnant a meaning.[33]

Such speculation is particularly relevant to *Last Poems*, but it may be applied as well to "Almond Blossom," in which Lawrence attempts to capture the sense of the spark of life "storming up from the dense underearth" to blossom in "flakes of rose-pale snow / Setting supreme annunciation to the world." Indeed, the general theory of form in thought, life and art that is suggested by Vivante is relevant to all of Lawrence's most successful poems —i.e., those in which he finds the rhythmic shape that seems to be inherent in any attempt to express a particular emotional experience in language. And this is a further development of Wordsworth's ambition to use the real language of men in a state of excitement, to come as close as possible to the facts of felt experience.

When he speaks of his vocation in "The Song of a Man Who Has Come Through," Lawrence employs the old Romantic metaphor of the wind of inspiration. In his use, however, this wind may be seen as the undiscovered purpose that is inherent in the present human situation, the "formless craving for form." It is the duty of the prophetic artist to be the wind's conscious instrument, to realize the new order in his life and his art. This Lawrence attempted to do.

His most significant forerunner in this task of prophecy had been Walt Whitman. We have seen already something of the way in which Lawrence's practice and theory are indebted to those of Whitman. Jessie Chambers writes:

> Whitman's *Leaves of Grass* was one of his great books. He would sometimes write, "I'm sending you a Whitmanesque poem", when he was enclosing his own.[34]

"Dreams Old and Nascent—Nascent" is such a poem. But the influence of Whitman was a long-range one, and few of the early poems are truly Whitmanesque. His is a stronger presence in *Look! We Have Come Through!* and the later poems.

The passage on the "delicious word Death" in Whitman's "Out of the Cradle Endlessly Rocking" must have affected the young Lawrence deeply:

A word then, (for I will conquer it)
The word final, superior to all,
Subtle, sent up—what is it?—I listen;
Are you whispering it, and have been all the time, you sea-
waves?
Is that it from your liquid rims and wet sands?

Whereto answering, the sea
Delaying not, hurrying not,

Whisper'd me through the night, and very plainly before day-
  break,
Lisp'd to me the low and delicious word death,
And again death, death, death, death,
Hissing melodious, neither like the bird nor like my arous'd
  child's heart,
But edging near as privately for me rustling at my feet,
Creeping thence steadily up to my ears and laving me softly
  all over,
Death, death, death, death, death.

Lawrence quotes this passage in his essay on Whitman. And it is
evident that he was impressed by Whitman's acceptance of death
as natural and good. In the poems about his mother he too speaks
of death in terms of the sea. And his poem "Blueness," which was
called "The Mystic Blue" in *Amores*, may have been inspired in
part by "the dark blue so mystic" in Whitman's great elegy for
Lincoln, "When Lilacs Last in the Dooryard Bloomed."
  Consider this passage from an inferior Whitman poem:

But O the ship, the immortal ship! O ship aboard the ship!
O ship of the body—ship of the soul—voyaging, voyaging,
  voyaging.

("Abroad at a Ship's Helm")

Again, this may have impressed itself upon Lawrence. The ship
of the soul voyaging to new discovery is a persistent metaphor in
Whitman's work, as it is in Shelley's. But Whitman does not ex-
clude the body; he exalts it as Lawrence does.
  Lawrence at first admired Whitman's "natural" attitudes and
his stress on male comradeship as the basis of a new civilization in
America. Later, however, he came to feel that Whitman's "splendid animality" was only mental. Whitman wanted to "know" everything in order to *be* everything; he was not properly aware of
"otherness." He wanted to contain within himself the whole cosmos. His way of merging with lovers and comrades (and, indeed,

all of humanity) must, Lawrence felt, lead inevitably to dissolution and death, since that is the only genuine merging that is possible. Whitman was not content to feel sympathy *with* other human beings; he had to make the attempt to feel *for* them. Like Wordsworth with the primrose, he ousted them from their own individuality in his poems. Everything became Walt.

Whitman's great positive achievement, for Lawrence, was his assertion that the human soul must go forward into the future on the open road. "The soul passing unenhanced, passing on foot and being no more than itself. And recognized, and passed by or greeted according to the soul's dictate. If it be a great soul, it will be worshipped in the road." [35] Unfortunately Whitman betrayed this vision in his attempt to possess others. But it is well to remember, in this context, that it is his own tendency to a kind of merging in the great female Mystery that makes Lawrence react so violently against Whitman. It is to right the balance in himself that he lays such stress on the "otherness" of things.

As late as 1920 Lawrence had this to say about Whitman's artistry:

> The greatest modern poet! Whitman, at his best, is purely himself. His verse springs sheer from the spontaneous sources of his being. Hence its lovely, lovely form and rhythm: at the best. It is sheer perfect *human* spontaneity, spontaneous as a nightingale throbbing, but still controlled, the highest loveliness of human spontaneity, undecorated, unclothed. The whole being is there, sensually throbbing, spiritually quivering, mentally, ideally speaking. It is not, like Swinburne, an exaggeration of the one part of being. It is perfect and whole. The whole soul speaks at once, and is too sure for mechanical assistance of rhyme and measure. The perfect utterance of a concentrated spontaneous soul. The unforgettable loveliness of Whitman's lines! [36]

Whitman is the model for Lawrence's "poetry of the present." As such, he is easily the most important influence on Lawrence's poetic development.

This is not to say that Lawrence's mature free verse closely resembles Whitman's. Louis Untermeyer, in a review of *Last Poems*, has pointed out the differences in their styles:

> Lawrence's rhythms are brusque and taut, shaped to the sentence rather than tuned to lengthy stanzas, whereas Whitman's are large and perfervid, flowing into great tidal movements. Lawrence's diction is direct, talk-patterned, unostentatious; Whitman's is florid, equivocal, crammed with gaudy and inappropriate neologisms.[37]

And W. H. Auden has indicated the difference in method between the two poets:

> Whitman quite consciously set out to be the Epic Bard of America and created a poetic *persona* for the purpose. . . . The more we learn about Whitman the man, the less like his *persona* he looks. On the other hand it is doubtful if a writer ever existed who had less of an artistic *persona* than Lawrence. . . . Then, Whitman looks at life extensively rather than intensively. No detail is dwelt upon for long; it is snapshotted and added as one more item to the vast American catalogue. But Lawrence in his best poems is always concerned intensively with a single subject, a bat, a tortoise, a fig tree, which he broods on until he has exhausted its possibilities.[38]

Because he was a very different individual Lawrence developed his own kind of free verse. But it was Whitman who guided his first steps in that direction.

In *Look! We Have Come Through!* "Wedlock," "New Heaven and Earth," "Manifesto," and "Craving for Spring" exhibit the Whitman influence. Unfortunately, they are slack and verbose, like "Song of Myself," not controlled and exact like "When Lilacs Last in the Dooryard Bloomed." Whitman's best poems flow along like music; his worst merely bore with their repetitious (and frequently pretentious) verbiage. In *Birds, Beasts and Flowers* Lawrence develops a manner that owes something to Whitman but is, in most respects, very much his own.

In this, he was undoubtedly aided by his personal association with the imagists, particularly H. D. and Richard Aldington.

"Don't you think," he wrote to Edward Marsh in 1917, "H. D.—Mrs. Aldington—writes some good poetry? I do—really very good." [39] What he admired about H. D.'s poems was their "non-human" quality, as this passage from a letter to Amy Lowell indicates:

> It is very surprising to me, now I have come to understand you Americans a little, to realize how much older you are than us, how much further you and your art are really developed, outstripping us by far in decadence and non-emotional aestheticism, how much beyond us you are in the last stages of human apprehension of the physico-sensational world, apprehension of things non-human, not conceptual. We still see with concepts. But you, in the last stages of return, have gone beyond tragedy and emotion, even beyond irony, and have come to the pure mechanical stage of physical apprehension, the *human* unit almost lost, the primary elemental forces, kinetic, dynamic—prismatic, tonic, the great, massive, active, *inorganic* world, elemental, never softened by life, that hard universe of Matter and Force where life is not yet known, come to pass again. It is strange and wonderful. I find it only in you and H. D., in English. . . .[40]

H. D. has been considered the purest of the imagists, but Lawrence's characterization of her work is hardly an orthodox description of imagism. It is closer to the theory of "non-human" character, influenced by Marinetti and the Italian Futurists, that he outlined to Edward Garnett. Nevertheless, it shows how interested he was in a kind of objectivism developed by the Americans. He did not consider himself an imagist at all, but it is likely that his development was aided by his association with Miss Lowell's group. Some of the general aims of the imagists—"to use the language of common speech, but to employ always the *exact* word," to "create new rhythms . . . as the expression of new moods," to "present an image," and to "produce poetry that is hard and clear, never blurred nor indefinite" [41]—are admirably realized in "After the Opera," which was almost certainly written after Lawrence's association with the imagists had begun, since it was first published in *The English Review* in June 1918. In *Birds, Beasts and Flowers* Lawrence continues to pursue these aims in an attempt to express the "non-human" forces at work in the natural world.

To do this, he had to leave the "Georgian" poetry of cheerful country scenes behind. But, then, he was never much of a Georgian anyhow, as his letters to Edward Marsh demonstrate. His contributions to the Georgian anthologies—"Snap-Dragon," "Cruelty in Love" ("Love on the Farm"), "Seven Seals," and "Snake"—stand out vividly for their powerful eroticism and flexible form. Edward Marsh, the "policeman" of poetry who lectured Lawrence about his free rhythms, obviously considered him something of a sport among his new immortals.

Nevertheless, Lawrence was the only poet deemed fit for inclusion by both the imagist and Georgian anthologists. Horace Gregory feels that "The Wild Common" is a Georgian poem, since it celebrates the healthy outdoors, and that "Snap-Dragon" successfully unites the Georgian ethos with the young man's psychological peculiarities. But even he remarks of "Snap-Dragon": ". . . no other Georgian could have written this entire poem, and, though its last two lines . . . are spoken with Georgian confidence, the ominous snap-dragon symbol remains a note of disharmony within the neatly clipped green-grass and sunlight pastures of Marsh's hopeful anthology." [42]

In *Look! We Have Come Through!* Lawrence turns definitely away from the Georgians and reveals his closer kinship with the imagists. In *Birds, Beasts and Flowers* he comes into his majority as a poet in work whose force, originality and authority makes very nearly meaningless any further discussion of influences and schools.

﹏ Three

The Rainbow Change:

Birds, Beasts and Flowers and

the Poems from *The Plumed Serpent*

I

Birds, Beasts and Flowers is an exploration of the "other," non-human world. Lawrence becomes Adam in a newly discovered universe, and he seeks to define the world outside himself, not in terms of his own merely "personal" emotions, but in terms of the elemental energies he can sense both in himself and in other living things. His method is, then, neither one involving the "pathetic fallacy" nor one that is objective in a scientific sense; it is a fusion of subjective and objective modes, as in all great poetry.

Lawrence is objective in his close observation of the thing and subjective in stressing (or, sometimes, stretching) the analogies between animal or plant life and human life. "Lawrence does not import an abstract symbolism into something already there, he *sees* things as themselves *and* as symbols," observes R. G. N. Salgādo.[1] This is possible because he believes that certain human qualities or states of mind and body and the qualities of plants and animals are manifestations of the same basic energy. Thus, for example, it has always been very natural and appropriate to regard fruits as female—they carry the seed. Such a belief is not mystical except in the sense defined in the late poem "Mystic"; it is a further development of Lawrentian realism.

The title of the book is probably taken from S. Baring-Gould's "Evening Hymn":

> Now the darkness gathers,
>   Stars begin to peep,
> Birds and beasts and flowers
>   Soon will be asleep.

If Lawrence did have this passage in mind, then he must have been moved by the vision of the whole creation moving into the invisible world of night. In *Birds, Beasts and Flowers* he attempts to see within the bright surface of things, to find and reveal "a dark and nude, vast heaven."

Apart from the jocular defence of drunkenness, which looks forward to "Medlars and Sorb Apples" and "Grapes," the note to the first section, "Fruits," is devoted to an assertion of the "female" quality of fruits, thus providing a link with the great female "Other" of "New Heaven and Earth." The mystery of generation is pre-eminently a female mystery for Lawrence, who tends to ignore the fact that the man also carries the seed of life. His ideal man is the prophet, intoxicated with his own singleness and essentially unconcerned about generation, as in "Medlars and Sorb Apples"; this man's concern is to bring down the old social world and to reveal a new and better world, as in "The Revolutionary."

The first poem, "Pomegranate," opens with a Whitmanesque assertion of the authority of the poet's intuitive vision:

> You tell me I am wrong,
> Who are you, who is anybody to tell me I am wrong?
> I am not wrong.

This seems to be addressed to a particular person. Indeed, the reader finds himself placed in this person's shoes. He finds himself engaged in conversation with Lawrence, a conversation in which

Lawrence insists that his reader recognize not only the female nature of the pomegranate but also the world within the world that such an apprehension opens up. There is, apparently, a necessary fissure in the universe itself, one that opens up the world of fiery vision that most men fear and would prefer to ignore. In this bold fashion, at the very beginning of his book, Lawrence upbraids his reader or average modern man, condemning him for his failure to see beyond appearances. This method combines a direct conversational attack with the subtle progression of imagery from the fissure of the pomegranate through the fissure of the setting sun to the fissure in a man's heart.

In "Medlars and Sorb Apples," a more complex poem, Lawrence changes his tactics. He no longer attacks the reader but addresses himself to the fruits. The delicious rottenness, the "brown morbidity" of these "Autumnal excrementa" makes him think of "white gods" and of the "wonderful" experiences of Orpheus and Dionysos in hell. This hell is not a place of torment but a mode of being:

A kiss, and a spasm of farewell, a moment's orgasm of rupture,
Then along the damp road alone, till the next turning.
And there, a new partner, a new parting, a new unfusing into
    twain,
A new gasp of further isolation,
A new intoxication of loneliness, among decaying, frost-cold
    leaves.

Going down the strange lanes of hell, more and more intensely
    alone,
The fibres of the heart parting one after the other
And yet the soul continuing, naked-footed, ever more vividly
    embodied
Like a flame blown whiter and whiter
In a deeper and deeper darkness
Ever more exquisite, distilled in separation.

The medlars and sorb apples give the "distilled essence of hell." Hell is identified with parting and individual integrity. Thus, it has a value equal to that of the heaven of sexual ecstasy. But both are parts of the larger process of life and growth. If Orpheus must part from Eurydice, he must also return to her. In autumn, the season of separation, silence and death, Lawrence celebrates the value of solitude and single being. As in "The Ship of Death," the separation of the fruit from the tree is a natural emblem of such a process in human life.

In an earlier version of this poem, published in *The New Republic*, Lawrence placed more emphasis on death as the ultimate separation or consummation of the single self: "I say, death was one of their intricate experiences / Intricate going asunder. / A kiss, a vivid spasm of farewell . . ." In both versions he expresses this idea in the myth of the descent of Orpheus into the Underworld, but this is greatly strengthened in the later version. "The distilled potion of departure" becomes "the distilled essence of hell," and "the secret of Orpheus and Hades" becomes the far more evocative "Orpheus, and the winding, leaf-clogged, silent lanes of hell." Moreover, in the later version Orpheus is fused with Dionysos, who does not appear at all in the earlier version. This lays stress on the "perfect drunkenness" of the single state; Lawrence deliberately gives hell a status equal to that of his heaven. This is the neglected "other" half of human existence—the necessary loneliness of man that is consummated finally in death.[2]

"Figs" returns to the subject of the female and the qualities that are precious in her. The fig is "a very sensitive fruit" resembling "the female part," and thus intensely female. The inward life of the fig is seen only when it bursts: "Like a prostitute, the bursten fig, making a show of her secret." And this is what happens, all too often, to the modern woman, asserts Lawrence. For once Eve got the fact of her nakedness "in her mind" she covered herself with fig-leaves. The modern woman still has sex on her mind; she does not accept it as a natural and instinctive part of her life, but seeks to control and manipulate it with her intelligence. Her sex is mentally induced and stimulated. She wishes to "burst into affirmation," to make love "free" perhaps, but Lawrence has no sympathy for suffragettes or flappers. "Ripe figs won't keep," he insists. The modern woman has lost the mystery he seeks in woman.[3]

The inner life of the fig is invisible, magic. Similarly, the grape suggests the world of touch that is more ancient and more profound than the superficial world of the eye:

Ours is the universe of the unfolded rose,
The explicit
The candid revelation.

But long ago, oh, long ago
Before the rose began to simper supreme,
Before the rose of all roses, rose of all the world, was even in
  bud,
Before the glaciers were gathered up in a bunch out of the un-
  settled seas and winds,
Or else before they had been let down again, in Noah's flood,
There was another world, a dusky, flowerless, tendrilled world
And creatures webbed and marshy,
And on the margin, men soft-footed and pristine,
Still, and sensitive, and active,
Audile, tactile sensitiveness as of a tendril which orientates and
  reaches out,
Reaching out and grasping by an instinct more delicate than
  the moon's as she feels for the tides.

Of which world, the vine was the invisible rose,
Before petals spread, before colour made its disturbance, before
  eyes saw too much.

In a green, muddy, web-foot, unutterably songless world
The vine was rose of all roses.*

Even now the grape keeps its power of invisibility; it is "blue-
black . . . globed in Egyptian darkness." As in "Medlars and
Sorb Apples," there is an argument by associations: because the
rose opens and spreads out, it can be an emblem for candour and
explicit revelation, but with its dark night-colour, its power of intoxication, and its sensitive reaching tendrils, the grape becomes
the symbolic embodiment of an older, more complete mode of
consciousness. Once God "was all negroid, as now he is fair."
Even the most primitive peoples have forgotten this ancient wisdom, but now the white man, who has never known it, is somehow on the brink of "re-remembrance," since his Christian vision
has proven itself inadequate:

Our pale day is sinking into twilight,
And if we sip the wine, we find dreams coming upon us
Out of the imminent night.
Nay, we find ourselves crossing the fern-scented frontiers
Of the world before the floods, where man was dark and
    evasive
And the tiny vine-flower rose of all roses, perfumed,
And all in naked communion communicating as now our
    clothed vision can never communicate.

America has adopted prohibition, Lawrence suggests (probably
quite seriously), because she is afraid of the discovery that she
must inevitably make.

Dusky are the avenues of wine,
And we must cross the frontiers, though we will not,

* *Complete Poems*, pp. 285–86. In the penultimate line of this passage I
have given "unutterably" where the *Complete Poems* of 1967 had "unutterly." In this case *Birds, Beasts and Flowers* (p. 23) has "unutterably"
and *Collected Poems* (p. 134) has "unutterly." But the latter is a misprint
and has been corrected for the new edition.

Of the lost, fern-scented world:
Take the fern-seed on our lips,
Close the eyes, and go
Down the tendrilled avenues of wine and the otherworld.

A good deal of Lawrence's myth of renewal and discovery is
expressed in "Grapes." It goes farther than "Medlars and Sorb
Apples" in its attempt to express the necessity of a descent by the
individual man into the "otherworld" of "audile, tactile" sensitivity. (It is noteworthy that Lawrence foresees a restoration of audile and tactile sensitivity a good many years before the advent of
Marshall McLuhan.) The "world within the world" that could
be detected in early poems such as "Snap-Dragon" and the poems
of grief for the mother may now be seen as the world that is created and discovered at once in the full experience of the senses.
One must feel with the whole body. For Lawrence's aim is the restoration of the whole man through the resurrection of the body.

His ideal world is antediluvian, as the reference to the glaciers
and Noah's flood indicates. In *Fantasia of the Unconscious* we are
given a fuller version of this unusual historical theory:

> In the period which geologists call the Glacial Period, the wa-
> ters of the earth must have been gathered up in a vast body on the
> higher places of our globe, vast worlds of ice. And the sea-beds of
> today must have been comparatively dry. So that the Azores rose
> up mountainous from the plain of Atlantis, where the Atlantic
> now washes, and the Easter Isles and the Marquesas and the rest
> rose loftily from the marvellous great continent of the Pacific.
> In that world men lived and taught and knew, and were in one
> complete correspondence over all the earth. Men wandered back
> and forth from Atlantis to the Polynesian Continent as men now
> sail from Europe to America. The interchange was complete, and
> knowledge, science was universal over the earth, cosmopolitan as it
> is today.
> Then came the melting of the glaciers and the world flood. The
> refugees from the drowned continents fled to the high places of
> America, Europe, Asia, and the Pacific Isles. And some degener-

ated naturally into cavemen, neolithic and paleolithic creatures, and some retained their marvellous innate beauty and life-perfection, as in the South Sea Islanders, and some wandered savage in Africa, and some, like Druids or Etruscans or Chaldeans or Amerindians or Chinese, refused to forget, but taught the old wisdom, only in its half-forgotten, symbolic forms. More or less forgotten, as knowledge: remembered as ritual, gesture, and myth-story.[4]

This is the Lawrentian version of the myth of the Golden Age. In its exaltation of a human creature golden in life-wisdom and power it is Rousseauistic: the brutish cave man is brushed aside as degeneration of Lawrence's man. Such a myth is very convenient, for it enables Lawrence to consider Egyptians, Greeks, Polynesians, and even Etruscans as remnants of a race who possessed a fuller wisdom. But it seems likely, whether or not one accepts his antediluvian world civilization as a possibility, that Lawrence's basic intuition about human development and the loss it has entailed is a valid one. In his impressive study of the development and purpose of instinctive behaviour patterns in animals and human beings Konrad Lorenz writes:

It is a curious paradox that the greatest gifts of man, the unique faculties of conceptual thought and verbal speech which have raised him to a level high above all other creatures and given him mastery over the globe, are not altogether blessings, or at least are blessings that have to be paid for very dearly indeed. All the great dangers threatening humanity with extinction are direct consequences of conceptual thought and verbal speech. They drove man out of the paradise in which he could follow his instincts with impunity and do or not do whatever he pleased. There is much truth in the parable of the tree of knowledge and its fruit, though I want to make an addition to it to make it fit into my own picture of Adam: that apple was thoroughly unripe! Knowledge springing from conceptual thought robbed man of the security provided by his well-adapted instincts long, long before it was sufficient to provide him with an equally safe adaptation. Man is, as Arnold Gehlen has so truly said, by nature a jeopardized creature.[5]

Lorenz believes further that "instinctive behaviour mechanisms failed to cope with the new circumstances which culture unavoidably produced even at its very dawn." [6] Man's survival is in jeopardy because he has yet to adapt the instinctive behaviour patterns that were once the guarantee of his survival to the difficult new circumstances of the awesome power that he has discovered by the use of his intellect. Thus Lawrence's search for the unified man is of the utmost relevance to the human situation today. But it is interesting that his acute insight takes the form that it does. Obviously, he is more indebted to Genesis than to science in his use of the world flood as the great divide. "I do not believe in evolution," he declares, "but in the strangeness and rainbow-change of ever-renewed creative civilizations." [7] After the flood, the rainbow, the promise of a new world.

In "Grapes" the story of Noah provides the same sort of structural skeleton for Lawrence's myth of the "otherworld" that is provided by the stories of Orpheus and Dionysos in "Medlars and Sorb Apples." These figures and others—most notably Pluto and Persephone, Christ, and Osiris—figure in some of Lawrence's finest poems as archetypal expressions of basic human experiences and insights. More important than this, however, is Lawrence's primary reliance on suggestive arrangements of sound and imagery to further his "argument."

In "Medlars and Sorb Apples" the unity achieved by the conjunction of rhythm and substance in the arrangement of the lines and by the disarming immediacy of the confidential and colloquial opening, expressed in dangling syntax and incomplete sentences, is greatly aided by the close texture of sound-effects running through the poem. Echoes, internal rhymes, assonances and alliterations abound: "flux . . . sucked"; "rambling sky-dropped grape"; "smack of preciosity / Soon in the pussyfoot West"; "Syracusan Muscat"; "So brown and soft and coming suave"; "Autumnal excrementa"; "Orphic, delicate / Dionysos of the Underworld"; "spasm . . . orgasm"; "exquisite distilled"; "decaying, frost-cold leaves." * Such effects help to knit the poem together and make it a single entity, a single order of sound.

Similarly, Lawrence's characteristic combination adjectives—"flesh-fragrant," "sky-dropped"—serve to fuse seemingly disparate thoughts, feelings, and sense-impressions so as to express and present them in the unified way one actually does experience them. The means may seem somewhat unusual (even somewhat baroque) for this writer, but the end is to preserve the immediacy of experience. A grape that is "sky-dropped" is one whose blue colour seems to be borrowed from the sky and whose shape is like a drop of water: thus does Lawrence condense those associations that come immediately into his mind when he observes the grape. There is no dissociation of sensibility in this poem, as there is in the less successful didactic passages of *Look! We Have Come Through!*

In "The Revolutionary" and "The Evening Land" Lawrence considers the possibility of a restoration of his otherworld, wondering in the latter poem whether America might not be the place where this will happen. It is well to remember, in considering his use of history here and elsewhere, that the new world is always potentially present. For the new world is not really a place or a particular era but a mode of being. It is the "mystic Now," the full sensuous experience of the present moment. Lawrence wishes to restore lost faculties, faculties he senses at times in himself. To do so he must end the dominance of the intellect and overthrow the temple of white bloodless idealism that has excluded the full life of the instincts. He wishes to heal the "split" between intellect and instinct, mind and body, the split that caused the war. He hopes that the death-flood may be followed by "rainbow-change."

In "The Revolutionary" Lawrence sees himself as the Samson who will pull down the pillars of "pale-face authority." This is

---

* This last somewhat resembles Robert Frost's "slow smokeless burning of decay" in "The Woodpile."

not merely atavistic; it is prophetic in its assumption that the house of western civilization is about to fall. The pale-faced modern man has "lips of metal" that are like "slits in an automatic machine." He is the robot of *Last Poems*. In *Psychoanalysis and the Unconscious* Lawrence argues that the most idealistic peoples— the Americans, for example—tend to become the most materialistic peoples because idealism tends to mechanism.

> This motivizing of the passional sphere from the ideal is the final peril of human consciousness. It is the death of all spontaneous, creative life, and the substitution of the mechanical principle. . . . Ideal and material are identical. The ideal is but the god in the machine—the little, fixed machine principle which works the human psyche automatically.[8]

But whole men are not machines. In "The Revolutionary" Lawrence speaks of the modern man's "visuality," and this word appears to have the same relation to "visual" as the word "religiosity" has to "religious." Something spurious is suggested. Again, one is reminded of Marshall McLuhan's use of the term "visual" to describe the abstract, purely mental nature of print technology. The world of visuality is, paradoxically, more blind than the Samson who challenges it. For his blindness is the truer vision of the body.* Lawrence concludes the poem with an arrogant assertion of his own superiority:

> See if your skies aren't falling!
> And my head, at least, is thick enough to stand it, the smash.

* In *The Utopian Vision of D. H. Lawrence* (pp. 104–105) Eugene Goodheart notes the similarity between some of Lawrence's ideas and those of Norman O. Brown in *Life Against Death:* Brown believes that the pregenital infantile organizations of the libido that were discovered and described by Freud are not biologically determined "but are constructed by the human ego, or rather they represent that distortion of the human body which *is* the human ego. . . ." Brown, like Lawrence before him, is at work at resurrecting the body—Brown calls it the Dionysian ego or reality." In *The Gutenberg Galaxy* Marshall McLuhan argues that electronic media tend to restore a tribal situation in which man regains his old audile and tactile sensitivity. Neither Brown nor McLuhan, however, properly acknowledges Lawrence's prophetic insight.

See if I don't move under a dark and nude, vast heaven
When your world is in ruins, under your fallen skies.
Caryatids, pale-faces.
See if I am not Lord of the dark and moving hosts
Before I die.

In the following poem, "The Evening Land," Lawrence wonders aloud whether the United States may not be the most appropriate setting for his psychic revolution. As the extreme expression of all that is wrong with European civilization, America is perhaps the most likely "grave of our day." But before he goes there, Lawrence feels, American must "cajole" his soul. He is afraid of such a "grave of mingling" as America, the home of Whitman's ideal, merging love. The extreme European idealism of America has merely produced the perfect machine-man. Despite these evils, Lawrence's soul is "half-cajoled." Something calls him, in spite of his condemnation of American society. This something is the spirit of place, the "demonish New World nature / Glimpsed now and then." Perhaps the American demon, the wild nature of an emotionally unsettled continent, will have his way in the end, speculates Lawrence. But his feelings are uncertain. Possibly Whitman's "States" may be taken as states of being, new modes of consciousness. Will the American, in the end, forsake his machines and submit to his demon? The prophet does not really know.

In "Cypresses," from the second section, "Trees," the theme of the "otherworld" is continued. The trees can suggest dark Etruscans because they are "softly swaying pillars of dark flame," living monuments to the last dark race. They do not, of course, *become* Etruscans; they "remain" what they are. But in their mysterious concentration of dark life they seem to Lawrence to be the perfect emblem for his sense of the mysterious Etruscans. The Romans called the Etruscans evil, but Lawrence is weary of Roman virtue. He is sure there is more than meets the eye in such "evil."

> For oh, I know, in the dust where we have buried
> The silenced races and all their abominations,
> We have buried so much of the delicate magic of life.

Lawrence distrusts the account of the victors, and feels that something uniquely valuable in human life may have been lost with the Etruscans:

> They say the fit survive,
> But I invoke the spirits of the lost.
> Those that have not survived, the darkly lost,
> To bring their meaning back into life again,
> Which they have taken away
> And wrapt inviolable in soft cypress-trees,
> Etruscan cypresses.
>
> Evil, what is evil?
> There is only one evil, to deny life
> As Rome denied Etruria
> And mechanical America Montezuma still.

In this conclusion Lawrence reminds us once again that the Americans, though they are obstinately mechanical, may have a unique chance to regain connection with the lost way of life of ancient peoples.*

---

* An earlier version of "Cypresses," published in *The Adelphi* (October 1923, pp. 368–70), contains the following lines:
> Among the cypresses
> To sit with pure, slim, long-nosed,
> Evil-called, sensitive Etruscans, naked except for their boots;
> To be able to smile back at them
> And exchange the lost kiss
> And come to dark connection.

This is open to obvious misunderstanding. Such a passage is probably best understood as the symbolic expression of an internal process by which Lawrence accepts and releases the qualities of his father which were driven underground in his youth. In *Sea and Sardinia* (pp. 122–23) he remarks: "Italy has given me back I know not what of myself, but a very very great deal. She has found for me so much that was lost: like a restored Osiris."

"Flowers" proceeds to the theme of resurrection. "Almond Blossom," one of Lawrence's most triumphant poems, begins surely and directly in short staccato bursts, like excited conversation, then brings itself to a temporary resolution in a longer stanza with longer, more cadenced lines:

> Even iron can put forth,
> Even iron.
>
> This is the iron age,
> But let us take heart
> Seeing iron break and bud,
> Seeing rusty iron puff with clouds of blossom.
>
> The almond-tree,
> December's bare iron hooks sticking out of earth.
>
> The almond-tree,
> That knows the deadliest poison, like a snake
> In supreme bitterness.
>
> Upon the iron, and upon the steel,
> Odd flakes as if of snow, odd bits of snow,
> Odd crumbs of melting snow.
>
> But you mistake, it is not from the sky;
> From out the iron, and from out the steel,
> Flying not down from heaven, but storming up,
> Strange storming-up from the dense under-earth
> Along the iron, to the living steel
> In rose-hot tips, and flakes of rose-pale snow
> Setting supreme annunciation to the world.

Before it has blossomed the tree suggests bare iron hooks and, by extension, the iron or mechanical-industrial age. The tree knows deadly poison "like a snake / In supreme bitterness." As we have

seen, the snake can suggest more positive qualities; here it is noteworthy that the almond-tree can proceed from "supreme bitterness" to the "supreme annunciation" of its blossoming. Thus,
even our poisonous iron age may break into blossom of new life.
But this new life is not from heaven; it is a "strange storming-up
from the dense under-earth," an impulse from the true source of
being

Like Lawrence himself, the trees are in exile. They suffer
through the long ages, like wandering Jews. There seems here to
be the suggestion that these trees, like the cypresses, belong to a
lost world, another order of being than that we normally experience. Having kept some secret, ancient wisdom, they are able to
renew themselves in blossom, even in the iron age:

> Iron, but unforgotten.
> Iron, dawn-hearted,
> Ever-beating dawn-heart, enveloped in iron against the exile,
>   against the ages.

> See it come forth in blossom
> From the snow-remembering heart
> In long-nighted January,
> In the long, dark nights of the evening star, and Sirius, and the
>   Etna snow-wind through the long night.
> Sweating his drops of blood through the long-nighted Geth-
>   semane
> Into blossom, into pride, into honey-triumph, into most exqui-
>   site splendour.
> Oh, give me the tree of life in blossom
> And the Cross sprouting its superb and fearless flowers!

Here again, the resolution of the process of "storming up" is expressed in long cadenced lines which convey the breathless excitement of the speaker in the presence of this miracle. Under the
iron there is a heart that is able to blossom. Perhaps, then, there is
new life hidden beneath the smooth surface of our superficial ma-

chine civilization. The almond-tree becomes a symbol of life unvanquished, "the tree of life in blossom," a cross "sprouting its superb and fearless flowers." The supreme bitterness of the crucifixion of life in a mechanical age is to be followed by the supreme triumph of life.

> Something must be reassuring to the almond, in the evening
>   star, and the snow-wind, and the long, long nights,
> Some memory of far, sun-gentler lands,
> So that the faith in his heart smiles again
> And his blood ripples with that untellable delight of once-
>   more-vindicated faith,
> And the Gethsemane blood at the iron pores unfolds, unfolds,
> Pearls itself into tenderness of bud
> And in a great and sacred forthcoming steps forth, steps out
>   in one stride
> A naked tree of blossom, like a bridegroom bathing in dew,
>   divested of cover,
> Frail-naked, utterly uncovered
> To the green night-baying of the dog-star, Etna's snow-edged
>   wind
> And January's loud-seeming sun.
>
> Think of it, from the iron fastness
> Suddenly to dare to come out naked, in perfection of blossom,
>   beyond the sword-rust.
> Think, to stand there in full-unfolded nudity, smiling,
> With all the snow-wind, and the sun-glare, and the dog-star
>   baying epithalamion.

After this climax there is a gradual falling-off of sound, a lessening of rhythmic intensity in a reversion to the choppy rhythms, the incomplete sentences and short lines that characterize both the opening and the brief stanzas that serve as connecting links between the passages of maximum intensity. The poem concludes in a dying fall.

As in all of his most exuberant poems, Lawrence makes considerable use of compound adjectives or epithets. Some of these— "fish-silvery," "snow-edged," "subtly-smiling," "snow-remembering," "honey-bodied," "hoar-frost-like"—are simply compound adjectives (or, occasionally, compound nouns), similar in their vivid descriptive effect to Hopkins' unhyphenated "rolling level underneath him steady air" in "The Windhover." Others (*e.g.*, "long-nighted January") have the formal quality of Homer's "wine-dark sea." Most serve, directly or implicitly, to yoke together separate things and qualities, utilizing the power of metaphor to unify the seemingly disparate elements of experience— *e.g.*, "rose-hot," "rose-pale," "honey-triumph," "sun-gentler," "dawn-tender," and the like. The effect, like that of Hopkins' and Joyce's word-play, is one of implosion. Sometimes the effectiveness of a particularly striking phrase, such as "January's loud-seeming sun," resulting as it does from the conjunction of the rhythm, the synaesthesia involved in the compound adjective and its noun, the alliteration, and the subtle assonantal rhyme, seems to defy final analysis.

If a poem of this length has centres of rhythmic and emotional intensity whose energy radiates outward to colour one's experience of the whole poem, then surely the stanzas which announce the tree as a bridegroom are the emotional climax of this poem. They resemble in their thematic centrality, their rhythmic intensity, and their emotional resonance the famous passage about the presence that "rolls through all things" in Wordsworth's "Tintern Abbey." In the image of the tree as bridegroom are concentrated and focused both the emotional core and the essential meaning of the poem. Here, the unfolding of the individual life is again seen in the light of marriage. Marriage, in this context, with the dog-star in the sky baying epithalamion, would seem to be an affirmation of the total unity of related but distinct beings in the universe. This is the cosmic marriage in which the lovers participate in "Moonrise." It is that union of life with life that is best expressed in the blossoming of the individual life within the context of the whole. This is the counterweight to the autumnal movement toward separation and death in "Medlars and Sorb Apples."

Lawrence's essay "The Spirit of Place" has a passage that seems related to "Almond Blossom":

> Every great locality expresses itself perfectly, in its own flowers, its own birds and beasts, lastly its own men, with their perfected works. Mountains convey themselves in unutterable expressed perfection in the blue gentian flower and in the edelweiss flower, so soft, yet shaped like snow-crystals. The very strata of the earth come to a point of perfect, unutterable concentration in the inherent sapphires and emeralds. It is so with all worlds and all places of the world. We may take it as a law.
>
> So now we wait for the fulfilment of the law in the west, the inception of a new era of living. At present there is a vast myriad-branched human engine, the very thought of which is death. But in the winter even a tree looks like iron. Seeing the great trunk of dark iron and the swaying steel flails of boughs, we cannot help being afraid. What we see of buds looks like sharp bronze studpoints. The whole thing hums elastic and sinister and faintly metallic, like some confused scourge of swinging steel thongs. Yet the lovely cloud of green and summer lustre is within it.
>
> We wait for the miracle, for the new soft wind. Even the buds of iron break into soft little flames of issue. So will people change. So will the machine-parts open like buds and the great machines break into leaf. Even we can expect our iron ships to put forth vine and tendril and bunches of grapes, like the ship of Dionysos in full sail upon the ocean.[9]

Here, as in "The Evening Land," Lawrence hopes that the spirit of place in America may transform our civilization. In "Almond Blossom" the miracle is not localized in this way. Nor does it need to be. In every country flowers restore lost worlds to Lawrence:

> It was spring in Western Australia, and a wonder of delicate blueness, of frail, unearthly beauty. The earth was full of weird flowers, star-shaped, needle-pointed, fringed, scarlet, white, blue,

a whole world of strange flowers. Like being in a new Paradise from which man had not been cast out.[10]

Similarly, in *The White Peacock*, Lettie feels in the snowdrops the suggestion of an old and elemental religion.[11] And Alvina, in *The Lost Girl*, senses in the small anemones the spirit of the wild Abruzzi: ". . . their red-purple silkiness had something pre-world about it, at last. The more she wandered, the more the shadow of the pagan world seemed to come over her." [12] It is sometimes difficult to determine whether Lawrence desires the restoration of pagan life-modes or the blossoming of new ones. He does not always distinguish between the two possibilities. While he finds in legend and history and in his own experience of the natural world the raw materials for his myth of renewal, he cannot really know what the future will be.

In "Purple Anenomes," a comic version of the world-in-the-flower theme, Lawrence combines satirical observations on suffragettes with the myth of Persephone. In the spring, when Persephone has come back to earth, she and her mother Ceres are "enfranchised women," but the dark husband Dis is after his independent bride. "Poor Persephone and her rights for women," mocks Lawrence. As in "Medlars and Sorb Apples," this particular hell is regarded as a desirable state. The cheerful flippancy of the poem provides a change of pace before Lawrence returns to the mysterious "pre-world" in "Sicilian Cyclamens."

The cyclamens suggest a certain moment in history (or, properly speaking, prehistory), that moment when the Pelasgi, a primitive Aegean and East-Mediterranean people, first saw them:

When he pushed his bush of black hair off his brow:
When she lifted her mop from her eyes, and screwed it in a
    knob behind
        —O act of fearful temerity!
When they felt their foreheads bare, naked to heaven, their
    eyes revealed:

When they felt the light of heaven brandished like a knife at
    their defenceless eyes,
And the sea like a blade at their face,
Mediterranean savages:
When they came out, face-revealed, under heaven, from the
    shaggy undergrowth of their own hair
For the first time,
They saw tiny rose cyclamens between their toes, growing
Where the slow toads sat brooding on the past.*

Like the almond blossoms, the cyclamens can represent the first
glimpse of a new day. As the poem develops, Lawrence makes a
pattern of images of revelation and awakening: the savages brush-
ing hair out of their eyes; the delicate cyclamens emerging from
earth "pricking their ears / Like delicate very young greyhound
bitches / Half-yawning at the open, inexperienced / Vista of day,
/ Folding back their soundless petalled ears"; the cyclamens "like
bunches of wild hares / Muzzles together, ear-aprick, / Whispering witchcraft / Like women at a well, the dawn-fountain." Thus
they may be seen as emblems expressive of "Greece and the
world's morning," even of "the unborn / Erechtheion marbles."
In its own awakening the rose cyclamen is an "ecstatic fore-runner" of these later manifestations of the creative urge, a living
thing whose tiny being is nevertheless close to the source of all
man's creative effort.

It is not surprising, perhaps, that in the most celebrated of the
Birds, Beasts and Flowers poems, those devoted to animals, there
are rather fewer overt symbolic connections of the kind found in
"Cypresses" and "Grapes." Instead, there is, in the best of these
poems, a closer, less impressionistic observation. The poems on
animals constitute a kind of research into man's evolutionary past;
they are not so much concerned, as the poems on plants were,

---

* *Complete Poems*, p. 310. I have altered "brandishing" to "brandished."
Both *Birds, Beasts and Flowers* (p. 60) and *Collected Poems* (p. 166) have
"brandished." This is corrected in the new edition.

with what the thing being observed signifies (or can signify) to us about our loss of meaningful contact with our natural environment (though this is certainly a part of their method and purpose), as with what the animal's life means to itself, and thus, by extension, what it means to the animal *in us*. In proceeding to the considerations of higher forms of life than plant life Lawrence must at least *attempt* to imagine the kind of consciousness that his animal subjects possess. If this is necessarily subjective, it is nevertheless an attempt to imagine oneself *without* human self-consciousness and emotional complexity, and is thus very far from conventional anthropomorphism. If there is incidental anthropomorphism in these few central poems (as in the ending of "Man and Bat" or the remarks about tortoise family connections), it is clearly comic or ironic in intent, and meant to convey the gulf between human and animal consciousness. Thus, in "Fish," Lawrence does not attempt to sustain his simile likening the young pike to "a lout on an obscure pavement," but is obliged instead to confess that he "didn't know him."

In *The Dyer's Hand* [13] W. H. Auden lists five ways in which animals have figured in literature: the beast fable, in which the actors have animals' bodies but human consciousness; the animal simile, in which a man's behaviour is described as being that typical of a certain animal; the animal as an allegorical emblem; the romantic encounter of man and beast; and the animal as an object of human interest and affection. This last is probably the category that will contain most of Lawrence's animal poems, but there are certainly traces of some of the other kinds in his work as well. "St. Mark," for instance, can be regarded as a satirical beast fable (like "The Nun's Priest's Tale"), since it has the lion of the senses and the Christian lamb as characters. And in some of the animal poems Lawrence does proceed from naturalistic description to emblematic significance: among the animal poems we find the tortoise sequence, which makes an interesting use of the cross on the tortoise's shell. For the most part, however, Lawrence is concerned to find and express the essential being of the animal itself. He sees his animals, as Auden has remarked in another context, "neither as numinous symbols nor as aesthetic objects but as neighbours." [14] Or perhaps, to put the matter more exactly, Lawrence's snake (to take one instance) is a "numinous symbol" only insofar as it embodies and expresses the godlike or kingly quality of sensuous life. There is no attempt to *impose* upon the creature a significance that it does not already possess. There is no falsification of its nature.

Why is Lawrence so fascinated by animals? Perhaps for the reasons that Rilke gives for his interest in the *Duino Elegies:*

> With all its eyes the creature-world beholds
> the open. But our eyes, as though reversed,
> encircle it on every side, like traps
> set round its unobstructed path to freedom.
> What *is* outside, we know from the brute's face
> alone; for while a child's quite small we take it
> and turn it round and force it to look backwards
> at conformation, not that openness
> so deep within the brute's face. Free from death.
> We only see death; the free animal
> has its decease perpetually behind it
> and God in front, and when it moves, it moves
> into eternity, like running springs.[15]

The animal does not brood on death but lives according to its nature, accepting the whole process of growth and decay, in full possession of Lawrence's "mystic Now." Without man's crippling self-division, it can enjoy the fulness of transcience. By imagining the life of an animal, Lawrence feels, man can perhaps achieve a better and saner balance within his own more complex mode of consciousness. Most of Lawrence's animals have a wholeness and integrity of being that man has lost. In his tortoise poems, however, he discovers that man's self-division is foreshadowed by sexual division in animals. Man must accept this cycle of experience, as he must accept his death.

In "Fish" Lawrence observes a creature whose consciousness is much harder for man to imagine than that of the tortoise. Consequently, the poem does not rise to climactic passages of emotional and rhythmic intensity like those found in "Tortoise Shout" and "Almond Blossom." The emotional energy is cumulative, dispersed throughout the poem, which is arranged, for the most part, in short stanzas and short lines:

> Fish, oh Fish,
> So little matters!
>
> Whether the waters rise and cover the earth
> Or whether the waters wilt in the hollow places,
> All one to you.
>
> Aqueous, subaqueous,
> Submerged
> And wave-thrilled.
>
> As the waters roll
> Roll you.
> The waters wash,
> You wash in oneness
> And never emerge.
>
> Never know,
> Never grasp.

In this opening Lawrence uses short, choppy rhythms and incomplete sentences to express the remoteness of the fish's wave-bound being from his own experience. The sexuality of the fish, unlike that of the tortoise or even the snake, is very remote from man's own:

Even snakes lie together.

But oh, fish, that rock in water,
You lie only with the waters;
One touch.
No fingers, no hands and feet, no lips;
No tender muzzles,
No wistful bellies,
No loins of desire,
None.

You and the naked element,
Sway-wave.
Curvetting bits of tin in the evening light.

To his rhythmic imitation of the close sway of the waves Lawrence here adds one of his striking descriptive metaphors, thus making it possible for the reader to perceive (or seem to perceive) the existence of the fish both from within and from without.

Lawrence admits, of course, in the most famous passage of the poem, that fishes are beyond his imaginative reach. Nevertheless, in the passage that enlarges upon this confession he is able to offer a kind of fish's-eye view of himself in his description of the encounter between man and fish:

I have waited with a long rod
And suddenly pulled a gold-and-greenish, lucent fish from
    below,
And had him fly like a halo round my head,
Lunging in the air on the line.

Unhooked his gorping, water-horny mouth,
And seen his horror-tilted eye,
His red-gold, water-precious, mirror-flat bright eye;

And felt him beat in my hand, with his mucous, leaping life-
     throb.
And my heart accused itself
Thinking: *I am not the measure of creation.*
This is beyond me, this fish.
His God stands outside my God.

And the gold-and-green pure lacquer-mucus comes off in my
     hand,
And the red-gold mirror-eye stares and dies,
And the water-suave contour dims.

In this passage the concentration of compound words (absent, for
the most part, from the earlier part of the poem) in longer, more
cadenced lines produces a slight intensification of the flow of
feeling, but nothing to equal the exaltation of the climax of "Almond Blossom" or the conclusion of "Tortoise Shout." Still,
there is pathos and even horror in the man's interference in the
fish's world. For Lawrence is able to see himself as the fish must
see him—as "a many-fingered horror of daylight." All his observation intensifies his sense of the gulf between man and fish. Man
is not the measure of creation when such strange creatures as this
exist in the world. The conclusion of the poem seems to suggest,
moreover, that Jesus, too, is beyond the poet's imaginative reach
—a rare creature living according to his nature, which is alien to
Lawrence's own.

The section "Reptiles" contains perhaps the most admired of
the animal poems—"Snake" and the tortoise sequence. The note
stresses Lawrence's belief in the importance of the Heracleitan
"tension of opposites" in living things and in the world at large.
The snake, it is suggested, is held down by the moist pull of the
earth, though the fire in him would like to rise. The tortoise,
however, found feet and made the dome of his house his heaven.
"Therefore it is charted out and is the foundation of the world."
Thus, the life of the tortoise may symbolize the pattern of higher

forms in the living universe. In "Fish," "Snake," and the tortoise poems Lawrence moves, by careful stages, closer to the human condition.

Keith Sagar has noted that "Snake" is "virtually a dialogue between the poet's two selves—the 'young man' and the 'demon', the voice of education and the voice of the spontaneous self." [16] The strange "otherness" of the creature poses a problem for the man. He sees that the snake belongs to the volcanic Sicilian land itself; it is closely associated not only with the earth's burning bowels but with "Etna smoking." The snake has come "from out the dark door of the secret earth," from some secret "other" realm, and he looks about him "like a god." He is not said to *be* a god, but it is evident that he is a unique expression of the divine Creative Mystery, and therefore to be reverenced. And yet, the voices of the man's human education tell him that gold snakes are venomous and must be killed. When Lawrence succumbs to these voices of society, the grandeur of the earth's dark door vanishes, and it becomes a horrid black hole that revolts him. Such an image suggests, as Sagar has indicated, a horror of sex. More than this, the horror aroused by the snake is ultimately a neurotic fear of life itself.

In *The Plumed Serpent* [17] Kate's submission in marriage to Don Cipriano is accompanied by a very similar incident:

> Suddenly before her she saw a long, dark soft rope, lying over a pale boulder. But her soul was softly alert at once. It was a snake, with a subtle pattern along its soft dark back, lying there over a big stone, with its head sunk down to earth.
>
> It felt her presence too, for suddenly, with incredible soft quickness, it contracted itself down by the boulder, and she saw it entering a little gap in the wall.
>
> The hole was not very big. And as it entered it quickly looked back, poising its little dark, wicked pointed head, and flickering a dark tongue. Then it passed on, slowly easing its dark length into the hole.
>
> When it had all gone in, Kate could see the last fold still, and

the flat little head resting on the fold, like the devil with his chin
on his arms, looking out of a loop-hole. So the wicked sparks of
the eyes looked out at her, from within the recess. Watching out
of its own invisibility.

So she wondered over it, as it lay in its hidden places. At all
the unseen things in the hidden places of the earth. And she wondered if it was disappointed at not being able to rise higher in
creation: to be able to run on four feet, and not keep its belly on
the ground.

Perhaps not! Perhaps it had its own peace. She felt a certain reconciliation between herself and it.

This is of some importance in the novel, since Kate had once
thought of Mexico as being "so heavy, so oppressive, like the
folds of some huge serpent that seemed as if it could hardly raise
itself." [18] And in the story "Sun" there is yet another related episode: the sun-bathing woman and her small son respond with natural ease to the sight of a black snake in Sicily. Here, as elsewhere, the encounter with the snake suggests a necessary
reconciliation with all forms of life.

One remembers Lawrence's conscious acceptance of the snake
in "River Roses" and the essay "The Reality of Peace." In
"Snake" he has momentarily succumbed to his social conditioning, to the training of his mother. But immediately he regrets it.
As a living creature, powerful in his own sphere, the snake must
be accepted and honoured, and the human education that suggests
such life is evil is, for Lawrence, both presumptuous and funda-
mentally mistaken.

And I thought of the albatross,
And I wished he would come back, my snake.

For he seemed to me again like a king,
Like a king in exile, uncrowned in the underworld,
Now due to be crowned again.

And so, I missed my chance with one of the lords

Of life.
And I have something to expiate;
A pettiness.

The snake recalls to Lawrence Coleridge's albatross. It is worth remembering, in this regard, not only that the mariner was punished for his sin against life in slaying the albatross, but also that the bird was released from around his neck when he blessed, without forethought or conscious intention, the water snakes playing beneath him.

"Snake" is more dramatic than most of Lawrence's poems. Not only the encounter of man and snake but the tensions in the man provide the drama. Graham Hough has described the way in which the snake's mode of being and the man's two voices are defined by the rhythms:

> In "Snake" . . . noone sensitive to the rhythms of English speech can fail to observe the lovely fluidity of movement (like that of the snake itself). . . . The rhythm trembles on the verge of regular iambic for a line or two, then lapses into a loose conversational run; yet the two are not inharmonious but united; just as the mood of the poem oscillates between the apprehension of a strange Orphic life and the prosaic voices of "accursed human education". And a formal articulation is provided by the punctuating of the longer passages of description or reflection with short two-line sentences.[19]

As Hough observes, the shaping rhythm from within the poet can have a mimetic tendency; this is a natural part of the man's physical and mental response to the creature.

The rhythm of "Snake," like that of "Fish," is so expressive of the felt experience that the reader forgets he is reading a poem and simply sees and feels himself what Lawrence sees and feels.

He reached down from a fissure in the earth-wall in the gloom
And trailed his yellow-brown slackness soft-bellied down, over
    the edge of the stone trough

And rested his throat upon the stone bottom,
And where the water had dripped from the tap, in a small
    clearness,
He sipped with his straight mouth,
Softly drank through his straight gums, into his slack long
    body,
Silently.

Someone was before me at my water-trough,
And I, like a second comer, waiting.

He lifted his head from his drinking, as cattle do,
And looked at me vaguely, as drinking cattle do,
And flickered his two-forked tongue from his lips, and mused
    a moment,
And stooped and drank a little more,
Being earth-brown, earth-golden from the burning bowels of
    the earth
On the day of Sicilian July, with Etna smoking.

Here one is immediately caught up in the event. Each line, in its
unobtrusive way, contributes something more to one's vision of
the scene. The two lines set by themselves and the slightly varied
repetition of "drinking . . . cattle" tend to emphasize the dreamlike quality of the encounter, as does the insistence on the snake's
slowness and silence. The last lines relate the dream to the whole
landscape. Only the combination of the exact descriptive phrase
with the exact rhythmic shape could produce such an effect of
transparency. Though the writing seems effortless, it is a considerable achievement of poetic art. It is the "poetry of the present"
realized.

The tortoise poems are very impressive as well. From the mi-
nutely observed experience of the tortoise Lawrence makes an important statement of the tension between the value of independent single being and the need to seek a further wholeness in a
larger union. The life-journey of the tortoise is seen as a proto-

type of the journey of man as it is expressed in the myths of Christ and Osiris.

In "Baby Tortoise" Lawrence sees the "tiny, fragile, half-animate bean" as a pioneer just barely free of the "ponderous preponderate / Inanimate universe." The baby tortoise carries on his shoulders his "little round house," a precarious order "in the midst of chaos." All life is carried on to a further stage in the life of this "Ulyssean atom" who, like the cyclamen, is an "invincible forerunner." He is a perfect example of that order that comes from within, from the Creative Mystery. Lawrence interprets the baby's stripes as an evidence that the symbol of the Cross was not handed down from on high, but was inherent in the developing life of the tortoise. The Cross goes right through the tortoise's "crosswise cloven psyche," as it does through man's. Thus, it is a symbol of division in the nature of both man and beast.

In "Tortoise Family Connections" Lawrence notes the healthy independence of the tortoises:

On he goes, the little one,
Bud of the universe,
Pediment of life.

Setting off somewhere, apparently.
Whither away, brisk egg?

His mother deposited him on the soil as if he were no more
than droppings,
And now he scuffles tinily past her as if she were an old rusty
tin.

A mere obstacle,
He veers round the slow great mound of her—
Tortoises always foresee obstacles.

It is no use my saying to him in an emotional voice:
"This is your Mother, she laid you when you were an egg."

He does not even trouble to answer: "Woman, what have I to
    do with thee?"
He wearily looks the other way,
And she even more wearily looks another way still,
Each with the utmost apathy,
Incognisant,
Unaware,
Nothing.

As for papa,
He snaps when I offer him his offspring,
Just as he snaps when I poke a bit of stick at him,
Because he is irascible this morning, an irascible tortoise
Being touched with love, and devoid of fatherliness.

Father and mother,
And three little brothers,
And all rambling aimless, like little perambulating pebbles scat-
    tered in the garden,
Not knowing each other from bits of earth or old tins.

Here, as in "Snake," Lawrence uses himself as a character, as an
active participant in the events of the poem, in order to stress the
incongruity of any application of human social norms to the life
and being of the animal. At the same time, there are respects in
which man's situation and experience are like those of the tortoise, and this too is stressed by the presence of the observer, in
this passage by his biblical allusion. For like Jesus, one of the
great spiritual explorers, the tortoise leaves his mother behind him
in order to carry out his task as "fore-runner."

The baby tortoise is splendid in his singleness:

To be a tortoise!
Think of it, in a garden of inert clods
A brisk, brindled little tortoise, all to himself—
Adam!

In a garden of pebbles and insects
To roam, and feel the slow heart beat
Tortoise-wise, the first bell sounding
From the warm-blood in the dark-creation morning.

Moving, and being himself,
Slow, and unquestioned,
And inordinately there, O stoic!
Wandering in the slow triumph of his own existence,
Ringing the soundless bell of his presence in chaos,
And biting the frail grass arrogantly,
Decidedly arrogantly.

This idyll is shattered in "Lui et Elle," however. For now the sexual desire of the adult male tortoise gives him no peace. The male is smaller than the female, dapper and a bit ridiculous beside her. The "lonely rambler, the stoic, dignified stalker through chaos" is now reduced to a foolish lover. In "Lui et Elle" Lawrence interprets the symbolic fates of Christ and Osiris in terms of psychic division as it is expressed in sexuality. Neither man nor tortoise is complete until he has sought his consummation beyond himself.

"Tortoise Gallantry" describes the dogged pursuit of the apathetic female by the male. "Tortoise Shout" considers the significance of their eventual mating. The tortoise screams in orgasm with an "inexpressible faint yell" that carries one back to "the primeval rudiments of life, and the secret." The scream of the tortoise in extremity seems to Lawrence the prototype of all speech, the basic expression of all need:

I remember, when I was a boy,
I heard the scream of a frog, which was caught with his foot
  in the mouth of an up-starting snake;
I remember when I first heard bull-frogs break into sound in
  the spring;

I remember hearing a wild goose out of the throat of night
Cry loudly, beyond the lake of waters;
I remember the first time, out of a bush in the darkness, a night-
    ingale's piercing cries and gurgles startled the depths of
    my soul;
I remember the scream of a rabbit as I went through a wood at
    midnight;
I remember the heifer in her heat, blorting and blorting through
    the hours, persistent and irrepressible;
I remember my first terror hearing the howl of weird amorous
    cats;
I remember the scream of a terrified, injured horse, the sheet-
    lightning,
And running away from the sound of a woman in labour, some-
    thing like an owl whooing,
And listening inwardly to the first bleat of a lamb,
The first wail of an infant,
And my mother singing to herself,
And the first tenor singing of the passionate throat of a young
    collier, who has long since drunk himself to death,
The first elements of foreign speech
On wild dark lips.

The cinematic quality of this long catalogue, moving rapidly as it
does from incident to related incident, is reminiscent of similar
catalogues of scenes and events in Whitman's "Song of Myself."
Whitman, however, employed this technique in order to suggest
that he could, in imagination, contain within himself, a representative American, all of the experience of his countrymen; Lawrence employs it in order to suggest that the universal human need
for some fulfilment beyond oneself is related to all attempts at
self-expression and communication in both animals and humans.

It is sex, the divisive need, that breaks the perfect silence of single being and forces man to seek his complement and completion:

The cross,
The wheel on which our silence first is broken,

Sex, which breaks up our integrity, our single inviolability, our
 deep silence,
Tearing a cry from us.

Sex, which breaks us into voice, sets us calling across the deeps,
 calling, calling for the complement,
Singing, and calling, and singing again, being answered, having
 found.

Torn, to become whole again, after long seeking for what is
 lost,
The same cry from the tortoise as from Christ, the Osiris-cry
 of abandonment,
That which is whole, torn asunder,
That which is in part, finding its whole again throughout the
 universe.

In this bold conclusion Lawrence asserts that the last cry of
Christ forsaken by God, and that of Osiris when he must be torn
apart, have essentially the same meaning as the cry of the tortoise.
At the heart of the meaning of the mysteries of Christ and Osiris,
Lawrence feels, is the paradox of the whole which is only part,
which becomes truly whole by being broken. This is not a sexual
reduction of Christ's experience, as Harold Bloom suggests; [20] it is
rather that sex and mysticism have in common the desire to lose
oneself in order to find a larger self. Only in self-abandonment,
whether that of sex or mystical religious experience (or even the
special utterance of art), can one become whole. In Lawrence
these ways come together. "The abandonment to life which is
coition," writes Keith Sagar, "is celebrated in these poems with
the same clarity and splendour as the abandonment to death in
The Ship of Death and *Bavarian Gentians.*" [21]
 The "Birds" poems have not the same intensity as the tortoise
sequence. But they combine sharp observation with Lawrentian
speculation about the past and the future. Birds, suggests Law-

rence, are the life of the skies, and reveal the thoughts of the skies. All his birds are American, so the thoughts they "reveal" are mostly concerned with the new world of the west.

"Humming-Bird" presents a vision of the distant past; its success lies in the ease with which we can imagine the giant humming-bird piercing "the slow vegetable veins" merely by changing the scale. Such a change is possible because Lawrence has presented the reader with a very real humming-bird—a "little bit chipped off in brilliance"—and described his movements effectively.

In "Eagle in New Mexico" Lawrence recalls the more recent American past, the time of blood-sacrifice to the sun, suggesting that blood-thirsty sun-worship is somehow appropriate to America. The poem's conclusion reminds us, however, that Lawrence does not admire primitive energy for its own sake, but for the creative potentiality inherent in it. Americans must appreciate the genius of their wild land and make of it a new civilization.

Some of the animal poems, too, become vehicles for Lawrentian doctrine. In "Elephant," for instance, a highly coloured re-creation of the Pera-hera in Kandy, Ceylon, is given a political significance. In this poem a contrast is gradually developed between the majesty of the dark, old elephants come to do homage, and the pale, sickly humility of the young Prince of Wales:

> Elephants after elephants curl their trunks, vast shadows, and
>   some cry out
> As they approach and salaam, under the dripping fire of the
>   torches,
> That pale fragment of a Prince up there, whose motto is *Ich
>   dien.*
>
> Pale, dispirited Prince, with his chin on his hands, his nerves
>   tired out,
> Watching and hardly seeing the trunk-curl approach and
>   clumsy, knee-lifting salaam

Of the hugest, oldest of beasts in the night and the fire-flare
    below.
He is royalty, pale and dejected fragment up aloft.
And down below huge homage of shadowy beasts; bare-foot
    and trunk-lipped in the night.

R. G. N. Salgādo has pointed out that the elephants did homage
not to the visiting Prince but to the Sacred Tooth Relic of the
Lord Buddha in the temple at Kandy.[22] Nevertheless, the contrast between modern royalty and old obeisance seems a valid
one. For Lawrence feels that the ancient, dark people cannot help
jeering at a ruler who is nothing but a "drudge to the public":

They begin to understand.
The rickshaw boys begin to understand.
And then the devil comes into their faces,
But a different sort, a cold, rebellious, jeering devil.

In elephants and the east are two devils, in all men maybe.
The mystery of the dark mountain of blood, reeking in hom-
    age, in lust, in rage,
And passive with everlasting patience,
Then the little, cunning pig-devil of the elephant's lurking eyes,
    the unbeliever.

The spectacle of the pale prince can only have roused the jeering
unbeliever, thinks Lawrence. He feels that he himself could make
a better show of monarchy:

I wish they had given the three feathers to me;
That I had been he in the pavilion, as in a pepper-box aloft and
    alone
To stand and hold feathers, three feathers above the world,
And say to them: *Dient Ihr! Dient!*
Omnes, vos omnes, servite.
Serve me, I am meet to be served.
Being royal of the gods.

And to the elephants:
First great beasts of the earth,
A prince has come back to you,
Blood-mountains.
Crook the knee and be glad.

If monarchy is to retain any significance, it must effectively symbolize the power and dignity that is appropriate to man, Lawrence feels. Having experienced the mob hysteria of the war years, he has completely lost faith in democracy and come to believe that only some form of strong hierarchical and probably theocratic leadership can save civilization. The new order is nowhere very clearly adumbrated, however, though *The Plumed Serpent* attempts and fails to imagine it as a social reality. Lawrence's problem is that he is not really interested in political institutions and methods; he was no more impressed by Mussolini's attempts to restore grandeur to Italy than he was by the Prince of Wales, and he would certainly have been appalled by Hitler. What he wanted was not a political revolution, but a "revolution for life" —a reinstatement of pride, a change of heart. His ideal state is an artist's dream-kingdom, like Yeats's Byzantium.*

"Bibbles" is primarily an attack on Whitmanesque love—the promiscuous, "democratic" refusal to discriminate. Bibbles, a small black bitch, loves anybody who will pet her but is loyal to none:

Me or the Mexican who comes to chop wood
All the same,
All humanity is jam to you.

* *Cf. Women in Love* (p. 200):
". . . every true artist is the salvation of every other."
"I thought they got on so badly, as a rule."
"Perhaps. But only artists produce for each other the world that is fit to live in."

Everybody so dear, and yourself so ultra-beloved
That you have to run out at last and eat filth,
Gobble up filth, you horror, swallow utter abomination and
    fresh-dropped dung.

You stinker.
You worse than a carrion-crow.

Reeking dung-mouth.
You love-bird.

Reject nothing, sings Walt Whitman.
So you, you go out at last and eat the unmentionable,
In your appetite for affection.

And then you run in to vomit it in my house!
I get my love back.
And I have to clean up after you, filth which even blind Nature
    rejects
From the pit of your stomach;
But you, you snout-face, you reject nothing, you merge so
    much in love
You must eat even that.

Lawrence thinks that Bibbles will not welcome the sexual attention of the big dogs. He promises her protection if she will learn
loyalty "rather than loving." The poem has its moments of comedy or lively observation, but is damaged by its lengthy and
rather too-insistent moralizing.

    "Mountain Lion" somewhat restores the balance between ob-
servation and moral. It belongs with the most successful of the
poems of "encounter." In "Fish" and the tortoise poems there are
passages that express the dramatic encounter of man and beast,
but these appear to be subservient to the poet's observation of the
animal itself in order to discern and demonstrate both the similarities and differences between the experiencing natures of man and

beast. In "Snake," however, the encounter is the central action of
the poem, and in "Mountain Lion" the element of realistic narrative is paramount, as it is also in "Man and Bat." In "Mountain
Lion" Lawrence encounters two Mexicans with a dead lion in the
Lobo Canyon. As in "Snake," the encounter gives birth to a
moral observation, and the moral of the piece is acceptable, since
it seems to proceed immediately from the facts at hand.

There is a very convincing re-creation of the natural scene and
the embarrassment of the human encounter:

> Climbing through the January snow, into the Lobo Canyon
> Dark grow the spruce-trees, blue is the balsam, water sounds
>   still unfrozen, and the trail is still evident.
>
> Men!
> Two men!
> Men! The only animal in the world to fear!
>
> They hesitate.
> We hesitate.
> They have a gun.
> We have no gun.
>
> Then we all advance, to meet.
>
> Two Mexicans, strangers, emerging out of the dark and snow
>   and inwardness of the Lobo valley.
> What are they doing here on this vanishing trail?

In this opening Lawrence sets the scene for us with impressive
precision and economy. The long first sentence suggests admirably the character of the vast New Mexican landscape, while the
short staccato sentences that follow serve to suggest, by contrast,
the nervous incongruous quality of the human meeting within this
natural context. Man, the most dangerous of animals, disturbs the

natural order with his mechanical instruments of death and his neurotic need to destroy. The final lines remind us of the context of the meeting at the same time serving as punctuation for the first movement of the poem much as the lines

> Someone was before me at my water-trough,
> And I, like a second comer, waiting

do in "Snake."

There follows the embarrassment of the Mexicans about their act and a vivid description of the bright frost-face of the beautiful lioness they have shot. Then the poem proceeds to its seemingly inevitable elegiac reflection and moral:

> They go out towards the open;
> We go on into the gloom of Lobo.
> And above the trees I found her lair,
> A hole in the blood-orange brilliant rocks that stick up, a little cave.
> And bones, and twigs, and a perilous ascent.
>
> So, she will never leap up that way again, with the yellow flash of a mountain lion's long shoot!
> And her bright striped frost-face will never watch any more, out of the shadow of the cave in the blood-orange rock,
> Above the trees of the Lobo dark valley-mouth!
>
> Instead, I look out.
> And out to the dim of the desert, like a dream, never real;
> To the snow of the Sangre de Cristo mountains, the ice of the mountains of Picoris,
> And near across at the opposite steep of snow, green trees motionless standing in snow, like a Christmas toy.
>
> And I think in this empty world there was room for me and a mountain lion.

And I think in the world beyond, how easily we might spare
  a million or two of humans
And never miss them.
Yet what a gap in the world, the missing white frost-face of
  that slim yellow mountain lion!

Here Lawrence's reflections on the nobility of the lion and its superiority, as a whole creature, to most men arise perfectly
naturally from his examination of the lion's habitat. The harmony
between lioness and landscape is suggested in a mildly subliminal
way by the very similar visual impressions made by the "blood-
orange brilliant rocks" and the "bright striped frost-face" of the
lioness. She belongs here, as the men do not.

There is a beautiful restraint in Lawrence's description of the
lion's cave and the view of desert, trees, and mountains. And his
compassion for the slain beast is completely genuine, never for a
moment forced or sentimental. There is an implicit contrast in
the poem between the nobility of the lion and the slinking of the
Mexican, who "smiles foolishly, as if he were caught doing
wrong." For the lion had a wholeness and thus a nobility that
men have not achieved. Of the closing lines, in which Lawrence
seems to prefer the lion to most humans, R. G. N. Salgādo observes that "far from being anti-human in the interest of an abstract blood-philosophy these lines are really a criticism of contemporary living *from the standpoint of that which makes for
genuine life*—as indeed is the whole poem. . . ." [23]

One might expect a piece called "The Red Wolf" to be a similar kind of New Mexican animal poem, but it is, in fact, a very
different sort of poem both in method and in intention. It is of
some importance in Lawrence's development, however, since it
looks forward to the poems from *The Plumed Serpent* and also
to the late poems of social prophecy. This development is something of a new departure for Lawrence, even in *Birds, Beasts and
Flowers*, in which most of the poems are highly original, but it is,

of course, related to those poems in which flowers and fruits open up to reveal a new world within the known world. The difference is that in these later poems Lawrence no longer begins with an examination of the life of a plant but instead introduces gods, demons, and other mythical personages in order to express his vision.

The red wolf is Lawrence himself. He speaks in the sunset to one of the "tall old demons, smiling / The Indian smile." In the description of the desert scene is the implicit suggestion that because the Christian era is ending Lawrence must find new sources of life in an examination of primitive vitality.

> Day has gone to dust on the sage-grey desert
> Like a white Christus fallen to dust from a cross;
> To dust, to ash, on the twilit floor of the desert.
>
> And a black crucifix like a dead tree spreading wings;
> Maybe a black eagle with its wings out
> Left lonely in the night
> In a sort of worship.

The demon Lawrence speaks with is called Harry or Old Nick. It seems likely, then, that he represents those energies that the Christians consigned to the devil—elemental forces with which Lawrence seeks a living contact. But he wins one concession only from the demon—the admission that he is, in fact, a red wolf and not a tame dog. It is interesting that he calls the demon "Father," for the primitive or "natural" man found throughout his writings bears a considerable resemblance to his own father. In seeking to restore the antediluvian, "dark," tactile way of consciousness suggested in "Grapes" Lawrence is seeking fulfilment and release for the father, the male element within his psyche. He identifies the maleness he desires with the decayed but suggestive wisdom of primitive or ancient peoples.

In "The Red Wolf" it is evident that his quest is not wholly successful. He feels that he must wait for the demon to return with a "new story," a new signal from life out of the American wilderness. This theme or "myth" is reinforced in this poem by the powerful evocation of the Taos desert at twilight in the opening stanzas. But "The Red Wolf" is primarily a mythic rather than a realistic poem, and in this it anticipates the mode of the poems from *The Plumed Serpent*.

The whole of "Ghosts," the concluding section of *Birds, Beasts and Flowers,* is devoted to the character and possibilities of America. In the note Lawrence speaks once again of the unhappy dead who "linger" on the trail to the land of the dead; they are "disconsolate, since even death can never make up for some mistakes."

In "Men in New Mexico" the land is seen as a place of sleep-walkers where the old potent gods are asleep, as the mountains are asleep. The Indians thought the white man could waken them, but the whites too are asleep, somnambulistic. The self-laceration of the Penitentes and the gun-fights of the horsemen—these are attempts to wake the land, but they have failed. In New Mexico men are born with a caul, a "dark membrane over the will."

In "Autumn at Taos" Lawrence describes the landscape in terms of wild beasts—tigress, wolf, otter, hawk, bear—but these beasts, too, are asleep. But if the powers of the wild land are not yet fully realized, it provides, nevertheless, a new perspective from which Lawrence can view England. In "Spirits Summoned West" he thinks of the old country as a land of the dead, asking that his mother and his "ideal" lovers be reconciled to his quest, and live at peace within him. For he hopes that the delicate emotional ties of the old way of love may find some place in the larger context of his new way. The woman essentially virgin has still a place in his affections.

"The American Eagle" suggests the ambivalence of American idealism. The dove of liberty has denounced eagles, but then hatched one herself. So far, this eagle has masqueraded as "a sort of prosperity gander / Fathering endless ten-dollar golden eggs." But an eagle ought to be true to its nature, Lawrence feels. He wonders when America will exercise its latent power.

It is perhaps unfortunate that he chose to conclude *Birds, Beasts and Flowers* with such a dubious appeal to the American appetite for power, but it is interesting that he lays stress on the idea that America may be the appropriate site for his new way of life. In *The Plumed Serpent* he attempts to imagine a revival of the sleeping gods, utilizing his own responses to the Taos Indians. The alien Christianity is retired, and a new version of the old religion is advocated. Whatever one thinks about Lawrence's particular interpretation of the spirit of place in America, the poems included in this novel express his new religion as directly as it could be expressed. In them the vision of "Grapes" and other such poems in *Birds, Beasts and Flowers* is extended.

It is somewhat unusual, of course, to include poems in a novel; few other instances come readily to mind. Why did Lawrence do so? One purpose seems clear. It appears that Lawrence had very little notion just what his religious revolution or reformation of consciousness would involve in the way of concrete social and political changes, and that the hymns and other poetic fragments provide one means of evading this rather thorny problem. His strategy is to distract the reader with image and rhetoric from the failure to present his revolution in conventional novelistic terms as a social reality. It is evident that the dramatic purpose of the poems in the novel is, usually, to lend an air of credibility to the rather stagy and sometimes barbarous rituals indulged in by Lawrence's heroes, Don Ramon and Don Cipriano. The poem beginning "I am Huitzilopochtli," for instance, immediately follows a dance in which Cipriano and his men, their bodies painted "in horizontal bars of red and black," prance about tossing torches into the air and catching them again. Several other poems about an emblematic grey dog of cowardice and the goddess Malintzi's pardon accompany a public execution in which Cipriano first pardons one prisoner simply because of the luck of the draw and then personally stabs three others in their hearts. It is interesting that, taken by themselves, these poems give expression to a system of values that Lawrence signally fails to dramatize in his story of two Mexican reformers. Even Don Ramon's hymns of Quetzalcoatl, which present quite effectively his beliefs and hopes for his country, do not serve to make him seem much more than a wooden and humourless ventriloquist's dummy for Lawrence. It would seem that Lawrence could satisfy the human need for ritual only in his language and not in a completely imagined action. For the poems themselves are eloquent expressions of his quarrel with Christianity and his belief in human renewal.

In "The Coming of Quetzalcoatl" Jesus is a star that is falling; he has spent his force, as in "The Red Wolf." Quetzalcoatl has been sleeping in a cave in "the place of the west . . . beyond the lashing of the sun's bright tail," but he is awakened by the song of the star:

> The star that was falling was fading, was dying.
> I heard the star singing like a dying bird;
> *My name is Jesus, I am Mary's Son.*
> *I am coming home.*
> *My mother the Moon is dark,*
> *Oh brother, Quetzalcoatl*
> *Hold back the dragon of the sun,*
> *Bind him with shadow while I pass*
> *Homewards. Let me come home.*

> I bound the bright fangs of the sun
> And held him while Jesus passed
> Into the lidless shade,
> Into the eye of the Father,
> Into the womb of refreshment.

And the breath blew upon me again.
So I took the sandals of the Saviour
And started down the long slope
Past the mount of the sun.
Till I saw beneath me
White breast-tips of my Mexico
My bride.

Jesus the Crucified
Sleeps in the healing waters
The long sleep.
Sleep, sleep, my brother, sleep.
My bride between the seas
Is combing her dark hair
Saying to herself: Quetzalcoatl.

Such a poem has not the technical subtlety or dramatic realism of "Snake" and "Mountain Lion." Instead, in clear, simple sentences Lawrence conveys his meaning by means of myth and symbol. Jesus' time is up, so Quetzalcoatl now descends from behind the sun, from the androgynous source of all energy and being ("the eye of the Father . . . the womb of refreshment"), to Mexico. In the last three lines there is a lovely lyric flow, culminating in the magic-sounding name, Quetzalcoatl, to accompany the image of annunciation.

Sometimes an element of comedy enlivens these poems. In "Quetzalcoatl Looks Down on Mexico," for example, the tone becomes increasingly colloquial and comic in tone as the god expresses his mystification at mechanized cities and foreign domination. He finds the Mexicans "glum and lumpish," stupefied, stone deaf. And he appoints a man (Don Ramon) to tell them of his wrath if they do not awake. "For the sun and the moon are alive, and watching with gleaming eyes." This world is ripe for a "spring cleaning." Despite the comedy, Quetzalcoatl's return is as serious and potentially violent as that of the strange beast in Yeats's "The Second Coming." The poem moves from the majestic to the comic to the prophetic in an easy way.

The later poems from *The Plumed Serpent* propose a descent into the "deeps that life cannot fathom," the innermost life beyond and before life, the "non-human," inorganic Mystery from which all life comes and to which it returns. This greater reality is said to include "our life and our death," for the universe itself is a vast beast that lives forever in the continual process of self-renewal that is symbolized in the replacement of Jesus by Quetzalcoatl. These poems are far more abstract in their dependence on symbols like the great "Breath" and the "Fountain" and on the various mythic personages that inhabit them than are the poems from *Birds, Beasts and Flowers,* but they are nevertheless highly suggestive and (some of them) quite successful on their own terms. As they are not intended to present an immediate experience in the way that "Snake" and "A Doe at Evening" do, it seems idle to complain that they have departed the substantial world of *Birds, Beasts and Flowers.* They are mythic or biblical in style and method.* On the whole, they are more effective when they do not employ rhyme. The tone and rhythm are conversational or hortatory, and the meaning is almost wholly expressed in image and symbol. Taken altogether, these poems constitute a vivid mythic expression of the psychic revolution or change of heart that Lawrence desired. In this they look forward to the prophetic theme of *Last Poems.* In *Last Poems,* too, Lawrence writes of the awakening and return of sleeping gods who seem personifications of lost faculties, lost powers. But such poems are,

---

* Some of the hymns may have been influenced by the translations of Aztec hymns in Lewis Spence's *The Gods of Mexico* (London: T. Fisher Unwin, 1923) but their spirit is decidedly Lawrentian. Indeed, the resemblance is very slight: the hymns are simple, brief, and straightforward; Lawrence's hymns develop their message in recurrent patterns of imagery and symbol.

of course, not so pure an attempt to achieve the "poetry of the present" as we find in *Birds, Beasts and Flowers*.

Birds, Beasts and Flowers is, indeed, a unique experience in modern poetry. As Graham Hough has written, the poems are so original that they defy traditional classification.[24] It seems to me that in the best of them Lawrence has achieved what he could not achieve in his early poems—a fusion of lyric, dramatic, prophetic, analytic, and descriptive modes. "Almond Blossom" and "Snake," for example, combine all these elements. Only a considerable discipline could produce such a flexible but precise idiom —the discipline of the exact observation, the appropriate symbol, and the shaping rhythm of the poet's own voiced feeling. But, of course, all of these aims are inherent in Lawrence's vision of the purely experienced present, the "mystic Now." As Kenneth Rexroth has written, "the craft is the vision and the vision is the craft." [25] Even the poet's antediluvian Golden Age (and, for that matter, his vision of the future in Mexico or America or wherever) is a vision he feels is inherent in man's immediate experience of the world. By attending to his own deep, sensuous apprehension of the present, Lawrence has done what he set out to do. He has "discovered" a new world within the known world, and thereby created a poetry of the present.

❧ Four

The Cosmic Swan:

Pansies, *Nettles*, and "More Pansies"

I cannot feel that *Pansies* is anything but a decline from his earlier poems, while *Nettles* is about the worst and most trivial thing he ever published. It seems to me that nearly all these Pansies and Nettles came out of Lawrence's nerves, and not out of his real self. They are one long hammer, hammer, hammer of exasperation. Sometimes they are like the utterances of a little Whitman, but without Walt's calm sostenuto quality; and sometimes they are like a little Blake raving, but without the fiery vision. Yet it is always Lawrence speaking, even in the most disconcertingly trivial or spiteful, but to me at least very much the Lawrence of off days, the Lawrence one could most easily do without. I don't say this of all the Pansies, but of a good many, and certainly of all the Nettles.[1]

(Richard Aldington)

The poems that Lawrence wrote at the end of his life have a peculiar quality of freshness and directness. The Whitmanesque rhetoric and the "ritual frenzy" that Blackmur condemns have now disappeared. We hear in these poems the voice of a very wise man who is also humorous, completely disillusioned yet never cynical, a man who loves life, but is saddened and embittered at the way in which it is being fouled and violated by mass "civilization". . . . In some of the poems, especially those written in the last months of his life, the voice is that of a seer with a majestic vision of God and life and earth. . . .

In all these later poems of Lawrence one gets the impression of a man who, like the Byron of *Don Juan,* is able to speak out his whole mind in verse with complete ease and without any sort of inhibition. . . . [Richard Aldington's condemnation] seems to me a gross exaggeration. Some of the pansies and nettles are written in a mood of exasperation, but many of them are brilliant and incisive commentaries on Western civilization. . . .[2]

(Vivian de Sola Pinto)

These remarks suggest the disagreement of critics about Lawrence's satirical poems. Most writers have inclined to Aldington's view, but it is my judgment that *Pansies* has many more successes (some of them very slight pieces, to be sure) than has generally been acknowledged. *Nettles* is a much shorter and inferior collection; nevertheless, it contains a forceful vision of the industrial world Lawrence detested. And the "More Pansies" part of *Last Poems* adds to its censure the renewed faith in a human future.

Most of the *Pansies,* written in the winter of 1928–1929, is devoted to those particular things Lawrence most disliked about modern industrial society. But there is also the basic underlying assumption that "our day is over":

Our day is over, night comes up
shadows steal out of the earth.
Shadows, shadows
wash over our knees and splash between our thighs,
our day is done;
we wade, we wade, we stagger, darkness rushes between our
      stones,
we shall drown.

Our day is over
night comes up.

Civilization is dying, Lawrence feels. The war did not usher in the new era; it merely exacerbated the disintegration of the old.

Moreover, the attempt to imagine a new civilization in America has not yet been a success—only the vision of the poems survives, and most men do not share it. In two other pansies, "Hark in the Dusk!" and "Twilight," both placed near the beginning of the collection, Lawrence employs the image of a rising flood of darkness that will overwhelm us all.

On the personal level, this vision is expressed in terms of the poet's own deteriorating health. For he feels that his increasing bodily weakness is due to his special sensitivity to the psychic climate of the time; he has consciously experienced in his own being the fatal self-division of Western man.* Now he feels his vitality ebbing with that of his world

> I have no desire any more
> towards woman or man, bird, beast or creature or thing.
>
> All day long I feel the tide rocking, rocking
> though it strikes no shore
> in me.
>
> Only mid-ocean.—
> ("Desire Goes Down into the Sea—")
>
> The sea dissolves so much
> and the moon makes away with so much more than we know—
>
> Once the moon comes down
> and the sea gets hold of us
> cities dissolve like rock-salt

---

* Cf. "Sick" and "Healing." In *Fantasia of the Unconscious* (p. 55) Lawrence writes: "On the upper plane, the lungs and heart are controlled from the cardiac plane and the thoracic ganglion. Any excess in the sympathetic mode from the upper centres tends to burn the lungs with oxygen, weaken them with stress, and cause consumption. So it is just criminal to make a child too loving. No child should be induced to love too much. It means derangement and death at last." Such dangerous loving must be balanced, he felt, by independence, insouciance, pure single being.

and the sugar melts out of life
iron washes away like an old blood-stain
gold goes out into a green shadow
money makes even no sediment
and only the heart
glitters in salty triumph
over all it has known, that has gone now into salty nothingness.

("The Sea, the Sea")

The most moving of these few very personal poems is "November by the Sea," which anticipates the poems about death in *Last Poems:*

Now in November nearer comes the sun
down the abandoned heaven.

As the dark closes round him, he draws nearer
as if for our company.

At the base of the lower brain
the sun in me declines to his winter solstice
and darts a few gold rays
back to the old year's sun across the sea.

A few gold rays thickening down to red
as the sun of my soul is setting
setting fierce and undaunted, wintry
but setting, setting behind the sounding sea between my ribs.

The wide sea wins, and the dark
winter, and the great day-sun, and the sun in my soul
sinks, sinks to setting and the winter solstice
downward, they race in decline
my sun, and the great gold sun.

All the poems I have quoted seem to me very successful. They are perfectly direct, with no trace of rhetoric or self-pity. They are sparer and tougher than the poems of Lawrence's middle years, and in this respect a further development of the idiom that is peculiarly his own; it is the almost matter-of-fact tone as much as the vision that gives even the briefest of these poetic thoughts its characteristic shape and unity.

What is it that the man and his civilization must do in their situation of extremity? "Desire Is Dead," a small and perfect lyric, gives Lawrence's personal response:

> Desire may be dead
> and still a man can be
> a meeting place for sun and rain,
> wonder outwaiting pain
> as in a wintry tree.

He has lost the physical well-being necessary to feel desire, but still he can be true to his organic nature as a living creature. He now asks the woman for fidelity and trust instead of passionate love. And he senses that his death will release new energies into the cosmos:

> When the ripe fruit falls
> its sweetness distils and trickles away into the veins of the earth.
>
> When fulfilled people die
> the essential oil of their experience enters
> the veins of living space, and adds a glisten
> to the atom, to the body of immortal chaos.
>
> For space is alive
> and it stirs like a swan
> whose feathers glisten
> silky with oil of distilled experience.
>
> > ("When the Ripe Fruit Falls—")

The cosmos is alive; our little cycle of life and death is only a part of its greater life. Even in death we can be used by life, and thus be fulfilled.

In other poems the symbol of the swan or goose stands for the elemental energy or "electron" that will create new life from what we call inorganic matter:

> Far-off
> at the core of space
> at the quick
> of time
> beats
> and goes still
> the great swan upon the waters of all endings
> the swan within vast chaos, within the electron.
> ("Swan")

In this poem Lawrence combines his intuitive feelings about the origin of life in the purposive "electron" or atomic activity of matter with the myth of Leda and the swan. A new and vital life will come, not from the spiritless men of today, but from the cosmos itself, the immortal animal.

In "Give Us Gods" Lawrence asks for gods more basic than any we have known, gods before Jehovah, Christ, Jove, Orpheus, the eagle, the ram, the beetle, or the serpent. But modern "scientific" man has failed to achieve the religious vision inherent in his discoveries. He believes he has mastered life, but life will take its own course, and proceed with its "formless—though not absolutely formless—craving for form." Here is Lawrence's response to the discoveries of modern physics:

> I like relativity and quantum theories
> because I don't understand them
> and they make me feel as if space shifted about like a swan that
> can't settle,

refusing to sit still and be measured;
and as if the atom were an impulsive thing
always changing its mind.

("Relativity")

Somehow, there is a basic, if unpredictable, purposive energy at work.

Man cannot know if he has a viable future. He may grow and develop, or he may continue to disintegrate, and in so doing contribute to the advent of some new and higher form of life. What should man do in this situation of uncertainty?

Tell me first, O tell me,
will the dark flood of our day's annihilation
swim deeper, deeper, till it leaves no peak emerging?
Shall we be lost, all of us
and gone like weed, like weed, like eggs of fishes,
like sperm of whales, like germs of the great dead past
into which the creative future shall blow strange, unknown
            forms?

Are we nothing, already, but the lapsing of a great dead past?
Is the best that we are but sperm, loose sperm, like the sperm
            of fishes
that drifts upon time and chaos, till some unknown future takes
            it up
and is fecund with a new day of new creatures? different from
us.

Or is our shattered Argosy, our leaking ark
at this moment scraping tardy Ararat?
Have we got to get down and clear away the debris
of a swamped civilisation, and start a new world for man
that will blossom forth the whole of human nature?

Must we hold on, hold on
and go ahead with what is human nature
and make a new job of the human world?

Or can we let it go?
O, can we let it go,
and leave it to some nature that is more than human
to use the sperm of what's worth while in us
and thus eliminate us?
Is the time come for humans
now to begin to disappear,
leaving it to the vast revolutions of creative chaos
to bring forth creatures that are an improvement on humans,
as the horse was an improvement on the ichthyosaurus?

Must we hold on?
Or can we now let go?

Or is it even possible we must do both?

("To Let Go or to Hold On—?")

Apparently, we must do our best and hope for the best in the full knowledge of the failure of our past and present civilization. John Middleton Murry writes:

> I imagine that what he means when he spoke of both "holding on and letting go" at the same time is that we should at once accept the possibility that the day of man is really over, and yet do our utmost, pitifully little though it must be, to awaken in ourselves and in others a new consciousness of the profound human crisis, and our responsibility in it.[3]

It is in this spirit that Lawrence launches his particular attacks on twentieth-century western society. He had been militantly optimistic in some of the *Birds, Beasts and Flowers* and *Plumed Serpent* poems, but he was bound to suffer considerable disillusionment, and one result of this is the attempt to develop an idiom even more colloquial and direct than that of his middle years in order to communicate with greater force his own cure for the world's ills. Some of the pansies may reflect exasperation and nerves. But the poems already cited indicate a much more serious and basic concern for the health of the human adventure in civilization. As Louise Bogan has written, Lawrence "gave us a prophetic vignette of modern Europe in ruins, and he gave us warnings against 'the police state' and 'spy government everywhere.'" In his pansies Lawrence advanced "so far into a future he saw with the utmost clarity that many of his more sentimental followers fell away from him in a state of shock." [4] In "Police Spies" Lawrence asserts that "official spying" is anarchy, and in "Now It's Happened," that only the sickly idealism of Dostoevski, Chekhov and Tolstoi allowed Lenin to impose such a system in Russia. But the capitalist system imposes mechanization on man just as bolshevism does. Each is a result of industrialism.

"How Beastly the Bourgeois Is—," one of the best known of the pansies, expresses Lawrence's dislike of the parasitic inflexibility of spirit of the mechanical modern man. It begins well, with an amusing play on the word "present," but becomes merely abusive after the basic point is made in the fourth stanza. One is too aware of Lawrence himself, as his voice grows more and more shrill. There is no drama, since the bourgeois is not made very real. There is not the good-natured acknowledgement of exaggeration and caricature that there is in "The Noble Englishman":

> I know a noble Englishman
> who is sure he is a gentleman,
> that sort—
>
> This moderately young gentleman
> is very normal, as becomes an Englishman,
> rather proud of being a bit of a Don Juan
> you know—

But one of his beloveds, looking a little peaked
towards the end of her particular affair with him
said: Ronald, you know, is like most Englishmen,
by instinct, he's a sodomist
but he's frightened to know it
so he takes it out on women.

Oh come! said I. That Don Juan of a Ronald!
Exactly, she said. Don Juan was another of them, in love with
    himself
and taking it out on women.

Even that isn't sodomitical, said I.
But if a man is in love with himself, isn't that the meanest form
    of homosexuality? she said.

Here we have two comic characters besides Ronald—the
"peaked" beloved and a sweetly reasonable Lawrence who refuses
to jump to conclusions. In an earlier version of this poem the
conversation given above did not take place. Lawrence was much
more sweeping in his attack, referring sarcastically to the "Rock
of Ages of his public school" and to the noble Englishman's "icy
contempt" for perverts, even though "he's an instinctive homosexual / Like almost all Englishmen." The later version is less
general, less widely vituperative, and more economical. Lawrence
has wisely introduced the conversation between himself and the
disillusioned woman, a conversation in which he plays straight
man and sets her up for an attack on Ronald. Her exaggeration of
the homosexual tendency in Englishmen is somehow more acceptable in this context, and in her lively account Ronald becomes far more real than ever the bourgeois was. Altogether, the
poem is made much more convincing and effective by its dialogue form.

As in *Birds, Beasts and Flowers*, one of Lawrence's chief concerns is the way in which people have forgotten how to experi-

ence anything at first hand. Thus he dislikes the cinema, and, as in "The Noble Englishman," it is false emotion that moves him to scorn. The cinema, he feels, can provide only a mental thrill; men have forgotten how to experience with their whole selves. At the circus they are uneasy at the reminder of the human body. Modern man has lost his body.

A number of poems deal with the question of man's relation to his artifacts. Lawrence believes that such things "live" only insofar as they are expressions of the maker's life. For men are transmitters of life in sex and creativity. A man should not fret about earning his living; he must earn his life by truly living it. And this is a matter for the people themselves. Napoleon and Lenin may announce themselves as saviours, but the people "have been saved so often / and sold" ("When Wilt Thou Teach the People—?").

But why put up with the modern life-denying political systems?

> why have the industrial system?
> why have machines, that we only have to serve?
> why have a soviet, that only wants to screw us all in as parts
>   of the machine?
> why have working classes at all, as if men were only embodied
>   jobs?
> why not have men as men, and the work as merely part of the
>   game of life?
>
> True, we've got all these things
> industrial and financial systems, machines and soviets, working
>   classes.
> But why go on having them, if they belittle us?
> Why should we be belittled any longer?

("Why—?")

In this way Lawrence dismisses both communism and capitalism as viable political and social systems. The psychic health of the individual, whole man demands that he be something more than a part of the social machine. Social and professional definition is essentially meaningless. Lawrence would like to eliminate class-struggle, to "abolish the working classes for ever / and have a world of men" ("O! Start a Revolution—").

Man's basic nature is hidden beneath the surface of his ordinary world:

> When the moon falls on a man's blood
> white and slippery, as on the black water in a port
> shaking asunder, and flicking at his ribs—
>
> then the noisy, dirty day-world
> exists no more, nor ever truly existed;
> but instead
> this wet white gleam
> twitches, and ebbs hitting, washing inwardly, silverily against
>   his ribs
> on his soul that is dark ocean within him.
>
> And under the flicking of the white whip-lash of the moon
> sea-beasts immersed lean sideways and flash bright
> in pure brilliance of anger, sea-immersed anger
> at the trashy, motor-driven transit of dirty day
> that has left scum on the sea, even in the night.
>
>   ("Moon Memory")

In "There Is Rain in Me—" Lawrence declares that the "old ocean within a man" is angry in its enforced exile. And in several poems he exhorts young men to fight against the worship of cash and to free the life within them. In "Don'ts" and "The Risen Lord" he envisions a resurrection of the flesh. Some of these poems employ the most ragged doggerel, but the message is very clear.

Several poems about the ways of nature offer a contrast to

man's behaviour. Probably the best is "The Elephant Is Slow to Mate":

> The elephant, the huge old beast,
>   is slow to mate;
> he finds a female, they show no haste
>   they wait
>
> for the sympathy in their vast shy hearts
>   slowly, slowly to rouse
> as they loiter along the river-beds
>   and drink and browse
>
> and dash in panic through the brake
>   of forest with the herd,
> and sleep in massive silence, and wake
>   together, without a word.
>
> So slowly the great hot elephant hearts
>   grow full of desire,
> and the great beasts mate in secret at last,
>   hiding their fire.
>
> Oldest they are and the wisest of beasts
>   so they know at last
> how to wait for the loneliest of feasts
>   for the full repast.
>
> They do not snatch, they do not tear;
>   their massive blood
> moves as the moon-tides, near, more near,
>   till they touch in flood.

Here is the perfect expression of a "natural" rather than a mentally induced sexuality. Like poetry, sexuality must always find its own rhythm.

The other "nature" poems are brief imagistic epigrams. At their best they express either *joie de vivre:*

> The tiny fish enjoy themselves
> in the sea.
> Quick little splinters of life,
> their little lives are fun to them
> in the sea.
>
> ("Little Fish")

or natural wisdom:

> The mosquito knows full well, small as he is
> he's a beast of prey.
> But after all
> he only takes his bellyful,
> he doesn't put my blood in the bank.
>
> ("The Mosquito Knows")

In "Self-Pity" Lawrence notes that wild things do not feel sorry for themselves. If only man could be less self-conscious, he might express himself with the cool fragrance of a new moon or the beautiful rage of spray. In "Many Mansions" he is seen to be inferior to a bird. But perhaps the poem that best captures Lawrence's sense of the social man's inadequacy is "Lizard":

> A lizard ran out on a rock and looked up, listening
> no doubt to the sounding of the spheres.
> And what a dandy fellow! the right toss of a chin for you
> and swirl of a tail!
>
> If men were as much men as lizards are lizards
> they'd be worth looking at.

Unlike the lizard man has not achieved his true individuality as a creature.

His problem is the unnatural dominance of the mind, or rather, the self-conscious ego:

> As a plant becomes pot-bound
> man becomes ego-bound
> enclosed in his own limited mental consciousness.
>
> Then he can't feel any more
> or love, or rejoice or even grieve any more,
> he is ego-bound,
> pot-bound
> in the pot of his own conceit,
> and he can only slowly die.
>
> Unless he is a sturdy plant.
> Then he can burst the pot,
> shell off his ego
> and get his roots in earth again,
> raw earth.
>
> ("Ego-Bound")

In another poem Lawrence sees his London friends as ships in bottles. Modern ego-bound young intellectuals are given only to the perverse mental thrills of imagined murder, suicide, rape; thus Lawrence is dismayed by his friend Aldous Huxley's *Point Counter Point*.

Somehow man must escape from the prison of his mental and social ego. In "Elemental" Lawrence asks why people don't "leave off being lovable . . . and be a bit elemental instead."

> Since man is made up of the elements
> fire, and rain, and air, and live loam
> and none of these is lovable
> but elemental,
> man is lop-sided on the side of the angels.

Such a poem reminds one of Frederick J. Hoffman's statement of Lawrence's quarrel with Freud: "Whereas Freud regarded the ego as the guardian (a badly confused guardian, it must be admitted) of the total self against its violation by the dark unconscious self, to Lawrence such a discipline caused interference with fundamental sources of emotional expression." [5] And Louise Bogan has remarked that Lawrence "succeeded in keeping the barrier between his unconscious forces and his consciousness extremely thin." [6] Such a life frightens most men, but it may be uniquely fulfilling. Lawrence believes that:

> If you will go down into yourself, under your surface person-
> ality
> you will find you have a great desire to drink life direct
> from the source, not out of bottles and bottled personal vessels.
> ("The Primal Passions")

Lawrence's view of the unconscious as the source of spontaneity and creativity is closer to Jung than to Freud. Like Jung he values the wholeness that may come from a fuller awareness of one's elemental psychic energies. These are physical and instinctive at bottom, as Jung notes:

> The deeper "Layers" of the psyche lose their individual unique-
> ness as they retreat farther and farther into darkness. "Lower down",
> that is to say as they approach the autonomous functional systems,
> they become increasingly collective until they are universalised
> and extinguished in the body's materiality, i.e. in chemical sub-
> stances. The body's carbon is simply carbon. Hence "at bottom"
> the psyche is simply "world." [7]

It is contact with this genuine "world" that is both within and without that Lawrence desires as a corrective for the modern man's exclusively "mental" awareness. Man must get beyond his own machines and technology in order to be truly at home in the world.

A number of poems attack the evils of buying and selling. Lawrence asks for a communism based not on economics but on a religion of life. Men have become wage-slaves, caged monkeys. Even our university "culture" has its roots "in the deep dung of cash" ("Nottingham's New University"). In "Wages" Lawrence feels that the scramble for money makes the world a prison. It is the competitive system that drives men to acquire more possessions than they need. Only mutual trust and a "revolution for fun" can restore man's sanity.

In a number of poems Lawrence employs the sun as a symbol of that basic energy that may bring about the resurrection of the flesh:

> A sun will rise in me,
> I shall slowly resurrect,
> already the whiteness of false dawn is on my inner ocean.

> A sun in me.
> And a sun in heaven.
> And beyond that, the immense sun behind the sun,
> the sun of immense distances, that fold themselves together
> within the genitals of living space.
> And further, the sun within the atom
> which is god in the atom.
>
> ("Sun in Me")

One is a part of the whole:

> Space, of course, is alive
> that's why it moves about;
> and that's what makes it eternally spacious and unstuffy.

> And sane where it has a wild heart
> that sends pulses even through me;
> and I call it the sun;

and I feel aristocratic, noble, when I feel a pulse go through me
from the wild heart of space, that I call the sun of suns.

("Space")

One must preserve one's sanity even in extremity in order to give
oneself to space. The universe itself is sane. Man today is insane
because he fears society; puritans and profligates divide the world
between them, each acting only in relation to social pressure, and
they are equally insane.

In "Sun-Men," "Sun-Women," "Democracy," "Aristocracy of
the Sun," "Conscience," "The Middle Classes," and "Immortality" Lawrence employs the sun to formulate once again his "natural" morality. Men must turn the sun in their breasts to the
great sun. Some women, perhaps, belong not to their men but to
the sun—they are chosen by life, like Leda. Class distinctions are
irrelevant; all that matters is whether a man has the sun in him.
The middle classes, however, are essentially sunless since they live
for position and money. They are inclined to be "sun-extinct /
and busy putting out the sun in other people."

Lawrence's comic sense reasserts itself in the poems about the
modern woman—"Volcanic Venus," "What Does She Want?,"
"Wonderful Spiritual Women," "Poor Bit of a Wench," "What
Ails Thee?," "It's no good!" and "Don't Look at Me." Modern
women are volcanoes of frustrated energy; they think they want
love but something more basic is wanting. Lawrence does not
spare himself in his comedy of the sexes. When the man attempts
to comfort his brooding woman, speaking like Mellors in dialect,
she tells him to "leave off putting the Robbie Burns touch over
me" and demands cigarettes ("What Ails Thee?").

On the other hand, the trivial squibs and ballads about class are
perhaps the worst because the least objective of the pansies.
Lawrence might have had something valuable to say about the
complicated class-consciousness of the English, or about his own
necessary loss of social context, but he is, for the most part, con-

tent with simple abuse. Similarly, the poems about the difficulties of *Lady Chatterley's Lover* are not very interesting. They are neither witty nor pointed enough to justify their doggerel shape. "To Clarinda" and "Henriette," which are related poems, are rather silly. "The Jeune Fille" is more sensible, but the jingling quatrains seem forced. "Censors" is much better than these, not only because it is more pointed, but because it has a natural rhythm. Censors are dead men casting a stern eye on the life that frightens them. Thus Lawrence repays the authorities who attacked not only *The Rainbow* and *Lady Chatterley's Lover* but *Pansies* as well.*

Unfortunately, most of *Nettles* is on the same level as the most trivial of the pansies. In "The People," however, Lawrence indicates a deeper and more personal involvement in the fate of modern man. As always, in his best work, he implicates himself as well as his enemies in the sickness and progressive emasculation of modern man caught up in the industrial and social machine. For he has not wholly escaped from the environmental conditioning of his Midlands childhood. "We Die Together," from the "More Pansies" part of *Last Poems*, makes this clear:

> Oh, when I think of the industrial millions, when I see some of them,
> a weight comes over me heavier than leaden linings of coffins
> and I almost cease to exist, weighed down to extinction
> and sunk into a depression that almost blots me out.

---

* Lawrence's difficulties with censors have occasioned some minor textual problems. The editors of *Complete Poems* of 1967 stated that their text of *Pansies* consisted of the poems published in the private definitive edition (p. 24). But their text seems to be that of the public edition with the fourteen poems published only in the private edition added to it. In at least one case they have kept the reading of the public edition: the version of "The Saddest Day" that appears in the private edition has "cat-piss" (p. 115), not "my eye," but the editors have retained the latter. Moreover, they preserved the order of poems of the public edition; that of the private *Pansies* is somewhat different. For the new edition they have gone back to the private *Pansies* of 1929.

Then I say to myself: Am I also dead? is that the truth?
Then I know
that with so many dead men in mills
I too am almost dead.
I know the unliving factory-hand, living-dead millions
is unliving me, living-dead me,
I, with them, am living-dead, mechanical at the machine.

And enshrouded in the vast corpse of the industrial millions
embedded in them, I look out on the sunshine of the South.
And though the pomegranate has red flowers outside the window
and oleander is hot with perfume under the afternoon sun
and I am "il Signore" and they love me here,
yet I am a mill-hand in Leeds
and the death of the Black Country is upon me
and I am wrapped in the lead of a coffin-lining, the living death
   of my fellow men.

Lawrence is involved in the sufferings of his fellows. For he is
flesh of their flesh, and he feels that his illness is a part of the illness of his civilization.

On the whole, "More Pansies" is a more even collection than
Pansies. It is also more hopeful in its assertion of an eventual ma-
chineless future. The personal and public themes recur: the desire
to be alone, "to possess one's soul in silence"; the false love of the
self-conscious and self-important ego; the end of the Christian
era; the evil of the factories; the deadness of censors and judges;
the "vast realms of consciousness still undreamed of"; the coming
of new (or perhaps old) gods.

"Image-Making Love" is a good expression of the failing Lawrence's need to escape from egotistical love. "Intimates" is a witty
(though probably somewhat unfair) response to his healthy
wife's demands:

Don't you care for my love? she said bitterly.

I handed her the mirror, and said:
Please address these questions to the proper person!
Please make all requests to headquarters!
In all matters of emotional importance
please approach the supreme authority direct!
So I handed her the mirror.

And she would have broken it over my head,
but she caught sight of her own reflection
and that held her spellbound for two seconds
while I fled.

Such a humorous treatment of a painful personal situation suggests that Lawrence has achieved a certain wisdom and detached
serenity, but without losing concern. More and more, he is sustained by his inner vision of the external world. He is dying, but
his vision of man and woman in organic relation to the universe
of life is his consolation. Thus, he can delight in his solitude:

I know no greater delight than the sheer delight of being alone.
It makes me realise the delicious pleasure of the moon
that she has in travelling by herself: throughout time,
or the splendid growing of an ash-tree
alone, on a hill-side in the north, humming in the wind.
                    ("Delight of Being Alone")

The ash-tree of "Discord in Childhood" is now remembered with
love; once a symbol of inner disharmony, it is now a symbol of
achieved peace and cosmic harmony.

In "Future Relationships," "Future Religion," "Future States,"
and "Future War" Lawrence asserts that once men touch one
another "the modern industrial form of machine civilisation will
melt away," there will be no more seeking after ideal "oneness,"
and there will be an infinite variety of individual men and states.
It requires only that men truly touch one another and sense the

life of the natural universe in the way that Lawrence does. Mass man needs to feel his "connection with the living cosmos" to be truly individual.

In "Free Will" Lawrence suggests that each man is free to "stay connected with the tree of life" or to become a machine or standard product—"self-centered, self-willed, self-motivated— / and subject, really, to the draught of every motor-car or the kicking tread of every passer-by." Such machine-men become "grinning and insatiable robots" ("Hold Back!"). Because he has lost his roots in the cosmos, the robot is incapable of love, and feels only "an endless grinding nihilistic hate" ("Robot Feelings"). Nevertheless, Lawrence envisages his redemption:

> If the robot can recognise the clean flame of life
> in the men who have never fallen in life
> then he repents, and his will breaks, and a great love of life
> brings him to his knees, in homage and pure passion of service.
>
> Then he receives the kiss of reconciliation
> and ceases to be a robot, and becomes a servant of life
> serving with delight and reverence those men whose flame
> of life undimmed delights him, so even he is lit up.
>
> ("Real Democracy")

John Middleton Murry has observed, "This miracle of regeneration happens through recognition of the god manifest. That, at another moment, Lawrence should define the robot as the man incapable of recognizing the manifest god is merely superficial contradiction: a form of the paradox inevitable in any statement of the necessity of spiritual rebirth." [8] An important point to remember in this context is that the battle between mechanization and spontaneity is *inside* Lawrence as well as in society at large. In the *Memoirs and Correspondence* Frieda Lawrence recalls that Lawrence identified himself both with Clifford Chatterley, the victim of the war, the purely intellectual author of spiteful stories about his acquaintances, and with the frail but vital natural man, Mellors. For he was both.

"The Triumph of the Machine" expresses Lawrence's faith that ultimately the machine "will never triumph." Instead, it will drive man mad by frustrating his animal impulses. But this madness will lead to the destruction of the machines themselves. And there are some hearts through which machines will never roll. Here is the paradox of the robot redeemed by the violent reaction of his own suppressed instincts.

The robot denies the gleam in the faces of men who have looked into the eyes of the gods. And who are the gods, we may ask?

What are the gods, then, what are the gods?

The gods are nameless and imageless
yet looking in a great full lime-tree of summer
I suddenly saw deep into the eyes of god:
it is enough.
                       ("What Are the Gods?")

Lawrence's gods do not need names:

I refuse to name the gods, because they have no name.
I refuse to describe the gods, because they have no form nor
    shape nor substance.

Ah, but the simple ask for images!
Then for a time at least, they must do without.

But all the time I see the gods:
the man who is mowing the tall white corn,
suddenly, as it curves, as it yields, the white wheat
and sinks down with a swift rustle, and a strange falling flat-
    ness,

ah! the gods, the swaying body of god!
ah the fallen stillness of god, autumnus, and it is only July
the pale gold flesh of Priapus dropping asleep.

("Name the Gods!")

Ernst Cassirer speaks of the primitive man's consciousness of "momentary deities":

> These beings do not personify any force of nature, nor do they represent some special aspect of human life; no recurrent trait or value is retained in them and transformed into a mythico-religious image; it is something purely instantaneous, a fleeting, emerging and vanishing mental content, whose objectification and outward discharge produces the image of the "momentary deity". Every impression that man receives, every wish that stirs in him, every hope that lures him, every danger that threatens him can affect him thus religiously. Just let spontaneous feeling invest the object before him, or his own personal condition, or some display of power that surprises him, with an air of holiness, and the momentary god has been experienced and created. In stark uniqueness and singleness it confronts us; not as a part of some force which may manifest itself here, there and everywhere, in various places and times, and for different persons, but as something that exists only here and now, in one indivisible moment of experience, and for only one subject whom it overwhelms and holds in thrall.[9]

Cassirer also observes that it is customary among the Algonquins, "when they note anything unusual in men, women, birds, beasts or fish, to exclaim: *Manitu!* that is: 'This is a god!' " [10] Such gods precede the representative deities of the classical Greeks. They are pure manifestations of wonder, or, to use Lawrence's earlier expression, "strange angels," gleaming impulses of life from within living beings. The god in Lawrence may be suddenly struck by the god in the lime-tree of summer. This, for Lawrence as for primitive man, is God.

"There Are No Gods" indicates his awareness that such a religious apprehension depends on the sensibility of the individual:

There are no gods, and you can please yourself
have a game of tennis, go out in the car, do some shopping, sit
        and talk, talk, talk
with a cigarette browning your fingers.
There are no gods, and you can please yourself—
go and please yourself—

But leave me alone, leave me alone, to myself!
and then in the room, whose is the presence
that makes the air so still and lovely to me?

Who is it that softly touches the sides of my breast
and touches me over the heart
so that my heart beats soothed, soothed, soothed and at peace?

Who is it smooths the bed-sheets like the cool
smooth ocean where the fishes rest on edge
in their own dream?

Who is it that clasps and kneads my naked feet, till they unfold,
till all is well, till all is utterly well? the lotus-lilies of the feet!

I tell you, it is no woman, it is no man, for I am alone.
And I fall asleep with the gods, the gods
that are not, or that are
according to the soul's desire,
like a pool into which we plunge, or do not plunge.

Because the expression is so much more direct than in the mythical poems from *The Plumed Serpent*, we see clearly that Lawrence's gods arise from one's inner strengths and resources; they
do not need names, though it is sometimes convenient to express
them in terms of myth. The spirit of "There Are No Gods," if
we forget the comedy of the opening, is close to that of a passage
in Yeats's "A Prayer for My Daughter":

. . . all hatred driven hence
The soul recovers radical innocence
And learns at last that it is self-delighting,
Self-appeasing, self-affrighting,
And that its own sweet will is Heaven's will. . . .

The true gods are within; they are those life-impulses with which
we have lost touch.

In "Terra Incognita" Lawrence writes of the "vast realms of
consciousness still undreamed of," the time

when at last we escape the barbed-wire enclosure
of *Know Thyself*, knowing we can never know,
we can but touch, and wonder, and ponder, and make our ef-
    fort
and dangle in a last fastidious fine delight
as the fuchsia does, dangling her reckless drop
of purple after so much putting forth
and slow mounting marvel of a little tree.

One may see glimpses of the gods in men, too, when they are
perfectly unself-conscious in the expression of their emotions. In
"For a Moment" Lawrence presents some human gods: a tram-
conductor, a girl, Frieda, Pino Orioli—as in "Manifesto," all can
be gods in expressing their genuine feelings. And in "God Is
Born" we see that divinity expresses itself in each new form that
is born of the cosmos.

In "Astronomical Changes" we are reminded again that Jesus
has had his day:

Dawn is no longer in the house of the Fish
Pisces, oh Fish, Jesus of the watery way,
your two thousand years are up.

And the foot of the Cross no longer is planted in the place of
    the birth of the Sun.

The whole great heavens have shifted over, and slowly pushed
    aside
The Cross, the Virgin, Pisces, the Sacred Fish
that casts its sperm upon the waters, and knows no intercourse;
pushed them all aside, discarded them, make way now for
    something else.

Even the Pole itself has departed now from the Pole Star
and pivots on the invisible,
while the Pole Star lies aside, like an old axle taken from the
    wheel.

Frederick Carter has recorded Lawrence's theosophical-astrologi-
cal notions of the astronomical "great year" that is to come:

> It interested him deeply that the old notion of the signs of the
> Zodiac as part of the arrangement of the great year, now indicated
> the near ending of our age. A little while yet and then the sun will
> open the year in a new sign. He saw the days of prophecy with us
> and the need for a declaration of the new dawn.[11]

> Yes, magic had a meaning to him, it was not a juggler's device.
> Acutely he sensed the vast power of imagination towards the mak-
> ing of a new age. Requiring a new way of life for the new time
> period that is coming on the world, he felt it in him to herald it
> and cry out news about the uprising of a new vision.[12]

Like Yeats, Lawrence was concerned to prophesy the new era
that would follow the Christian era. As in the case of Yeats, this
is not merely mumbo-jumbo from Madame Blavatsky; it is the
deep desire for a thorough reorientation of values. Christ, the Sacred Fish that knows no intercourse, is no longer an adequate
symbol for the resurrected whole man; the Christian ideal of purity has made man "lop-sided on the side of the angels." Thus
Lucifer, the lower sensual man, must have his part in godhead, or
else "you cut off your god at the waist." [13] The true church
must teach the resurrection of the flesh.

Jesus, of course, has become a villain only because he has been a great hero. Coming at the end of an era that had been unbalanced in the direction of sensual excess and lust for power, he offered a way into the new era:

> That's why they called Jesus: The Fish. Pisces. Because he fell, like the weariest river, into the great Ocean that is outside the shore, and there took on a new way of knowledge. . . .
>
> In the great ocean of the End, most men are lost. But Jesus turned into a fish, he had the other consciousness of the Ocean which is the divine End of us all. And then like a salmon he beat his way up stream again, to speak from the source. . . .
>
> We are in the deep, muddy estuary of our era, and terrified of the emptiness of the sea beyond. Or we are at the end of the great road, that Jesus and Francis and Whitman walked. We are on the brink of a precipice, and terrified at the great void below.[14]

It is now time for a new saviour:

> From time to time, the Great God sends a new saviour. Christians will no longer have the pettiness to assert that Jesus is the only Saviour ever sent by the Everlasting God. There have been other saviours, in other lands, at other times, with other messages. And all of them Sons of God. All of them sharing the Godhead with the Father. All of them showing the Way of Salvation and the Right. Different Saviours. Different Ways of Salvation. Different pole-stars, in the great wandering Cosmos of time. And the Infinite God, always changing, and always the same infinite God, at the end of the different Ways.[15]

Here, as in *The Plumed Serpent*, Lawrence proclaims his cyclic theory of ever-renewed creative change. Probably he sees himself as one of the chief prophets of the new era that is about to begin.

It seems to me that the best of Lawrence's pansies justify themselves formally in the way in which the line-arrangement points the rhythm and the content. Some, like "The White Horse" or "Lizard," are slight imagist pieces; most provide direct personal insights, observations, or experiences, as in "November by the Sea" or "There Are No Gods." In these poems the rhythmic and

the verbal development reach a climax with the full resolution of
the thought or argument:

> The wide sea wins, and the dark
> winter, and the great day-sun, and the sun in my soul
> sinks, sinks to setting and the winter solstice
> downward, they race in decline
> my sun, and the great gold sun.

* * *

> I tell you, it is no woman, it is no man, for I am alone.
> And I fall asleep with the gods, the gods
> that are not, or that are
> according to the soul's desire,
> like a pool into which we plunge, or do not plunge.

In the first of the passages quoted above a very striking effect of
finality is achieved by such artful means as the separation of
"dark" and "winter"; the separation of "solstice" and "downward"; the repetition of the words "sun," "sinks," and "winter";
the partial echo of "great day-sun" in "great gold sun"; the subtle
play of patterns of alliteration and assonance found throughout
the passage; and the clinching half-rhyme of "decline" with
"sun." In the second passage the general effect, created by the
phrases "it is no woman, it is no man," "that are not, or that are"
and "into which we plunge, or do not plunge," and by the repetition of "the gods," is one of balance created from the tension of
conflicting opposites; the importance of the balancing line "according to the soul's desire" is reinforced by the faint echo of
"are" in "desire," which makes one pause momentarily. Thus the
conflict of materialistic and religious attitudes is transcended in
the organization of language. Such poems are very far from being
"jottings"—they are, in truth, highly patterned.

The best of the pansies—"November by the Sea," "Desire Is
Dead," "The Elephant Is Slow to Mate," "Intimates," "Andraitx

—Pomegranate Flowers," "There Are No Gods," "Terra Incognita," "For a Moment," and a few others—deserve a place with the best poems Lawrence wrote. They may be termed *pensées* in the sense in which Lawrence uses the word:

> Thought, I love thought.
> But not the jiggling and twisting of already existent ideas
> I despise that self-important game.
> Thought is the welling up of unknown life into consciousness,
> Thought is the testing of statements on the touchstone of the
> conscience,
> Thought is gazing on to the face of life, and reading what can
> be read,
> Thought is pondering over experience, and coming to a conclusion.
> Thought is not a trick, or an exercise, or a set of dodges,
> Thought is a man in his wholeness wholly attending.
>
> ("Thought")

Such a thought as Lawrence describes is not something final or fixed or abstract; it is the momentary focus or concentration of a man's whole physical and mental attention. Lawrence believes that the rhythm and feeling of such a momentary experience or "thought-adventure" can best be achieved in free verse. It is, as before, a matter of attending to the shaping rhythm of the felt experience itself when it is first voiced. The reader is not obliged to agree or disagree with the thought, as he would be if it were expressed in expository prose, but he *is* obliged, when the pansy is successful, to feel the authenticity of the experience. Or, to put it another way, the reader of these poems, whatever his own views and experience, will be hard put to deny that Lawrence has truly and deeply felt the exhilarating presence of gods and the equally depressing limitations of social man. Thus, at the very least, the reader is offered a fresh experience, a new perspective on important human experience. As an anonymous reviewer wrote in *The Times Literary Supplement,* "the effect of a thought is not to state a final truth but to set off trains of more thoughts. The best of the short Pansies are like mottoes, with a seed which goes on growing, even if we begin by instinctively reacting against what looks like an opinion." [16]

For the most part, Lawrence's pansies are not the result of nervous exasperation but the attempt of a dying visionary to speak with a new clarity and directness to his people. *Birds, Beasts and Flowers* is more optimistic and less urgent in tone, and the poems from *The Plumed Serpent* are symbolic and somewhat self-enclosed in reference, but these poems are addressed directly and forcefully to the reader. Lawrence's illness has intensified his concern for the health of man at large. But even as he castigates the modern machine-civilization he is preparing himself in serene confidence for death.

❧ Five

The Psychic Mariner:
The Last Poems

We left the heat of Florence for the Tegernsee to be near Max Mohr. We had a rough peasant house, it was autumn. Lawrence rested a good deal. My sister Else came to see him, and Alfred Weber. When he was alone with Alfred Weber, he said to him: "Do you see those leaves falling from the apple tree? When the leaves want to fall you must let them fall." . . . In the dim dawn an enormous bunch of gentians I had put on the floor by his bed seemed the only living thing in the room.[1]

The sun rose magnificently opposite his bed in red and gold across the bay and the fishermen standing up in their boats looked like eternal mythological figures dark and alive against the lit-up splendour of the sea and sky. . . .[2]

(Frieda Lawrence)

In the last months of his life, in Bavaria and then at Beau Soleil, Bandol, Lawrence wrote his finest poems—poems that embody with astonishing radiance and clarity a few closely interrelated themes: the potential splendour of man; the body of God inherent in all struggling life; the supreme beauty of the physical world; the mechanical self-enclosed ego as the sole principle and only source of evil; and the acceptance of death as the last and deepest consummation of the marriage with the cosmos.

Some of the poems are very personal re-creations of Greek myth. In "The Greeks Are Coming," "The Argonauts," "Middle of the World," "For the Heroes Are Dipped in Scarlet," "Maximus," and "The Man of Tyre" one feels that the poet has gone farther than ever before into a world of pure vision. This is not the excited expression of the heaving flux of elemental energies, as in a Van Gogh landscape, that was attempted at times in *Look! We Have Come Through!* and *Birds, Beasts and Flowers,* but it is still a world found within the known world. It is the world of eternal beauty shining in and through the ordinary:

> . . . now that the moon who gives men glistening bodies
> is in her exaltation, and can look down on the sun
> I see descending from the ships at dawn
> slim naked men from Cnossos, smiling the archaic smile
> of those that will without fail come back again,
> and kindling little fires upon the shores
> and crouching, and speaking the music of lost languages.
>
> And the Minoan Gods, and the Gods of Tiryns
> are heard softly laughing and chatting, as ever;
> and Dionysos, young, and a stranger
> leans listening on the gate, in all respect.
>
> ("Middle of the World")

This is a gentler Dionysos than we have come to expect from Lawrence. In all these mythological poems, as in "For a Moment" and "There Are No Gods" in "More Pansies," the poet's inner conflict is transcended by an act of attention more complete and pure than he had performed before.

The returning Greeks are ruddy. For vermilion is the colour of man's "sacred or potent or god body. Apparently it was so in all the ancient world. Man all scarlet was his bodily godly self." [3] This vision, probably reinforced for Lawrence by the fishermen standing up in the sun, is expressed in "For the Heroes Are

Dipped in Scarlet," in which Lawrence celebrates the splendid
natural creature that man may be, even in the day of P & O liners.
It is also a vision of himself restored to the physical and mental
wholeness of the hardy fishermen or the ancient warriors—or his
miner father.

"The Man of Tyre" demonstrates the way in which Lawrence
finds magic in the ordinary:

The man of Tyre went down to the sea
pondering, for he was Greek, that God is one and all alone
    and ever more shall be so.
And a woman who had been washing clothes in the pool of
    rock
where a stream came down to the gravel of the sea and sank in,
who had spread white washing on the gravel banked above the
    bay,
who had lain her shift on the shore, on the shingle slope,
Who had waded to the pale green sea of evening, out to a shoal,
pouring sea-water over herself
now turned, and came slowly back, with her hair back to the
    evening sky.

Oh lovely, lovely with the dark hair piled up, as she went
    deeper, deeper down the channel, then rose shallower,
    shallower,
with the full thighs slowly lifting of the wader wading shore-
    wards
and the shoulders pallid with light from the silent sky behind
both breasts dim and mysterious, with the glamorous kindness
    of twilight between them
and the dim blotch of black maidenhair like an indicator,
giving a message to the man—

So in the cane-brake he clasped his hands in delight
that could only be god-given, and murmured:
Lo! God is one god! But here in the twilight

> godly and lovely comes Aphrodite out of the sea
> towards me.

In the wholeness of twilight, between night and day, the naked woman is a goddess. The ease of movement in the poem, from the comic connection of "I'll sing you one-O!" with Greek rationalism at the opening to the delicate description of the woman's body, is very remarkable. Lawrence is in complete control of his own very flexible idiom. Thus he can *show* us that a heightened intensity of sensuous perception enables one to sense God in the wonder of his individual and distinct manifestations. "God is one god" but each living thing may be god as well.

In *Etruscan Places* Lawrence writes:

> To the Etruscan all was alive; the whole universe lived; and the business of man was himself to live amid it all. He had to draw life into himself, out of the wandering huge vitalities of the world. The cosmos was alive, like a vast creature. The whole thing breathed and stirred. Evaporation went up like breath from the nostrils of a whale, steaming up. The sky received it in its blue bosom, breathed it in and pondered on it and transmuted it, before breathing it out again. Inside the earth were fires like the heat in the hot red liver of a beast. Out of the fissures of the earth came breaths of other breathing, vapours direct from the living physical under-earth, exhalations carrying inspiration. The whole thing was alive, and had a great soul, or *anima:* and in spite of one great soul, there were myriad roving, lesser souls: every man, every creature and tree and lake and mountain and stream, was animate, had its own peculiar consciousness. And has it to-day.[4]

Thus, there are many gods; in "Maximus," another of the mythological poems, Lawrence feels that Hermes, the guide of souls into the land of death, is seated at his hearth.

"God is the great urge that has not yet found a body," writes Lawrence in "The Body of God." Jesus was not Jesus till he was born from a womb, ate soup and bread, and became a unique individual with "a body and with needs, and a lovely spirit." The mystery of creation is not a mind but a "tremendous creative yearning" or intrinsic purposiveness, as in the delightfully comic "Red Geranium and Godly Mignonette." Here, as in the early poem "Corot," the body of the world is perceived as the body of the becoming God. But how much more substantial and satisfying this poem is in its skilful manipulation of image and tone of voice. Such a light but responsible treatment of an extremely important subject is very rare. Alfred Alvarez writes:

> It is hard to know whether to emphasize more the ease and originality of the piece, or its tact. There is neither a jot of pretentiousness in the poem, nor of vulgarity, though the opportunity for both certainly offered. Lawrence uses his wit not in the modern fashion, to save his face, but to strengthen the seriousness of what he has to say. There is no disproportion between the colloquial liveliness of the opening and the equally alive tenderness of the close. The wit is not a flourish; it is one of the poetic means; it preserves the seriousness from sentimentality and overstatement, as the seriousness keeps the wit from flippancy.[5]

In "They Say the Sea Is Loveless" and "Whales Weep Not!" Lawrence celebrates the living creatures of the sea, finding in their world a contagious joy that was completely absent from "The Sea" and "Fish" (though it was prefigured in *Pansies* in "Little Fish"):

> They say the sea is cold, but the sea contains
> the hottest blood of all, and the wildest, the most urgent.
>   ("Whales Weep Not!")

In a passage strongly influenced by one of his favourite books, *Moby Dick*, the poet celebrates the holy dalliance of archangelic whales:

> And over the bridge of the whale's strong phallus, linking the
>   wonder of whales
> the burning archangels under the sea keep passing, back and
>   forth,

keep passing, archangels of bliss
from him to her, from her to him, great Cherubim
that wait on whales in mid-ocean, suspended in the waves of
    the sea
great heaven of whales in the waters, old hierarchies.

These too are gods: Aphrodite is "the wife of whales"

and Venus among the fishes skips and is a she-dolphin
she is the gay, delighted porpoise sporting with love and the sea
she is the female tunny fish, round and happy among the males
and dense with happy blood, dark rainbow bliss in the sea.

As in "Almond Blossom" it is the eternal triumph of life that is
cause for jubilation. The sea of death is also the sea of life abun-
dant and inexhaustible. In "Whales Weep Not!" Lawrence expresses with a greater particularity and coherence and power the
vision of the early poem "Blueness," in which the dolphins leaped
from the sea of midnight, shaking it to fire.

In *Etruscan Places* Lawrence relates his happy dolphin both to
the phallus and to his idea of the resurrection of the flesh:

> The dolphin which gives up the sea's rainbows only when he
> dies. Out he leaps; then, with a head-dive, back again he plunges
> into the sea. He is so much alive, he is like the phallus carrying
> the fiery spark of procreation down into the wet darkness of the
> womb. The diver does the same, carrying like a phallus his small
> hot spark into the deeps of death. And the sea will give up her
> dead like dolphins that leap out and have the rainbow within
> them.[6]

And in *Apocalypse*, in a much-quoted passage, the dying poet is
able to express with compelling force the wonder and beauty of
all that he is losing:

> Man wants his physical fulfilment first and foremost, since now,
> once and once only, he is in the flesh and potent. For man, the vast
> marvel is to be alive. For man, as for flower and beast and bird,

the supreme triumph is to be most vividly, most perfectly alive. Whatever the unborn and the dead may know, they cannot know the beauty, the marvel of being alive in the flesh. The dead may look after the afterwards. But the magnificent here and now of life in the flesh is ours, and ours alone, and ours only for a time. We ought to dance with rapture that we should be alive and in the flesh, and part of the living, incarnate cosmos.[7]

Here, as in the poems of celebration, Lawrence would rather speak to and for all living men than mourn his own loss. There is no intrusion of the merely personal ego into his last poems.

In considering the poems that follow, it is well to remember the "rainbow bliss" of "Whales Weep Not!" For only a man who has truly lived can prepare himself with such calm faith for the experience of oblivion. "Invocation to the Moon," "Butterfly," and "Bavarian Gentians"—these are progressive explorations of the probable imminence of the soul's final journey.

"Invocation to the Moon" suggests the possibility (or the hope) of some kind of renewal. In *Apocalypse* the moon is said to control the nerves, as the sun controls the blood, so it seems possible that Lawrence is asking for the restoration of his full sensuous awareness. He writes:

Oh, the moon could soothe us and heal us like a cool great Artemis between her arms. But we have lost her, in our stupidity we ignore her, and angry she stares down on us and whips us with nervous whips. Oh beware of the angry Artemis of the night heavens, beware of the spite of Cybele, beware of the vindictiveness of horned Astarte. [8]

If we get out of contact and harmony with the sun and the moon, then both turn into great dragons of destruction against us.[9]

How is one to restore one's proper relationship with the cosmos, and thus become whole? Only, Lawrence feels, by "a sort of worship." [10] In "Invocation to the Moon" he offers this worship. He has left the earth and the sun and Venus behind as stages in a kind of rite of passage or initiation, and has now come to the mansion of the "glorious lady":

> Now, lady of the moon, now open the gate of your silvery
>   house
> and let me come past the silver bells of your flowers, and the
>   cockle-shells
> into your house, garmentless lady of the last great gift:
> who will give me back my lost limbs
> and my lost white fearless breast
> and set me again on moon-remembering feet
> a healed, whole man, O Moon!

This is reminiscent of the journey of the dead in the *Plumed Serpent* poems.

The moon's house is the "last house down the long, long street of the stars." The speaker knows he has come almost to a point of no return. And in "Butterfly" the tiny creature blows in the wind from the warm house to the sea. Lawrence sees in this an emblem of his own situation and wonders (though never openly) if this is to be his fate. If the time has come, one must accept the inevitable.

"Bavarian Gentians" is the climax of this brief series. Less explicit in its statement than "The Ship of Death," it is nevertheless a powerful mythic expression of the acceptance of death:

> Not every man has gentians in his house
> in soft September, at slow, sad Michaelmas.
>
> Bavarian gentians, big and dark, only dark
> darkening the day-time, torch-like with the smoking blueness
>   of Pluto's gloom,
> ribbed and torch-like, with their blaze of darkness spread blue
> down flattening into points, flattened under the sweep of white
>   day

torch-flower of the blue-smoking darkness, Pluto's dark-blue
daze,
black lamps from the halls of Dis, burning dark blue,
giving off darkness, blue darkness, as Demeter's pale lamps give
off light,
lead me then, lead the way.

Reach me a gentian, give me a torch!
let me guide myself with the blue, forked torch of this flower
down the darker and darker stairs, where blue is darkened on
blueness
even where Persephone goes, just now, from the frosted September
to the sightless realm where darkness is awake upon the dark
and Persephone herself is but a voice
or a darkness invisible enfolded in the deeper dark
of the arms Plutonic, and pierced with the passion of dense
gloom,
among the splendour of torches of darkness, shedding darkness
on the lost bride and her groom.

The gentians are torchlike; they seem to shed darkness rather
than light, and they are suggestive of Pluto's realm, of the underworld. As the poem proceeds the flower *becomes* a torch, a lamp
from the halls of Dis, and it is suggested that the lamp that sheds
darkness is more vital than "Demeter's pale lamps" that give off
light. In the latter part of the poem the myth of Demeter, Persephone, and Pluto (or Dis) is invoked as a parallel to the
speaker's descent, with flower for torch, into the underworld.

"Bavarian Gentians" has the basic pattern of many of Lawrence's finest poems. As in "Snap-Dragon," "Green," "Almond
Blossom," and "Sicilian Cyclamens," the opening of a flower is a
revelation to the poet—a doorway to an "other" world, to unknown modes of being. Even death may be associated in this way
with revelation and adventure. The descent into the underworld

of matter, though opposite to the "strange storming-up" of life into the almond tree, is a part of the whole process of life, and is thus accorded the same dignity and majesty that belonged to the unfolding almond blossom. Moreover, the descent is seen, as was the unfolding, in terms of marriage—the marriage of Persephone and Pluto, of two darknesses. The word "darkness" itself seems to assume a tangible reality in the last lines of the poem. Darkness is a kind of flame opposite to that of Demeter's pale lamps. We are in a world where darkness has more meaning than light, a world in which the darkness in the poet, his anima or soul, is wed finally and forever to the dark mystery of the "other" world, to the larger world of life (the cosmic swan of *Pansies*, the atomic electron states of the physicists) that exists before and after what we know as the organic. This marriage is as much a union with life as was that expressed in the blossoming of the almond tree. It is man's ultimate consummation in its ultimate grandeur.

The suggestion here, as in "The Ship of Death" and many other poems, is that one ought to give oneself freely and wholly to natural experience—whether it be sexual love, self-expression, or the surrender to death. One ought to live in the present wonder. Lawrence's mother failed to do this when she failed to accept her husband as the natural man he was; in his persistent use of the myth of Persephone and Pluto Lawrence has perhaps been motivated by the need to reconcile the dark, subterranean man and the aspiring, spiritual woman within himself. But this is only part of a larger reconciliation. For the voyaging and searching soul must be wed to the whole universe of life, of which death is a part. Cosmic marriage, then, can be taken to mean a commitment to the most profound participation in present experience in order to be whole and to avoid the rigidity of the limited, self-centred mental consciousness.

The process of deeper and deeper awareness may be seen in the development of the poem itself from its first sketchy version to its full realization. But it was never merely a description of the gentians. Already, in the ink version of "Glory of Darkness," Lawrence speaks of having embarked on the flowers' "dark blue fringes," and sees this as a journey of his soul. The pencil version of "Glory of Darkness" appears to be an attempt to enlarge upon the journey motif; it may well have been intended as an addition to the ink version. In it Lawrence speaks of "the dark doorway" to Hades opened up by the flower, and of the wedding of Persephone and Pluto. The other "Bavarian Gentians" is fairly close to the final version, but it is slacker, unnecessarily detailed, and a bit *too* repetitious, mentioning marriage several times. The final version is more economical, nothing too much, just the right number of repetitions of "darkness." And its rhymed conclusion does not seem to be merely tacked on, as does the last brief stanza of the previous version; because the last nine lines are one flowing sentence, it proceeds directly and with seeming inevitability from what went before.

None of the brief poems that follow "Bavarian Gentians" have the same degree of compressed power. "Lucifer" is a small celebration of the dark self or demon gleaming within one's normal self. The devil of the flesh that was rejected by the Christians and driven underground is nevertheless the source of vitality, the gleam or dark god within. His return as the Morning Star or Son of the Morning is the sign of a new era for Lawrence.

More important than any such symbolic embodiment of instinct, however, is the great God of the cosmos itself. In "The Breath of Life," "Silence," "The Hands of God," "Pax," "Abysmal Immortality," and "Only Man" Lawrence speaks again of the need to keep a rooted connection with the cosmos. To fall out of the hands of the living God is to fall into the knowledge of oneself in isolation, the sterile state of alienation, when the self pivots on the hub of the ego. This fall is opposite to the descent into a deeper consciousness of connection that is symbolized by Lucifer and Persephone.

The following poems, which are mainly concerned with the esoteric symbolism explained in *Apocalypse*, are rather obscure. What, one wonders, can be the meaning of "Return of Returns"?

> Come in a week
> Yes, yes, in the seven-day week!
> for how can I count in your three times three
> of the sea-blown week of nine.

> Come then, as I say, in a week,
> when the planets have given seven nods
> "It shall be! It shall be!" assented seven times
> by the great seven, by Helios the brightest
> and by Artemis the whitest
> by Hermes and Aphrodite, flashing white glittering words,
> by Ares and Kronos and Zeus,
> the seven great ones, who must all say yes.

> When the moon from out of the darkness
> has come like a thread, like a door just opening
> opening, till the round white doorway of delight
> is half open.

> Come then!
> Then, when the door is half open.
> In a week!
> The ancient river week, the old one.
> Come then!

In *Apocalypse* we learn that the "Greeks of the sea had a nine-day week." [11] But the seven-day week is more significant to Lawence, since seven "is the number of the seven ancient planets, which began with the sun and moon, and included the five great 'wandering' stars, Jupiter, Venus, Mercury, Mars and Saturn." [12] These planets, Lawrence believes, have an incalculable psychic effect on human beings:

The great sun that makes day and makes all life on earth, the moon that sways the tides and sways our physical being, unknown, sways the menstrual period in women and the sexual rhythm in a man, then the five big wandering stars, Mars, Venus, Saturn, Jupiter, Mercury, these, which are also our days of the week, are as much our rulers now as ever they were: and as little. We know we live by the sun; how much we live by the others, we don't know. We reduce it all to simple gravitation-pull. Even at that, strange fine threads hold us to the moon and stars. That these threads have a psychic pull on us, we know from the moon. But what of the stars? How can we say? We have lost that sort of awareness.[13]

Seven is also the number of the "great psychic centres of the human body."[14] In the process of rebirth or regeneration that, in Lawrence's opinion, underlies the confused symbolism of the book of Revelation, the bodily centres figure prominently:

We are witnessing the opening, and conquest of the great psychic centres of the human body. The old Adam is going to be conquered, die, and be re-born as the new Adam: but in stages, and then a climax, seven. For man has seven levels of awareness, deeper and higher; or seven spheres of consciousness. And one by one those must be conquered, transformed, transfigured.[15]

We may infer from all of this, I think, that the mysterious "return" in "Return of Returns" involves some such process. With the cooperation of the seven great planets over seven days Lawrence will welcome back the powers he has lost. Apparently, he identifies this with the sea-faring Greeks of "The Greeks Are Coming," since he speaks of their "sea-blown week of nine," but surely these must also be lost faculties or powers that man once possessed and may still possess in his own body.

In the process of renewal man must encounter his suppressed self:

The old nature of man must yield and give way to a new nature. In yielding, it passes away down into Hades, and there lives on, undying and malefic, superseded, yet malevolent-potent in the underworld. . . . The worship of the underworld powers, the

chthonoi, was perhaps the very basis of the most ancient Greek religion. When man has neither the strength to subdue his underworld powers—which are really the ancient powers of his old, superseded self—nor the wit to placate them with sacrifice and the
burnt holocaust, then they come back at him, and destroy him
again. Hence every new conquest of life means a "harrowing of
Hell." [16]

These underworld powers are closely akin to the angry dead of
the war poems and to the aggressive urges driven into the obscu-
rity of the unconscious by Christianity. Probably, Lawrence
hopes for a peaceful reconciliation with the powers denied for so
long. The main concern of "Return of Returns," then, would
seem to be a rebirth both personal and general. But the poem remains obscure.

Another poem, "Lord's Prayer," offers a much clearer indication of the nature of Lawrence's new man. When all the mythol-
ogy is left behind, it becomes evident that what Lawrence
desires is a liberation and new expression of the instinctive urge
to power and sensual gratification. This urge will provide the
counterweight to the Christian ideal of self-sacrificial love. Every
natural creature has such an urge, he feels, and can only be whole
if it is allowed an expression.

This need is not unrelated to magic and to poetry:

> We have lost almost entirely the great and intrinsically devel-
> oped sensual awareness, or sense-awareness, and sense-knowledge,
> of the ancients. It was a great depth of knowledge arrived at di-
> rect, by instinct and intuition, as we say, not by reason. It was a
> knowledge based not on words but on images. The abstraction was
> not into generalisations or into qualities, but into symbols. And
> the connection was not logical but emotional. The word "there-
> fore" did not exist. Images or symbols succeeded one another in a
> procession of instinctive and arbitrary physical connection—some
> of the Psalms give us examples—and they "get nowhere" because
> there was nowhere to go to, the desire was to achieve a consumma-
> tion of a certain state of consciousness, to fulfil a certain state of
> feeling-awareness. Perhaps all that remains to us to-day of the an-

cient way of "thought-process" are games like chess and cards. Chessmen and card-figures are symbols: their "values" are fixed in each case: their "movements" are non-logical, arbitrary, and based on the power-instinct.[17]

To get at the Apocalypse we have to appreciate the mental working of the pagan thinker or poet—pagan thinkers were necessarily poets—who starts with an image, sets the image in motion, allows it to achieve a certain course of circuit of its own, and then takes up another image. The old Greeks were very fine image-thinkers, as the myths prove. Their images were wonderfully natural and harmonious. They followed the logic of action rather than of reason, and they had no moral axe to grind. But still they are nearer to us than the orientals, whose image-thinking often followed no plan whatsoever, not even the sequence of action. We can see it in some of the Psalms, the flitting from image to image with no essential connection at all, but just the curious image-association. The oriental loved that.[18]

The poet and the magician know the power of pattern and non-logical connection, but modern man is emotionally impoverished, Lawrence feels: he has lost the necessary respect for magic. Though man still thinks, in the first instance, in images, he robs them of their emotional value by subjecting them to a rigid chain of logical circumstances. But the ancient oracles

were not supposed to say something that fitted plainly in the whole chain of circumstance. They were supposed to deliver a set of images or symbols of the real dynamic value, which should set the emotional consciousness of the inquirer, as he pondered them, revolving more and more rapidly, till out of a state of intense emotional absorption the resolve at last formed; or, as we say, the decision was arrived at. As a matter of fact, we do very much the same in a crisis. When anything very important is to be decided we withdraw and ponder and ponder until the deep emotions are set working and revolving together, revolving, revolving, till a centre is formed and we "know what to do." [19]

Conceptual thought and verbal speech, as Konrad Lorenz has observed, have posed major obstacles to the proper functioning of man's instinctive life. It is this basic insight that underlies and makes valuable all the theorizing about cycles of gods, dragons, and civilizations in *Apocalypse* and in the poems closely related to it. Man must regain contact with his own elemental nature, the demon that continues to haunt him, in order to be truly whole and at home in the universe.

The man who denies magic is dead; his cosmos is lost, and his cities are full of angry dead:

> Groan, then groan.
> For the sun is dead, and all that is in heaven
> is the pyre of blazing gas.
>
> And the moon that went
> So queenly, shaking her glistening beams
> is dead too, a dead orb wheeled once a month round the park.
>
> And the five others, the travellers
> they are all dead!
> In the hearse of night you see their tarnished coffins
> travelling, travelling still, still travelling
> to the end, for they are not yet buried.
>
> ("Stoic")

> In Minos, in Mycenae
> in all the cities with lion gates
> the dead threaded the air, lingering
> lingering in the earth's shadow
> and leaning towards the old hearth.
>
> In London, New York, Paris
> in the bursten cities
> the dead tread heavily through the muddy air
> through the mire of fumes
> heavily, stepping weary on our hearts.
>
> ("In the Cities")

Such a city cannot escape wrath. If man denies his "underworld powers" they will have their revenge.

In "Walk Warily" a new version of the death of our era is given:

> The angels are standing back, the angels of the Kiss.
> They wait, they give way now
> to the Sunderers, to the swift ones
> the ones with the sharp black wings
> and the shudder of electric anger
> and the drumming of pinions of thunder
> and hands like salt
> and the sudden dripping down of the knife-edge cleavage of
>   the lightning
> cleaving, cleaving.

"Things fall apart; the centre cannot hold." Our civilization, it seems, is undergoing a process of disintegration in which the balanced elements of fire and water are separated by the salty Sunderers. One doubts, however, if this is a particularly apt way of symbolizing the breakdown Lawrence sees ahead. Probably it is more expressive of his own feeling of physical disintegration.

In the following very neat and effectively colloquial poem he explains his "mysticism":

> They call all experience of the senses *mystic*, when the experi-
>   ence is considered.
> So an apple becomes *mystic* when I taste in it
> the summer and the snows, the wild welter of earth
> and the insistence of the sun.
>
> All of which things I can surely taste in a good apple.
> Though some apples taste preponderantly of water, wet and
>   sour
> and some of too much sun, brackish sweet
> like lagoon-water, that has been too much sunned.

If I say I taste these things in an apple, I am called *mystic*,
    which means a liar.
The only way to eat an apple is to hog it down like a pig
and taste nothing
that is *real*.

But if I eat an apple, I like to eat it with all my senses awake.
Hogging it down like a pig I call the feeding of corpses.

("Mystic")

Here again, one sees that Lawrence is essentially a literalist of the
imagination. He is always happier with a concrete sense-experience (however he may "extend" it with mythic parallels) than he
is with an abstract symbolism. Thus, in "Anaxagoras" he accuses
the philosopher of "mental conceit and mystification" in his argument for the blackness of snow; the infallible senses tell us that
snow has a "lovely bloom of whiteness upon white" or is "blue-
aloof" in the sun.

In "Kissing and Horrid Strife" Lawrence reaffirms his faith
both in the process of growth and in the process of disintegration. It is grey neutrality that he detests:

I have been defeated and dragged down by pain
and worsted by the evil world-soul of today.

But still I know that life is for delight
and for bliss
as now when the tiny wavelets of the sea
tip the morning light on edge, and spill it with delight
to show how inexhaustible it is . . .

And life is for dread,
for doom that darkens, and the Sunderers
that sunder us from each other
that strip us and destroy us and break us down . . .

Life is for kissing and for horrid strife.
Life is for the angels and the Sunderers.
Life is for the daimons and the demons,
those that put honey on our lips, and those that put salt.
But life is not
for the dead vanity of knowing better, nor the blank
cold comfort of superiority, nor silly
conceit of being immune,
nor puerility of contradictions
like saying snow is black, or desire is evil.

Neither desire nor death are evil; both are natural. But Lawrence's illness is caused, he feels, by the evil atmosphere of his time.* What is this evil? It is a third thing; it has no proper place in life:

Evil has no home,
only evil has no home,
not even the home of demoniacal hell.
Hell is the home of souls lost in darkness,
even as heaven is the home of souls lost in light.
And like Persephone, or Attis
there are souls that are at home in both homes.
Not like grey Dante, colour-blind
to the scarlet and purple flowers at the doors of hell.

("Evil Is Homeless")

What then is evil? In the poem of that name Lawrence says that "the wheel is the first principle of all evil." Machines are parts of the evil world-soul, as are the robots. The evil world-soul that has robbed Lawrence of his health is an impulse from ego-bound so-

---

* *Cf. Letters* (pp. 1211–12): "I say, as the ancients said, there is an evil world soul which sometimes overpowers one, and with which one has to struggle most of the time, to keep oneself clear. I feel so strongly as if my illness weren't really me—I feel perfectly well and all right, *in myself*. Yet there is this beastly torturing chest superimposed on me, and it's as if there was a demon lived there, triumphing, and extraneous to me."

cial men that "wishes to blaspheme the world into greyness"
("The Evil World-Soul").

Unlike the wheel, the cosmos is a wanderer in space: earth, sun
and planets are wandering in heaven, not turning in a fixed cycle.
Man ceases to wander when he falls into the egotism of purely
mental consciousness:

> Only the human being, absolved from kissing and strife
> goes on and on and on, without wandering
> fixed upon the hub of the ego
> going, yet never wandering, fixed, yet in motion,
> the kind of hell that is real, grey and awful
> sinless and stainless going round and round
> the kind of hell grey Dante never saw
> but of which he had a bit inside him.
> ("Death Is Not Evil, Evil Is Mechanical")

Lawrence rejects Dante's vision of a hell of tormented passion.
Heaven and hell, spirit and senses, balance one another. If there is
a "hell" of evil, it is not that of natural passion but that of emotion neutralized and perverted by the mental consciousness.

In "Murder" Lawrence distinguishes between passionate anger
and violence that is evil. The war was evil, for it was cold-blooded
murder and not a passionate struggle and communion. Weapons
are evil, for they make strife impersonal and obscene. Men must
depart from such abstractions from life as machines, finance, politics, contemporary science and education, jazz and film and wire-
less. For the "evil will in many men makes an evil world-soul,
which proposes to reduce the world to grey ash" ("Departure").
Loathing second-hand experience, the collective consciousness
and mechanical impersonal violence so much as he did, what
would Lawrence have made of Hiroshima, television, and Ausch-
witz? In some respects, he seems already to belong to another era.
But if he failed to see that such new media as jazz and the cinema
had in them the power to express and represent human passion as

authentically as poetry or the novel, his larger insight into the possible horrors and special problems of a scientific and technological society was surely very profound. The modern man is still in danger of being merely a part of the social machine; his tastes, habits, beliefs and emotions mass-produced for him.

How is one to avoid this? One must, says Lawrence, return to life's essentials and live in rooted connection with the wandering cosmos. One must be flexible, responsive to new life-impulses from within and from without. This requires an acceptance of the whole of the life-process—man must accept disintegration as he rejoiced in growth, and cast off the hysterical fear of death that drives him to make a fortress of the ego till he becomes paralyzed, insulated forever against all deep or meaningful experience. Instead of a fortress of mental conceit, man must build a ship of death for the longest journey. Then, paradoxically, he may be truly alive.

"The Ship of Death" is the culmination of the theme of death and resurrection in Lawrence's whole work. The death of the self in the flood of oblivion is related to the death of our era in the great Flood. Lawrence's own sickness, of which he will be purged in the flood, has been imposed upon him by a sick civilization. Both must die and be reborn. In the poem Lawrence becomes a Noah of the imagination, navigating his ship towards a possible rainbow of hope.

What is this ship of death, this ark that we are offered by a dying prophet? It is, of course, suggested by the small ship Lawrence saw in an Etruscan tomb, and it owes something to the Egyptian ship of death and to the mythical crossing of the Styx or the Acheron, but it becomes also, in Lawrence's treatment, an ark. For the myth of Noah has always fascinated him. In the essay "Books" he writes:

> When you come to think of it, Noah matters more than the deluge, and the ark is more than all the world washed out.
> Now we've got the sulks, and are waiting for the flood to come

and wash out our world and our civilization. All right, let it come. But somebody's got to be ready with Noah's Ark.[20]

The monasteries were the ark of the Dark Ages, keeping alive the knowledge of a better life. Today this is the task of the visionary artist.

In *Etruscan Places* it is suggested that Noah's Ark is the *arx* or womb of all the world, and thus the source of its creatures. It carries the "mystery of eternal life." It is "where life retreats in the last refuge." [21] We may infer from this that Lawrence's ship of death ("the fragile ship of courage, the ark of faith") is founded upon that sense of reverence and wonderful mystery that has enabled him boldly to live in the full use of the senses, to sail knowingly upon the dark ocean of death and renewed life, the mysterious "Greater Day" of the fragment "The Flying Fish." Thus in *Lady Chatterley's Lover* Mellors and Connie, alienated from the surrounding world of mines and mechanism, are alone "in a little ark in the Flood." [22] Their sense of reverence for life in the flesh has saved them. Lawrence himself is now incapable of the full experience of Mellors and Connie, but he accepts his death as a part of the larger process of life. For the ship of death is really the ship of life.

The sense of a larger, greater life, containing both life and death, has been with Lawrence at least since the time of his mother's death, and it has usually been seen in terms of the dark sea. It is expressed in his last years in such passages as this from *The Man Who Died:*

> The man who had died looked nakedly on life, and saw a vast resoluteness everywhere flinging itself up in stormy or subtle wave-crests, foam-tips emerging out of the blue invisible, a black and orange cock or the green flame-tongues out of the extremes of the fig tree. They came forth, these things and creatures of spring, glowing with desire and with assertion. They came like crests of foam, out of the blue flood of the invisible desire, out of the vast

invisible sea of strength, and they came coloured and tangible, eva-
nescent, yet deathless in their coming.[23]

This is the condition of Lawrence in his last years. Living close
to the experience of death, having nearly died and yet returned
to life a number of times, he is nevertheless able to contemplate
the sea of darkness with a profound inner peace and joy. This is
because he knows that the sea of death is also the sea of renewed
life. And it is precisely this knowledge, this faith in the ultimate
goodness and wisdom of the cosmic processes of life and death,
that he wishes to impart to his fellow men. This faith *is* his ship
of death, and he believes that it could save and renew civilization,
if men could perceive and appreciate it. Thus the significance of
his most powerful poem's closing admonition, to build a ship of
death, is more than personal. Going beyond even the simple wisdom of resignation to death, it is a call to more vivid and meaningful life. Like Lawrence, we must learn to live in the fulness of
the present wonder, since the full life in the flesh is ours "once
and once only." Having lived deeply and well, man will trust to
the larger life, and so surrender gladly to death when the time
comes.

The poem itself begins and proceeds with impressive simplicity
and clarity:

Now it is autumn and the falling fruit
and the long journey towards oblivion.

The apples falling like great drops of dew
to bruise themselves an exit from themselves.

And it is time to go, to bid farewell
to one's own self, and find an exit
from the fallen self.

The tone is precisely right, neither pathetic nor grandiloquent; it is a restrained but vividly imagined statement of the case. The time has come for the fruit to leave the tree. In Part II the imminence of general catastrophe is suggested. The flow of feeling rises to a somewhat higher intensity when the poet speaks directly to the reader:

> Have you built your ship of death, O have you?
> O build your ship of death, for you will need it.
>
> The grim frost is at hand, when the apples will fall
> thick, almost thunderous, on the hardened earth.
>
> And death is on the air like a smell of ashes!
> Ah! can't you smell it?
>
> And in the bruised body, the frightened soul
> finds itself shrinking, wincing from the cold
> that blows upon it through the orifices.

In Part III Lawrence rejects suicide as a means of avoiding the flood, and achieving quiet; in IV he asks the basic question:

> O let us talk of quiet that we know,
> that we can know, the deep and lovely quiet
> of a strong heart at peace!
>
> How can we this, our own quietus, make?

The answer is given in V:

> Build then the ship of death, for you must take
> the longest journey, to oblivion.
>
> And die the death, the long and painful death
> that lies between the old self and the new.

Already our bodies are fallen, bruised, badly bruised,
already our souls are oozing through the exit
of the cruel bruise.

Already the dark and endless ocean of the end
is washing in through the breaches of our wounds,
already the flood is upon us.

Oh build your ship of death, your little ark
and furnish it with food, with little cakes, and wine
for the dark flight down oblivion.

As before, the restrained tone and the vivid physical imagery give
an immediate power to the poet's admonition. The flood is upon
us, but the possible achievement of a new self is suggested. Pre-
sumably, this would involve the death of the self-important ego
and the birth of the whole man; in any case, the reference seems
to be both general and personal, as does that of the following section:

Piecemeal the body dies, and the timid soul
has her footing washed away, as the dark flood rises.

We are dying, we are dying, we are all of us dying
and nothing will stay the death-flood rising within us
and soon it will rise on the world, on the outside world.

We are dying, we are dying, piecemeal our bodies are dying
and our strength leaves us,
and our soul cowers naked in the dark rain over the flood,
cowering in the last branches of the tree of our life.

This resembles the brief poems about the dark flood at the beginning of *Pansies*. Section VII is even more powerfully moving in
its combination of myth and intimate domestic detail:

We are dying, we are dying, so all we can do
is now to be willing to die, and to build the ship
of death to carry the soul on the longest journey.

A little ship, with oars and food
and little dishes, and all accoutrements
fitting and ready for the departing soul.

Now launch the small ship, now as the body dies
and life departs, launch out, the fragile soul
in the fragile ship of courage, the ark of faith
with its store of food and little cooking pans
and change of clothes,
upon the flood's black waste
upon the waters of the end
upon the sea of death, where still we sail
darkly, for we cannot steer, and have no port.

In VIII comes the point of deepest darkness: "It is the end, it is
oblivion." But IX brings a reprieve that is "cruel" to the man
who was prepared to die:

And yet out of eternity, a thread
separates itself on the blackness,
a horizontal thread
that fumes a little with pallor upon the dark.

Is it illusion? or does the pallor fume
a little higher?
Ah wait, wait, for there's the dawn,
the cruel dawn of coming back to life
out of oblivion.

Wait, wait, the little ship
drifting, beneath the deathly ashy grey
of a flood-dawn.

Wait, wait! even so, a flush of yellow
and strangely, O chilled man soul, a flush of rose.

A flush of rose, and the whole thing starts again.

It seems virtually certain that Lawrence is here describing his own waking at Bandol to another day of life. If it is an idea of the resurrection of the body or the awakening into an afterlife that he is attempting to express, then it is significant that he does so in these terms. For it seems that the only afterlife that he can imagine must be a physical one:

The flood subsides, and the body, like a worn sea-shell
emerges strange and lovely.
And the little ship wings home, faltering and lapsing
on the pink flood,
and the frail soul steps out, into her house again
filling the heart with peace.

Swings the heart renewed with peace
even of oblivion.

Oh build your ship of death, oh build it!
for you will need it.
For the voyage of oblivion awaits you.

Each dip into oblivion renews the heart, and gives it peace. In order to be ready for the final flood, all men must live in the knowledge of the womb of oblivion from which they have come and to which they must return. Lawrence's whole ambition, in this and in all his work, has been to act as a guide of souls, a Noah for the twentieth century.

"The Ship of Death" has a beautiful economy of structure, with its clear narrative line and its skilful use of two basic and vividly realized symbols—the little ship and the fruit falling from the tree of life. The earlier, somewhat longer version of MS. B is much less well formed. Its first line, "I sing of autumn and the falling fruit," seems rather more grandiloquent than "Now it is autumn. . . ." It has no divisions, and contains a good deal of the material that is reworked in "The Houseless Dead," "Beware the Unhappy Dead" and several other related poems. There is no development in this MS. B "Ship of Death" of the falling-fruit imagery, but there is a marvellous evocation of the sea voyage, in which memories of experience, accoutrements, and even the ship itself all melt away into the great womb. Lawrence's exclusion of such impressive material in order to achieve the majestic simplicity and very definite structure of the last version is the final proof (if it is needed) of his skill as a craftsman in verse.

The problem of the unhappy dead is the concern of the following poems. This theme was apparent in the early poem "Brother and Sister" and in several of the war poems. It is necessary, says Lawrence, to appease the unwilling and unhappy dead so that they may continue their journey across the dark sea. The unhappy dead are those who have not truly lived, those who have not known wonder. One must help them to build a ship of death. In this poem Lawrence is almost certainly thinking of the effect of his own mother's frustration and possessive love on himself. He believes, as we have seen, that to make a child too dependent and loving is to encourage a tendency to consumption. Such possessive, egotistical, harmful loving is an expression of the evil world-soul. He had attempted and partially succeeded in appeasing the unhappy spirit of his mother, but there are so many unappeased dead from the war that the modern atmosphere is poisoned. This it is, he believes, that has dragged him down. Only kindness and honour to their dead can save the living now. And this demands that they live in awareness of the mystery of death. Thus they may appease the dead within them and live a fuller life. For "Without the song of death, the song of life / becomes pointless and silly" ("Song of Death").

The remaining poems of *Last Poems*—"The End, the Beginning," "Sleep," "Sleep and Waking," "Fatigue," "Forget," "Know-All," "Tabernacle," "Shadows," "Change," and "Phoenix"—express a longing for oblivion but also a belief in the renewal that comes from the experience of oblivion. "Shadows" is the most substantial and moving of these poems:

> . . . if, as autumn deepens and darkens
> I feel the pain of falling leaves, and stems that break in storms
> and trouble and dissolution and distress
> and then the softness of deep shadows folding, folding
> around my soul and spirit, around my lips
> so sweet, like a swoon, or more like the drowse of a low, sad
>   song
> singing darker than the nightingale, on, on to the solstice
> and the silence of short days, the silence of the year, the
>   shadow,
> then I shall know that my life is moving still
> with the dark earth, and drenched
> with the deep oblivion of earth's lapse and renewal.

He hopes still for natural renewal, and feels that God may send him forth "on a new morning, a new man." One senses that Lawrence was prepared either for absorption into the greater life of the cosmos or for the possibility of recovery and new vitality. Neither here nor in "The Ship of Death" is there, in my opinion, any speculation about the traditional Christian idea of an afterlife. Lawrence did not pretend to know any more than that the dead persist in the living. It was, as we know from the famous passage in *Apocalypse*, "life in the flesh," given "once and once only," that he valued. Frieda Lawrence has written that her husband did not want to die, but he seems to have known (as his remark to Alfred Weber indicates) that the body, like the leaves, has its own wisdom in these matters.

The best of Lawrence's last poems—"Middle of the World,"

"The Man of Tyre," "Red Geranium and Godly Mignonette," "Whales Weep Not!," "Invocation to the Moon," "Bavarian Gentians," "Mystic," "The Ship of Death," and "Shadows"—have an absolute sureness of tone and movement. Their "flowing" quality is the final result of Lawrence's concern for truth to the felt experience of perception:

> . . . a man who sees, sees not as a camera does when it takes a snapshot, not even as a cinema-camera, taking its succession of instantaneous snaps; but in a curious rolling flood of vision, in which the image itself seethes and rolls. . . .[24]

This passage from *Etruscan Places* suggests the impulse behind the varied repetition of phrase and rhythm that is so marked a feature of Lawrence's style. He wishes the reader to feel in his use of language the full body and movement of a sense-experience. As Christopher Hassall has noted, the theory and practice of the poet are implicit in Lawrence's remarks about Etruscan painting:

> The subtlety of Etruscan painting, as of Chinese and Hindu, lies in the wonderfully suggestive *edge* of the figures. It is not outlined. It is not what we call "drawing". It is the flowing contour where the body suddenly leaves off, upon the atmosphere. The Etruscan artist seems to have seen living things surging from their own centre to their own surface. And the curving and contour of the silhouette-edge suggests the whole movement of the modelling within.[25]

The last poems have a similar "suggestive edge"; they seem to flow from within, "surging from their own centre to their own surface." Thus Lawrence makes an inner darkness seem palpable in "Bavarian Gentians" and Part VII of "The Ship of Death." And in all of the poems mentioned above there is a purposive and flowing rhythmic shape, an immediate communication of idea and feeling.

The last poems are a considerable achievement. Two of them, "Bavarian Gentians" and "The Ship of Death," are very great poems, magnificent both in theme and execution. All of them are triumphant expressions of undiminished faith and courage. They are the final testament of a man who wished to celebrate all of life's great occasions.

Conclusion:

The Future Kingdom

I

The essential quality of poetry is that it makes a new effort of attention, and 'discovers' a new world within the known world. Man, and the animals, and the flowers, all live within a strange and for ever surging chaos. The chaos which we have got used to we call a cosmos. The unspeakable inner chaos of which we are composed we call consciousness, and mind, and even civilization. But it is, ultimately, chaos lit up by visions, or not lit up by visions. Just as the rainbow may or may not light up the storm. And, like the rainbow, the vision perisheth.[1]

[Modern poets] show the desire for chaos, and the fear of chaos. The desire for chaos is the breath of their poetry. The fear of chaos is in their parade of forms and technique.[2]

This opening, and this alone, is the essential act of attention, the essential poetic and vital act. . . . In this act, and this alone, we truly *live*: in that innermost naive opening of the soul, like a flower, like an animal, like a coloured snake, it does not matter, to the sun of chaotic livingness.[3]

To see the world with new eyes, without the evasion of an imposed philosophy or an imposed form: this was surely the first concern of Lawrence the poet. He wished to capture the visions that appear and disappear in the creative chaos that surrounds and inhabits us. These are, of course, *his* visions and not necessarily those of any other man. But insofar as they are true to his own felt experience they have an objective validity as well. Despite the abnormal intensity of his emotional life (or, really, because of it), Lawrence may be regarded as a representative man. He suffered and enjoyed basic human experiences—alienation, love, marriage, death—with a searching intensity that illuminates for us their underlying complexity and our own ambivalence. His poems, like Wordsworth's *Prelude* and Whitman's finest poems, have as their central theme the journey of the human soul to maturity and wisdom.

In the early poems a young man, bound to his dying mother but with an unconscious affection for his rejected father, struggles to escape from a static, introverted "ideal" love and to achieve a meaningful and flexible relationship with the substantial "other" in order that he may define himself in relation to it. This involves the reconciliation of the conflicting tendencies of spirit and flesh within himself (the marriage of Persephone and Pluto) as a way to whole being (the restoration of the fragmented Osiris). In *Look! We Have Come Through!* the conflict and the resolution are given their most intense personal expression, and in *Birds, Beasts and Flowers* the honest exploration of the "otherness" of the natural world constitutes an extension of this solution —a marriage of man with the living "non-human" cosmos. In "New Heaven and Earth" Lawrence identifies the body of the bride with the body of the world; in "Almond Blossom" a tree becomes a naked bridegroom, and the dog-star bays epithalamion: this is the union of life with life that has its purpose and meaning in the blossoming of the individual life within the context of the whole. In the purely experienced present of "Manifesto" the spirit moves in perfect harmony with matter; in "Grapes" the "mystic Now," the full sensual experience of the fruit ("how black, how blue-black, how globed in Egyptian darkness") suggests a vision of the "dark and evasive" man in full possession of those faculties that modern man has lost.

Why has he lost them, and how might they be regained? This aspect of the problem becomes a major concern in the *Plumed Serpent* poems, in *Pansies*, and in *Last Poems*. It is, Lawrence feels, the condemnation of the body and the banishment of Lucifer by the Christians that has left man divided against himself: he believes that the Manichean heresy has been the dominant force in Christian civilization, and that this has led to the substitution of the mechanical principle for the spontaneous expression of the "instant whole man." [4]

> This motivizing of the passional sphere from the ideal is the final peril of human consciousness. It is the death of all spontaneous, creative life, and the substitution of the mechanical principle. . . . Ideal and material are identical. The ideal is but the god in the machine—the little, fixed machine principle which works the human psyche automatically. [5]

Somehow man must come to terms with the dark powers locked within himself. Lawrence speaks, at different times, of the Tuatha de Danaan, the Greeks, the "strange angels," the angry dead, and the sleeping gods of Mexico: but all these are surely symbolic expressions of those faculties or instincts that man has suppressed and frustrated by his exaggerated dependence on the intellect. The mature Lawrence believes that the Christian civilization is doomed and that it is his duty, even as he is himself "dragged down" by the evil world-soul, to give expression to the vision of restored life that he discerns in the creative chaos of a time of great change.

This, then, is the "myth" or basic pattern of Lawrence's poems: an interpretation of experience that emphasizes again and again, both on the personal and the universal plane, the necessity of the death of the old self and the birth of the new. The figure in the carpet is the Christ of *The Man Who Died*—the crucified man restored to physical and mental health by his union with the priestess of Isis. Here, as in the tortoise sequence, Christ is blended with Osiris (and, indeed, with Lucifer, Quetzalcoatl, and Dionysos). Breaking through "the prison-house of a dead form," Lawrence offers a new image of man—one that fuses the Christian ideal of spiritual love with the ancient physical pride and splendour of Mediterranean man.

The new man is, like the poet, open "to the sun of chaotic livingness," wedded to the whole universe of life. Like a flower or a coloured snake, he is responsive to the natural rhythms within and without. It is significant that the opening of the world within the world to the sensitive human soul is a recurrent event in the poems. "Piano" is a good early example; it presents the basic pattern of most of Lawrence's finest poems. A present and immediate experience—a woman singing—opens the doorway to another world, in this case the world of memory, of childhood love and security. As usual, the poet gives himself up, though here somewhat unwillingly, to the deeper reality opened up by his immediate sensual experience. The singing woman has the same magical power as the cypresses, the grapes, the almond blossom, and the blue gentians: she suggests relationships that carry the poet beyond his immediate experience while he is yet immersed in it. The point of the poem is that one's past emotional experience continues to live in the present. It is never really past.

Thus the "flood of remembrance" in this poem may be regarded as symbolically equivalent to the marriage-chamber of the deep from which the moon emerges in "Moonrise," to the underground world of "Snake" and that of "Bavarian Gentians," and, for that matter, to the seemingly opposite sea of darkness and oblivion upon which the poet embarks in "The Ship of Death." These are all ways of expressing the reality of another, partly hidden world that not only underlies but informs the world of living things that we see. This is expressed throughout the poems in the recurrent metaphors of blossoming, in the revelation afforded by the observation of animals like the snake and the tor-

toise, and in the recurrent use of the words "dark" and "darkness." The revelation can be expressed, as it frequently is, in
terms of marriage because the opening of the dark and potent
world underlying the ordinary world of our daytime consciousness involves a recognition of man's ultimate kinship with all
other distinct living things—the "love-unison." Lawrence's world
is a world of divine vitality and total relationship. This is the vision that illuminates chaos.

II

> . . . it is obvious that the poetry of the instant present cannot
> have the same body or the same motion as the poetry of the before
> and after. It can never submit to the same conditions. It is never
> finished. There is no rhythm which returns upon itself, no serpent
> of eternity with its tail in its own mouth. There is no static
> perfection, none of that finality which we find so satisfying be-
> cause we are so frightened.[6]
>
> ("Poetry of the Present")

From the beginning Lawrence moved uncertainly towards a
poetic form that could render the immediate experience with perfect naturalness. The roughness and metrical irregularity of "The
Wild Common" suggest this very strongly; there appears to be
an uneasy (and unhappy) compromise between traditional and
expressive form.

> The common flaunts bravely; but below, from the rushes
> Crowds of glittering king-cups surge to challenge the blossom-
>   ing bushes;
> There the lazy streamlet pushes
> His bent course mildly; here wakes again, leaps, laughs, and
>   gushes
>
> Into a deep pond, an old sheep-dip,
> Dark, overgrown with willows, cool, with the brook ebbing
>   through so slow;

Naked on the steep, soft lip
Of the turf I stand watching my own white shadow quivering
to and fro.

In the first quatrain the long second line without a pause has the breathless urgency appropriate to the surging king-cups. By contrast, the brief third line and the breaking of the third and fourth lines at "pushes" serve to emphasize the laziness of the stream. The quickness and lightness of "here wakes again, leaps, laughs, and gushes" in the latter part of the fourth line signals the quickening of the stream. Similarly, the number of pauses in the second line of the second stanza suggests the slow and broken progress of the brook. In each case it is evident that Lawrence wishes the movement of the verse to express the movement in the natural scene. Unfortunately, both the heavy rhymes and the fact that the lines have been arranged in quatrains lead one to expect a greater regularity of rhythm. One principle of form is in conflict with another, so that their efforts are neutralized. An effect of awkwardness is unavoidable. What is lost in the compromise with imposed form is that "flowing contour where the body suddenly leaves off, upon the atmosphere" that the late Lawrence admires in the Etruscan paintings. The king-cups of "The Wild Common" may be felt "surging from their own centre to their own surface," but the young poet has imposed an artificial limitation on their movement, thus robbing them of their "wonderfully suggestive edge." The flow of the whole experience is crudely broken by the artificial chimes and arbitrary stanzaic divisions of the rhyming quatrains. It is significant that in this matter of the rhythmic flow Lawrence's revisions of the early poems make little or no difference—when they are most successful the revisions do much to heighten one's sense of the poet's situation and to clarify his emotional response (as in the cases of "Piano" and "The Wild Common"), but they do not involve a fundamental departure from the norm of rhymed, metrical verse.

The advantages (for Lawrence) of a looser organization may be seen in the opening of "End of Another Home Holiday":

When shall I see the half-moon sink again
Behind the black sycamore at the end of the garden?
When will the scent of the dim white phlox
Creep up the wall to me, and in at my open window?

Why is it, the long, slow stroke of the midnight bell
 (Will it never finish the twelve?)
Falls again and again on my heart with a heavy reproach?
The moon-mist is over the village, out of the mist speaks the
 bell,
And all the little roofs of the village bow low, pitiful, beseech-
 ing, resigned.
—Speak, you my home! what is it I don't do well?

Ah home, suddenly I love you
As I hear the sharp clean trot of a pony down the road,
Succeeding sharp little sounds dropping into silence
Clear upon the long-drawn hoarseness of a train across the
 valley.

It is interesting that these four stanzas contain only one obvious rhyme ("bell" and "well") and that this rhyme is the one jarring note in the passage. It makes one suddenly conscious of the language in a passage whose general effect is one of perfect transparency. The rhythms are the natural rhythms of the speaking voice as it expresses its response to the environment. In the last stanza, for example, the "sharp clean trot" of the pony and the "long-drawn hoarseness of a train across the valley" are perfectly rendered in the largely monosyllabic second line and in the long final line. The poet has begun to attend to the shaping rhythm (with its mimetic tendency) that is inherent in his immediate response to the world about him.

In "After the Opera" the tendency to a more flexible and expressive form has been carried further.

> Down the stone stairs
> Girls with their large eyes wide with tragedy
> Lift looks of shocked and momentous emotion up at me.
> And I smile.
>
> Ladies
> Stepping like birds with their bright and pointed feet
> Peer anxiously forth, as if for a boat to carry them out of the
>   wreckage;
> And among the wreck of the theatre crowd
> I stand and smile.
> They take tragedy so becomingly;
> Which pleases me.

Here Lawrence uses rhyme subtly and well—since the poem is "free," the occasional rhymes are unexpected and they serve to underline the pleasant absurdity of the birdlike ladies who take tragedy "so becomingly." Moreover, each stanza is effectively punctuated by a brief, ironic line expressing the speaker's amusement at the "momentous" emotion of the ladies. One would not have suspected that the young Lawrence could achieve such a control of tone.

In "After the Opera" the arrangement of the lines constitutes a kind of picture-making that is occasionally made more pointed by a rhyme. This is accomplished even more subtly in "A Doe at Evening":

> As I went through the marshes
> a doe sprang out of the corn
> and flashed up the hill-side
> leaving her fawn.

On the sky-line
she moved round to watch,
she pricked a fine black blotch
on the sky.

I looked at her
and felt her watching;
I became a strange being.
Still, I had my right to be there with her.

The action of the first stanza is advanced a bit further with each line; the completion of the action is lightly underscored with the partial rhyme of "corn" and "fawn." In the second stanza the vivid picture of the silhouetted doe on the sky-line is reinforced by the rhyme of "watch" and "blotch." And the less obvious rhyme of "watching" and "being" in the third stanza makes one pause momentarily just at the point where the poem moves from description to magic.

In these imagistic poems Lawrence has evolved a free-verse technique that is obviously quite distinct from that of such Whitmanesque poems as "New Heaven and Earth" and "Manifesto." This later cadenced verse has a flowing quality and a more urgent feeling:

Green streams that flow from the innermost continent of the
    new world,
what are they?
Green and illumined and travelling for ever
dissolved with the mystery of the innermost heart of the con-
    tinent,
mystery beyond knowledge or endurance, so sumptuous
out of the well-heads of the new world.—
The other, she too has strange green eyes!
White sands and fruits unknown and perfumes that never
can blow across the dark seas to our usual world!

And land that beats with a pulse!
And valleys that draw close in love!
("New Heaven and Earth")

Every man himself, and therefore, a surpassing singleness of
    mankind.
The blazing tiger will spring upon the deer, undimmed,
the hen will nestle over her chickens,
we shall love, we shall hate,
but it will be like music, sheer utterance,
issuing straight out of the unknown,
the lightning and the rainbow appearing in us unbidden, un-
    checked,
like ambassadors.
("Manifesto")

Not I, not I, but the wind that blows through me!
A fine wind is blowing the new direction of Time.
If only I let it bear me, carry me, if only it carry me!
If only I am sensitive, subtle, oh, delicate, a winged gift!
If only, most lovely of all, I yield myself and am borrowed
By the fine, fine wind that takes its course through the chaos
    of the world
Like a fine, an exquisite chisel, a wedge-blade inserted;
If only I am keen and hard like the sheer tip of a wedge
Driven by invisible blows,
The rock will split, we shall come out at the wonder, we shall
    find the Hesperides.
("The Song of a Man Who Has Come Through")

In each of these passages the "argument" is carried forward by
incantation and metaphor. There is no immediate physical scene,
as there is in "After the Opera" and "A Doe at Evening." Instead,
we are given the poet's immediate feeling as it wells up from
within and assumes a rhythmic shape of its own. It would seem,
then, that in the "poetry of the present" the poet's effort of at-

tention may be given primarily to the external scene at one time
and at another time to the internal emotional pressure. Sometimes,
in "Almond Blossom," for instance (and in "End of Another
Home Holiday," for that matter), one finds both a careful objective description and a rising and falling rhythmic urgency. In
"Almond Blossom" the external object and the feeling from
within are perfectly fused. In all his poems Lawrence's aim is to
be faithful at once to his own feeling and to the objective reality
—i.e., to the whole felt experience. But the emphasis may rest in
particular poems with one or the other.

"Bat" is a good example of the picture-making kind of free
verse:

> When the tired flower of Florence is in gloom beneath the
>   glowing
> Brown hills surrounding . . .
> When under the arches of the Ponte Vecchio
> A green light enters against stream, flush from the west,
> Against the current of obscure Arno . . .
>
> Look up, and you see things flying
> Between the day and the night;
> Swallows with spools of dark thread sewing the shadows to-
>   gether.
>
> A circle swoop, and a quick parabola under the bridge arches
> Where light pushes through;
> A sudden turning upon itself of a thing in the air.
> A dip to the water.
>
> And you think:
> "The swallows are flying so late!"
>
> Swallows?
>
> Dark air-life looping
> Yet missing the pure loop . . .

A twitch, a twitter, an elastic shudder in flight
And serrated wings against the sky,
Like a glove, a black glove thrown up at the light,
And falling back.

Never swallows!
Bats!
The swallows are gone.

Here, as in "After the Opera" and "A Doe at Evening," each line
contributes something definite to the whole picture. The rhythm
is that of excited talk, conversational rather than incantatory. The
other, more cadenced kind of free verse may be found, in *Birds,
Beasts and Flowers*, not only in "Almond Blossom" but in
"Snake" and in such passages as the conclusion of "Tortoise
Shout" and that of "Mountain Lion." In both kinds of poem
Lawrence uses the device of repetition of words and phrases—in
the conversational poems as a kind of stitching and in the more
incantatory ones as an attempt to go beyond conceptual statement in the progressive discovery of his own deep feelings.

It is obvious that most of the pansies are talk-patterned, just as
the most celebrated of the last poems, "Bavarian Gentians,"
"Whales Weep Not!," "Shadows," and "The Ship of Death," are
incantatory. But the pansies are also a new departure for Lawrence: there is not so much of the picture-making that one finds in
such earlier conversational poems as "Bat" and "Fish." Instead,
the poet speaks directly to the reader; if the effect is not one of
perfect transparency, neither is it one of pure exhortation or argument. In the best of these poems the speaker invites us to share
another kind of immediate experience—the thought-adventure
that involves image-thinking rather than abstract concepts:

When we get out of the glass bottles of our own ego,
and when we escape like squirrels from turning in the cage of
our personality

and get into the forest again,
we shall shiver with cold and fright
but things will happen to us
so that we don't know ourselves.

Cool, unlying life will rush in,
and passion will make our bodies taut with power,
we shall stamp our feet with new power
and old things will fall down,
we shall laugh, and institutions will curl up like burnt paper.

("Escape")

It is the combination of the natural speaking voice and the vivid imagery that makes this an authentic experience. We are persuaded—not necessarily that the "thought" is correct but that it is a genuine effort of attention on the part of this man. Who touches these poems touches a man, as Whitman says. The pansies offer an experience that is just as immediate, in its own way, as that afforded by "Snake" or "Bavarian Gentians." Having discovered and explored a "sacramentalized, objective world" in *Look! We Have Come Through!* and *Birds, Beasts and Flowers*, Lawrence now wished to express, more directly and sparely than before, his interpretation of his experience and the criticism of modern civilization that arises naturally from that experience.

Finally, in "More Pansies" and the last poems, Lawrence was able to express all his thoughts, feelings, and sense-experiences with a perfect fluid ease. He had come a long way from the rough originality of "The Wild Common" and the obscure rhetoric of some of the marriage poems. His free verse was more flexible and versatile than that of Whitman, and more whole, more deeply felt and imagined than the picturesque exercises of most of the other imagists. In *Birds, Beasts and Flowers, Pansies,* and *Last Poems* he had in truth carried free verse farther than any poet before him. Because he had the courage to explore an inner and outer chaos he discovered a new "body" and a new "motion" in the attempt to open up new areas of experience to poetry; his chaos was lit up by visions.

III

Dr. Leavis has come, apparently, to believe that D. H. Lawrence and T. S. Eliot represent the two warring and irreconcilable poles of modern literature. The best contemporary English verse, however, shows that their influences can be creatively reconciled. In the seriousness of what I have called the new depth poetry, the openness to experience, the psychological insight and integrity of D. H. Lawrence would, ideally, combine with the technical skill and formal intelligence of T. S. Eliot. If this were to happen, we would have contemporary work which, like Coleridge's Imagination, would reconcile "a more than usual state of emotion with more than usual order." [7]

These remarks, taken from the introduction to Alfred Alvarez's anthology *The New Poetry*, suggest the way in which the best poets of today, particularly Robert Lowell and Ted Hughes, may have benefited from the Lawrentian discipline of truth to feeling as well as from the formal fastidiousness of T. S. Eliot. Alvarez suggests that the doctrine of impersonality in poetry that was established by the critical followers of Eliot may be modified and corrected by an acquaintance with Lawrence's work.

The dominant voice in the English poetry of the early twentieth century was indisputably that of T. S. Eliot. But Lawrence's work has not been without a certain underground influence, which has manifested itself in a variety of ways. On the death of Lawrence, for instance, a fellow imagist, William Carlos Williams, wrote:

Green points on the shrub
and poor Lawrence dead.
The night damp and misty
and Lawrence no more in the world

to answer April's promise
with a fury of labor
against waste, waste and life's
coldness.

Once he received a letter—
he never answered it—
praising him: so English
he had thereby raised himself
to an unenglish greatness.
Dead now and it grows clearer
what bitterness drove him.

This is the time.
The serpent in the grotto
water dripping from the stone
into a pool.
Mediterranean evenings. Ashes
of Cretan fires. And to the north
forsythia hung with
yellow bells in the cold.

Poor Lawrence
worn with a fury of sad labor
to create summer from
spring's decay. English
women. Men driven not to love
but to the ends of the earth.
The serpent turning his
stone-like head,
the fixed agate eyes turn also.

And unopened jonquils
hang their folded heads. No
summer. But for Lawrence
full praise in this

half cold half season—
before trees are in leaf and
tufted grass stars
unevenly the bare ground.

Slowly the serpent leans
to drink by the tinkling water
the forked tongue alert.
Then fold after fold,
glassy strength, passing
a given point,
as by desire drawn
forward bodily, he glides
smoothly in.
   ("An Elegy for D. H. Lawrence")

Here is a conversational verse not unlike Lawrence's own in its rapid, shorthand movement and its concentration on small, natural details, Though Dr. Williams' language and rhythms are different—more laconic, more American—his poetic aims are very similar to Lawrence's: he seeks an effect of perfect transparency and a rhythm that is inherent in basic speech patterns. Today his followers in America—Charles Olson, Robert Creeley, Denise Levertov, Kenneth Rexroth, and others—have carried Williams' theory and practice further: the so-called Black Mountain school of poets writing a "projective verse" have become a major force in contemporary North American poetry. Some of them, most notably Kenneth Rexroth, acknowledge a debt to Lawrence as well as to Williams. But none of the Black Mountain poets has the passion and prophetic insight of a Lawrence: written according to theory, their work suffers from a homogeneous imagistic flatness.

    In England the young W. H. Auden was influenced by Lawrence's ideas, though not by his manner. This is evident in one of his most famous early poems, "Petition." This sonnet, now available only in earlier editions of Auden's poems, echoes Hopkins' "Thou art indeed just, Lord, if I contend" in technique and method: the compressed syntax, the plea for refreshment and renewal, the use of the terms "Sir" and "enemy"—all are derived from the Hopkins sonnet. But while it seems obvious that Auden wrote with Hopkins in mind, the "Sir" that he petitions is certainly not the God of his fathers; it appears instead to be some kind of Freudian energy or Lawrentian life-impulse that might cure all the modern neuroses. It is probable that certain neo-Freudian theories of psychosomatic illness have been adopted (for the moment) by the poet. But Auden's enemies in this poem are Lawrence's enemies: those who "will" the "negative inversion" of the power within themselves; the "intolerable neural itch" of the exclusively cerebral consciousness; "the distortions of ingrown virginity"; "the rehearsed response." Like Lawrence, the young Auden longs for a harrowing of hell, a reawakening of the dark powers buried within us, and thus for a "change of heart." Cowardice, dishonesty, obsessive mother-love, and the death-wish are to be decisively routed.

But Lawrence's way of self-renewal involved a confessional kind of verse: he would re-enact the drama of his love for his mother and the related conflict with his wife with a complete and naked honesty in his poems. The young Auden declined to give such a personal expression to his inner conflicts. "I must confess that I find Lawrence's love poems embarrassing," he wrote later; "they make me feel a peeping Tom." [8] He did not attempt the personal exploration that has recently been the concern of such poets as Robert Lowell and Sylvia Plath. Nor did he attempt to use language with a Lawrentian transparency and immediacy in his own work. He has remained a very gifted formal poet.

It has been argued that both Hart Crane and Dylan Thomas were strongly influenced by Lawrence. But here again the influence was a partial one. These poets, both of them very fine rhetoricians, shared Lawrence's cosmic consciousness but not his attitude to language. Crane wrote:

Take this Sea, whose diapason knells
On scrolls of silver snowy sentences,
The sceptered terror of whose sessions rends
As her demeanours motion well or ill,
All but the pieties of lovers' hands.

And onward, as bells off San Salvador
Salute the crocus lustres of the stars,
In these poinsettia meadows of her tides,—
Adagios of islands, O my Prodigal,
Complete the dark confessions her veins spell.

Mark how her turning shoulders wind the hours,
And hasten while her penniless rich palms
Pass superscription of bent foam and wave,—
Hasten, while they are true,—sleep, death, desire,
Close round one instant in one floating flower.
                                        ("Voyages II")

Compare this to Lawrence's "The Sea":

You who take the moon as in a sieve, and sift
Her flake by flake and spread her meaning out;
You who roll the stars like jewels in your palm,
So that they seem to utter themselves aloud;

You who steep from out the days their colour,
Reveal the universal tint that dyes
Their web; who shadow the sun's great gestures and expressions
So that he seems a stranger in his passing . . .

or to the lines in "Moonrise," when the moon throws

Confession of delight upon the wave,
Littering the waves with her own superscription
Of bliss, till all her lambent beauty shakes towards us
Spread out and known at last . . .

Not only the spirit but also some of the diction and imagery of Crane's poem seem rather Lawrentian.* But the two Lawrence poems are much clearer in meaning (though looser and less finished) because less compressed in their use of language.

Similarly, when Dylan Thomas expresses a Lawrentian cosmic piety in Lawrentian terms the differences are as striking as the similarities:

Never until the mankind making
Bird beast and flower
Fathering and all humbling darkness
Tells with silence the last light breaking
And the still hour
Is come of the sea tumbling in harness . . .
   ("A Refusal to Mourn the Death,
    by Fire, of a Child in London")

The rhetorician achieves power by a strict formal compression that is alien to Lawrence. There is no attempt to make poetry of natural speech.

Like Crane, Thomas has evolved a far more elaborate imagery than is compatible with Lawrence's dramatic realism. Compare, for example, Lawrence's "Wedding Morn" with Thomas's "On the Marriage of a Virgin."

The morning breaks like a pomegranate
 In a shining crack of red;
Ah, when tomorrow the dawn comes late
 Whitening across the bed

---

* I am indebted to D. S. Savage (*The Personal Principle*, p. 138) and Bernice Slote (*Start with the Sun*, p. 9) for pointing out similarities between Lawrence's and Crane's poems.

It will find me watching at the marriage-gate
   And waiting while light is shed
On him who is sleeping satiate
   With a sunk, unconscious head.

In this dramatic monologue the girl wonders whether her lover will mean joy or misery to her. Thomas deals with the consummation:

No longer will the vibrations of the sun desire on
Her deepsea pillow where once she married alone,
Her heart all ears and eyes, lips catching the avalanche
Of the golden ghost who ringed with his streams her mercury
   bone,
Who under the lids of her windows hoisted his golden luggage,
For a man sleeps where fire leapt down and she learns through
   his arm
That other sun, the jealous coursing of the unrivalled blood.

Here there is no attempt, as there is in Lawrence's poem, to give the girl's thoughts or her perhaps complex feelings about her new situation. The sun here is not part of a dramatic scene but a mythic or ghostly lover, who has been replaced by the other sun in a man's blood. This last is, of course, a Lawrentian idea, but Lawrence would have put it much more straightforwardly. In his poems the myth arises from the observed object or the realistic situation—the tortoise or the blue gentian or the woman longing for her children; it is never imposed upon the material by means of thundering rhetoric or overelaborate metaphor. In the early poems this sometimes means that the poem lacks the full significance that a further reflection and a greater compression of language might achieve (though this is sometimes accomplished in revision), but it is usually very faithful to the immediate situation.

Alfred Alvarez calls Lawrence "the foremost emotional realist of the century." [9] Perhaps it is this that separates him from the most talented of his contemporaries. The doctrine of strict impersonality that was so important to the followers of Eliot discouraged younger poets from any further psychological exploration, even though Eliot himself, in "The Waste Land," had followed,

with great precision and delicacy, the movement of a psyche, not just of a society, in the process of disintegration. Eliot's talk of classicism, like his use in the poem of literature and theology, was an elaborate and successful defence which forced impersonality on a deeply personal and painful subject. But during the later twenties and thirties in America, Eliot's technical achievements and the radical revaluation of literary tradition that went with them seemed so bewilderingly impressive that the urgently personal uses this technique was put to were overlooked. A whole school of criticism was developed to prove technically that there was no necessary or even significant connexion between art and its roots in the artist's life. During the forties, however, when English poetry was at its nadir, there arose in the States a new generation of poets, the most important of whom were Robert Lowell and John Berryman. They had assimilated the lesson of Eliot and the critical thirties: they assumed that a poet, to earn his title, had to be very skilful, very original and very intelligent. But they were no longer concerned with Eliot's rearguard action against the late Romantics; they were, I mean, no longer adherents of the cult of rigid impersonality. So they were able to write poetry of immense skill and intelligence which coped openly with the quick of their experience, experience sometimes on the edge of disintegration and breakdown. Robert Lowell's latest book, *Life Studies*, for example, is a large step forward in this new direction. It may contain no single poem as impressive as the "Quaker Graveyard in Nantucket", but the total impact of the book as a whole is altogether more powerful. Where once Lowell tried to externalize his disturbances theologically in Catholicism and rhetorically in certain mannerisms of language and rhythm, he is now, I think, trying to cope with them nakedly, and without evasion.[10]

I have followed Alvarez's argument thus far because it suggests an affinity, if no more, between Lawrence and such recent "emotional realists" as Robert Lowell and Sylvia Plath. Indeed, these two poets write of parents, marriage, and extreme alienation with a frankness that makes Lawrence seem sentimental. Consider this passage from Lowell's "Man and Wife":

> Tamed by *Miltown*, we lie on Mother's bed;
> the rising sun in war paint dyes us red;
> in broad daylight her gilded bed-posts shine,
> abandoned, almost Dionysian.
> At last the trees are green on Marlborough Street,
> blossoms on our magnolia ignite
> the morning with their murderous five days' white.
> All night I've held your hand,
> as if you had
> a fourth time faced the kingdom of the mad—
> its hackneyed speech, its homicidal eye—
> and dragged me home alive . . .

Here, as in *Look! We Have Come Through!* we have Mother, marital war, Dionysian abandon, and the unstable man's dependence on the stronger female—and all in one poem. In other poems in *Life Studies* Lowell examines his family and background with ruthless precision in a search for the source of his emotional tensions. This was Lawrence's procedure in many of his early poems. Of course, Lawrence moved from such beginnings to an exploration of the plant and animal kingdoms and thence to the cosmic vision and social polemic of *Pansies* and *Last Poems;* it seems highly unlikely that Robert Lowell will develop along precisely these lines (though his present interest in politics and the psychic health of America is not unlike the concern for civilization evinced by the later Lawrence).

The only recent poet who shares Lawrence's ability to evoke the mysterious forces of the "non-human" world of life to any significant degree is Ted Hughes. Like Lawrence, whom he greatly admires, Ted Hughes can focus his poetic lens on the life of a tiny flower:

> this harebell,
>
> That trembles, as under threats of death,
> In the summer turf's heat-rise,
> And in which—filling veins
> Any known name of blue would bruise
> Out of existence—sleeps, recovering,
>
> The maker of the sea.
>
> ("Still Life")

Here, as in "Sicilian Cyclamens," the Lawrentian notion of creative and purposive force in the smallest form of life is expressed. Similarly, Hughes's close examination of animals and birds, and his ability to feel his way into their consciousness, makes one think immediately of Lawrence's middle period.

But there are differences, of course. Ted Hughes is notably lacking in Lawrence's ultimate optimism about natural processes. "Ghost Crabs," a very impressive Hughes poem, presents a symbolic vision of the universe not unlike that of Lawrence's swan poems, but these ghost crabs are infinitely more sinister than Lawrence's cosmic swan:

> These crabs own this world.
> All night, around us or through us,
> They stalk each other, they fasten on to each other,
> They mount each other, they tear each other to pieces,
> They utterly exhaust each other.
> They are the powers of this world.
> We are their bacteria,
> Dying their lives and living their deaths.
> At dawn, they sidle back under the sea's edge.
> They are the turmoil of history, the convulsion

In the roots of the blood, in the cycles of concurrence.
To them, our cluttered countries are empty battleground.
All day they recuperate under the sea.
Their singing is like a thin sea-wind flexing in the rocks of a
    headland,
Where only crabs listen.

They are God's only toys.

It is possible that the atrocities and disasters of recent western
history have engendered in Ted Hughes a more profoundly pessi-
mistic view of natural processes than Lawrence held, just as they
drove Robert Lowell and Sylvia Plath to a more extreme psychological realism. In any case, these three poets (and others) are, in
a very real sense, Lawrence's heirs.

It is perhaps one measure of Lawrence's achievement that each
of the poets I have mentioned can equal it only in part. They
have, of course, their own peculiar qualities and excellences, but
one does not find in their poems the scope, the range of experience, and the passionate reflection upon that experience that are
to be found in Lawrence's poems. There is a largeness about him,
a largeness that may be felt even in his less successful work. Both
his failures and his triumphs in poetry are part of a sustained effort to begin anew—to find and express a necessary human renewal from within. Like Yeats and Pound and Eliot, he was extremely sensitive to the deep disturbance, the disintegration of
values, the mass madness, and the senseless violence of our time.
But he did not wish to establish, like them, a new version of or-
thodoxy in art and society—he sought instead release and a new
direction for the human soul. His art is not a monumental gesture
in the face of death and disintegration, or an otherworldly rejection of this life, or an evasion of life's complexity in Utopian social theorizing. It is, in the poems no less significantly than in the
novels, an honest investigation of those biological, psychological

and cultural forces that have produced our diseased civilization, and an attempt to realize, in form as in substance, a better and fuller way of life. In this approach to the problem Lawrence stands virtually alone. Other poets may have achieved a more uniform level of quality, but no other poet in our time has seen so far or so much. If Lawrence was mistaken, as he may well have been, in his belief that man may be saved merely by the release and the fuller expression of the instinctive life within him, he was nevertheless closer than any of his contemporaries to the heart of the problem, and closer as well to the necessary ground of its solution. He sought a new way into the interior. If there is a future kingdom for poetry or for civilization, then Lawrence must long be remembered as one of its first explorers.

Reference Notes

Introduction

1. D. H. Lawrence, *Complete Poems*, p. 849.
2. Edward Thomas, "More Georgian Poetry," *The Bookman*, XLIV (April 1913), p. 47.
3. *The Letters of Ezra Pound*, pp. 52–53.
4. *Poetry*, II (1913), pp. 149–51.
5. O. Shakespear, "The Poetry of D. H. Lawrence," *The Egoist*, May 1, 1915, p. 81.
6. *The Times Literary Supplement*, November 22, 1917, p. 571.
7. Conrad Aiken, "The Melodic Line," *The Dial*, LXVII (1919), pp. 97–100.
8. Conrad Aiken, *A Reviewer's abc* (New York: Meridian Books, 1958), pp. 256–61.
9. Louis Untermeyer, "Strained Intensities," *The Bookman* (New York), LIX (1924), pp. 219–22.
10. "Some Books of the Week," *The Spectator*, September 29, 1928, p. 403.
11. J. C. Squire, *The Observer*, October 7, 1928, p. 6.
12. E. B. "What are those golden builders doing?" *The Nation and Athenaeum*, XLIV (1928), p. 216.
13. *The Times Literary Supplement*, November 15, 1928, p. 852.
14. John Middleton Murry, *The New Adelphi*, II (1928–1929), pp. 165–67.
15. John Gould Fletcher, "Night Haunted Lover," *The New York Herald Tribune Books*, July 14, 1929, pp. 1, 6.
16. Louis Untermeyer, "Hot Blood's Blindfold Art," *The Saturday Review of Literature*, VI (1929), pp. 17–18.

17. Affable Hawk (Desmond MacCarthy), "Books in General," *The New Statesman*, XXXII (1928), p. 51.
18. Richard Church, "Three Established Poets," *The Spectator*, August 3, 1929, pp. 164–65.
19. *The Times Literary Supplement*, July 4, 1929, p. 532.
20. Mark Van Doren, *The New York Herald Tribune Books*, December 15, 1929, p. 15.
21. Humbert Wolfe, *The Observer*, August 14, 1932, p. 6. *The Times Literary Supplement*, September 29, 1932, pp. 673–74. Alan Pryce-Jones, *The London Mercury*, XXVI (1932), pp. 454–56. V. S. Pritchett, *The Fortnightly Review*, October 1, 1932, pp. 534–35.
22. Yvonne ffrench, *The London Mercury*, XXVIII (1933), pp. 262–64.
23. Lord David Cecil, "Lawrence in His Poems," *The Spectator*, August 4, 1933, p. 163.
24. Lawrence, *Collected Letters*, p. 413.
25. Quoted in F. O. Mathiessen, *The Achievement of T. S. Eliot*, pp. 89–90, 96.
26. T. S. Eliot, "Introduction," *Revelation*, pp. 30–31.
27. I. A. Richards, *Science and Poetry*, pp. 72–83.
28. R. P. Blackmur, *The Double Agent*, 1935.
29. Keith Sagar, *The Art of D. H. Lawrence*, p. 242.
30. *Ibid.*, p. 241.
31. Vivian de Sola Pinto, "Introduction," *Complete Poems*, p. 2.
32. Blackmur, *The Double Agent*, pp. 110–11.
33. Harold Bloom, *A D. H. Lawrence Miscellany*, 1959.
34. David Daiches, *Poetry in the Modern World*, pp. 51–53.
35. Richard Ellmann, *The Achievement of D. H. Lawrence*, p. 260.
36. R. G. N. Salgādo, "The Poetry of D. H. Lawrence" (Ph.D. dissertation, University of Nottingham, 1955).
37. Alfred Alvarez, *The Shaping Spirit*, 1958.
38. Pinto, "Introduction," *Complete Poems*, pp. 1–21. Cf. *The Critical Quarterly*, III (1961), pp. 5–18, 164–67, 267–70, 368–69; IV (1962), p. 81.
39. *The Times Literary Supplement*, August 26, 1965, pp. 725–27.
40. Salgādo in *The Critical Quarterly*, VII (1965), 389–92.
41. D. J. Enright, *Conspirators and Poets*.

One: The Blindfold Art: Lawrence's Early Poems

1. Lawrence, *Complete Poems*, p. 27.
2. *Ibid.*, p. 28.

3. Alvarez, *The Shaping Spirit*, p. 141.
4. Kenneth Rexroth, *Selected Poems*, p. 6.
5. Lawrence, *Collected Letters*, p. 234.
6. Kenneth Rexroth, *Selected Poems*, p. 2.
7. Lawrence, *Collected Letters*, pp. 243–44.
8. MS. 1479, *Amores*, pp. 4–6.
9. MS. 1479, *Love Poems and Others*, pp. 38–39.
10. Lawrence, *Sons and Lovers*, p. 162.
11. MS. 1479.
12. John Middleton Murry, *Love, Freedom and Society*, p. 62.
13. Lawrence, *Fantasia of the Unconscious*, pp. 25–26.
14. MS. 1479.
15. Salgādo, "The Poetry of D. H. Lawrence," p. 66.
16. Lawrence, *Love Poems and Others*, p. 25.
17. Harry T. Moore, *The Intelligent Heart*, p. 83.
18. Rexroth, *Selected Poems*, pp. 6–7.
19. Lawrence, *Sons and Lovers*, p. 411.
20. *Ibid.*, p. 419.
21. Lawrence, *The Symbolic Meaning*, pp. 72–73.
22. Rainer Maria Rilke, *Duino Elegies*, p. 87.
23. Lawrence, *Complete Poems*, p. 849.
24. MS. 1479.
25. Pinto, "Introduction," *Complete Poems*, p. 8.
26. Jessie Chambers, *D. H. Lawrence: A Personal Record*, p. 139.
27. MS. 1479.
28. Lawrence, *Collected Letters*, p. 282.
29. *Ibid.*, p. 288.
30. Lawrence, "Chaos in Poetry," *Phoenix*, p. 255.
31. Lawrence, *Collected Letters*, p. 282.
32. Frieda Lawrence, *The Memoirs and Correspondence*, p. 316.
33. Lawrence, *New Poems*, pp. 54–58.
34. Lawrence, *Collected Letters*, pp. 427–28.
35. Lawrence, *Women in Love*, p. 298.
36. Vivian de Sola Pinto, *D. H. Lawrence: Prophet of the Midlands*, p. 9.
37. Chambers, *A Personal Record*, p. 116.
38. *Ibid.*, p. 52.
39. W. H. Auden, *The Dyer's Hand*, p. 285.
40. Lawrence, *Complete Poems*, p. 28.
41. *Ibid.*, p. 183.
42. *Ibid.*, p. 184.

Two: Sufficiency of Death: *Look! We Have Come Through!*
and the War Poems

1. *The New York Times Review of Books*, April 20, 1919, p. 215.
2. Rexroth, "Introduction," *Selected Poems*, p. 11.
3. Moore, *The Intelligent Heart*, p. 124.
4. Lawrence, *Complete Poems*, p. 419.
5. Frieda Lawrence, *The Memoirs and Correspondence*, p. 330.
6. Lawrence, *Twilight in Italy*, p. 30.
7. *Ibid.*, p. 31.
8. Lawrence, *Look! We Have Come Through!*, p. 102.
9. Lawrence, *Collected Poems*, p. 78.
10. Lawrence, *Complete Poems* (1957), Vol. I, p. 234.
11. *Cf.* Raphael Levy, *The Explicator*, February 1964, Vol. XXII, No. 6, Item 44.
12. Earl and Achsah Brewster, *Reminiscences and Correspondence*, p. 28.
13. Lawrence, *Collected Letters*, p. 291.
14. *Ibid.*, p. 221.
15. Horace Gregory, *Pilgrim of the Apocalypse*, p. 31.
16. Rexroth, *Selected Poems*, p. 14.
17. Anais Nin, *D. H. Lawrence: An Unprofessional Study*, pp. 135–38.
18. Lawrence, *Complete Poems*, p. 185.
19. Murry, *Love, Freedom and Society*, p. 60.
20. Lawrence, *Kangaroo*, p. 215.
21. Murry, *Between Two Worlds*, p. 334.
22. Murry, *Love, Freedom and Society*, p. 47.
23. Lawrence, *Collected Letters*, p. 375.
24. *Ibid.*, p. 378.
25. *Ibid.*, p. 366.
26. *Ibid.*, p. 487.
27. Edward Nehls, *A Composite Biography*, Vol. I, pp. 315–16. (Quoted from Herbert Asquith, *Moments of Memory*, New York: Charles Scribner's Sons, 1938).
28. Lawrence, *Phoenix II*, p. 400.
29. *Ibid.*, pp. 447–48.
30. Lawrence, *Phoenix*, p. 256.
31. Lawrence, *Phoenix II*, pp. 598–99.
32. Lawrence, *The Rainbow*, p. 441.
33. Leone Vivante, *A Philosophy of Potentiality*, p. 83.
34. Chambers, *A Personal Record*, p. 122.

35. Lawrence, *Studies in Classic American Literature*, p. 168.
36. Lawrence, *The Symbolic Meaning*, p. 240.
37. *The Saturday Review of Literature*, IX (1933), pp. 523–24.
38. Auden, *The Dyer's Hand*, pp. 287–88.
39. Edward Marsh, *A Number of People*, p. 232.
40. S. Foster Damon, *Amy Lowell*, pp. 387–88.
41. Lawrence, *Some Imagist Poets* (1915), pp. vi–vii.
42. Gregory, *Pilgrim of the Apocalypse*, pp. 8–9.

Three: The Rainbow Change: *Birds, Beasts and Flowers* and the Poems from *The Plumed Serpent*

1. Salgādo, "The Poetry of D. H. Lawrence," p. 127.
2. *The New Republic*, Vol. XXV, No. 318, January 5, 1921, p. 169.
3. The word "convert" in line 7 of stanza 11 of the 1967 edition of the *Complete Poems* should read "covert." *Birds, Beasts and Flowers* (p. 19) and *Collected Poems* (p. 130) have "covert."
4. Lawrence, *Fantasia of the Unconscious*, p. 7.
5. Konrad Lorenz, *On Aggression*, pp. 204–205.
6. *Ibid.*, p. 205.
7. Lawrence, *Fantasia of the Unconscious*, p. 8.
8. *Ibid.*, p. 207.
9. Lawrence, *The Symbolic Meaning*, p. 30.
10. Lawrence, *The Boy in the Bush*, p. 93.
11. Lawrence, *The White Peacock*, pp. 128–29.
12. Lawrence, *The Lost Girl*, p. 345.
13. Auden, *The Dyer's Hand*, pp. 300–303.
14. Auden, "Some Notes on D. H. Lawrence," *The Nation*, April 26, 1947, pp. 482–84.
15. Rilke, *Duino Elegies*, p. 67.
16. Sagar, *The Art of D. H. Lawrence*, p. 120.
17. Lawrence, *The Plumed Serpent*, p. 423.
18. *Ibid.*, p. 18.
19. Graham Hough, *The Dark Sun*, p. 207.
20. *A D. H. Lawrence Miscellany*, p. 367.
21. Sagar, *The Art of D. H. Lawrence*, p. 128.
22. Salgādo, "The Poetry of D. H. Lawrence," p. 183.
23. *Ibid.*, p. 181.
24. Hough, *The Dark Sun*, pp. 205–206.
25. Rexroth, *Selected Poems*, p. 15.

Four: The Cosmic Swan: *Pansies, Nettles* and "More Pansies"

1. Richard Aldington, "Note to *Last Poems*," *Complete Poems*, p. 595.
2. Pinto, "Introduction," *Complete Poems*, p. 15.
3. Murry, *Love, Freedom and Society*, p. 109.
4. *The New Yorker*, March 20, 1948, p. 106.
5. Frederick J. Hoffman, *The Achievement of D. H. Lawrence*, p. 127.
6. *The New Yorker*, March 20, 1948, p. 106.
7. C. G. Jung, *Memories, Dreams, Reflections*, p. 420.
8. Murry, *Love, Freedom and Society*, p. 101.
9. Ernst Cassirer, *Language and Myth*, pp. 17–18.
10. *Ibid.*, p. 71.
11. Frederick Carter, *D. H. Lawrence and the Body Mystical*, p. 6.
12. *Ibid.*, p. 58.
13. Lawrence, "Introduction" to *Pansies*, *Complete Poems*, p. 418.
14. Lawrence, *Phoenix*, pp. 721–22.
15. *Ibid.*, p. 729.
16. *The Times Literary Supplement*, August 26, 1965, p. 727.

Five: The Psychic Mariner: The Last Poems

1. Frieda Lawrence, "*Not I, But the Wind . . .*," pp. 199–200.
2. *Ibid.*, p. 288.
3. Lawrence, *Etruscan Places*, p. 42.
4. *Ibid.*, p. 49.
5. Alvarez, *The Shaping Spirit*, p. 158.
6. Lawrence, *Etruscan Places*, p. 53.
7. Lawrence, *Apocalypse*, pp. 222–23.
8. *Ibid.*, p. 49.
9. *Ibid.*, p. 50.
10. *Ibid.*, p. 53.
11. *Ibid.*, p. 197.
12. *Ibid.*, p. 192.
13. *Ibid.*, pp. 102–103.
14. *Ibid.*, p. 108.
15. *Ibid.*, pp. 108–109.
16. *Ibid.*, p. 129.
17. *Ibid.*, pp. 86–87.
18. *Ibid.*, pp. 96–97.

19. *Ibid.*, pp. 91–92.
20. Lawrence, *Phoenix*, p. 733.
21. Lawrence, *Etruscan Places*, p. 14.
22. Lawrence, *Lady Chatterley's Lover*, p. 271.
23. Lawrence, *The Man Who Died*, p. 10.
24. Lawrence, *Etruscan Places*, p. 72.
25. *Ibid.*, p. 68.

Conclusion: The Future Kingdom

1. Lawrence, *Phoenix*, p. 255.
2. *Ibid.*, p. 257.
3. *Ibid.*, p. 261.
4. Lawrence, *Complete Poems*, p. 184.
5. Lawrence, *Fantasia of the Unconscious*, p. 207.
6. Lawrence, *Complete Poems*, p. 184.
7. Alvarez, "Beyond the Gentility Principle," *The New Poetry*, pp. 31–32.
8. Auden, *The Dyer's Hand*, p. 288.
9. Alvarez, *The Shaping Spirit*, p. 141.
10. Alvarez, *The New Poetry*, pp. 28–29.

Selected Bibliography

I. WORKS BY D. H. LAWRENCE

(a) *Poems*
   (i) Manuscripts
   MS. 1479, University of Nottingham Library.
   (ii) Books and Pamphlets
   Georgian Poetry 1911–12. London: The Poetry Bookshop, 1912.
   Love Poems and Others. London: Duckworth; New York: Mitchell Kennerly, 1913.
   Some Imagist Poets. Boston, New York: Houghton Mifflin; London: Constable, 1915.
   Georgian Poetry 1913–15. London: The Poetry Bookshop; New York: G. P. Putnam's Sons, 1915.
   Amores. London: Duckworth; New York: B. W. Huebsch, 1916.
   Look! We Have Come Through! London: Chatto and Windus; New York: B. W. Huebsch, 1917.
   New Poems. London: Martin Secker, 1918; New York: B. W. Huebsch, 1920.
   Bay. London: Cyril W. Beaumont, 1919.
   Tortoises. New York: Thomas Seltzer, 1921.
   Birds, Beasts and Flowers. New York: Thomas Seltzer; London: Martin Secker, 1923.
   The Collected Poems of D. H. Lawrence. London: Martin Secker, 1928; New York: Jonathan Cape and Harrison Smith, 1929.
   Pansies. London: privately printed, 1929.
   Pansies. London: Martin Secker; New York: Alfred A. Knopf, 1929.
   Nettles. London: Faber and Faber, 1930.

Imagist Anthology 1930. New York: Covici, Friede; London: Chatto and Windus, 1930.

The Triumph of the Machine. London: Faber and Faber, 1930.

Birds, Beasts and Flowers. London: The Cresset Press, 1930.

Last Poems. Florence: G. Orioli, 1932; New York: The Viking Press; London: Martin Secker, 1933.

Fire and Other Poems. San Francisco: printed at the Grabhorn Press for the Book Club of California, 1940.

Selected Poems. New York: New Directions, 1947.

The Complete Poems of D. H. Lawrence. Collected and Edited with an Introduction and Notes by Vivian de Sola Pinto and Warren Roberts. London: Heinemann; New York: The Viking Press, 1967.

(b) *Prose Works*

(i) Books Published by Heinemann (original publishers listed in parentheses)

The White Peacock, 1955 (London: Heinemann; New York: Duffield, 1911).

The Trespasser, 1955 (London: Duckworth; New York: Mitchell Kennerly, 1912).

Sons and Lovers, 1961 (London: Duckworth; New York: Mitchell Kennerly, 1913).

The Rainbow, 1955 (London: Methuen; New York: B. W. Huebsch, 1915)

Twilight in Italy, 1956 (London: Duckworth; New York: B. W. Huebsch, 1916).

Women in Love, 1954 (New York: privately printed, 1920; London: Martin Secker, 1921).

The Lost Girl, 1955 (London: Martin Secker, 1920; New York: Thomas Seltzer, 1921).

Sea and Sardinia, 1956 (New York: Thomas Seltzer, 1921; London: Martin Secker, 1923).

Aaron's Rod, 1954 (New York: Thomas Seltzer; London: Martin Secker, 1922).

Fantasia of the Unconscious and Psychoanalysis and the Unconscious, 1961 (*Psychoanalysis and the Unconscious*, New York: Thomas Seltzer, 1921; London: Martin Secker, 1923. *Fantasia of the Unconscious*, New York: Thomas Seltzer, 1922; London: Martin Secker, 1923).

Studies in Classic American Literature, 1964 (New York: Thomas Seltzer, 1923; London: Martin Secker, 1924).

Kangaroo, 1955 (London: Martin Secker; New York: Thomas Seltzer, 1923).

The Plumed Serpent, 1955 (London: Martin Secker; New York: Alfred A. Knopf, 1926).

Lady Chatterley's Lover, 1963 (privately printed, 1928; London: Martin Secker; New York: Alfred A. Knopf, 1932).

The Short Novels, 1956 (*The Man Who Died,* as *The Escaped Cock;* Paris: Black Sun Press, 1929; London: Martin Secker; New York: Alfred A. Knopf, 1931).

Etruscan Places, 1956 (London: Martin Secker; New York: The Viking Press, 1932).

Phoenix, 1968 (London: Heinemann; New York: The Viking Press, 1936).

The Complete Short Stories (London: Heinemann; New York: The Viking Press, 1955).

Collected Letters (London: Heinemann; New York: The Viking Press, 1962).

Phoenix II. London: Heinemann; New York: The Viking Press, 1968.

(ii) Other Prose Works

The Boy in the Bush. London: Martin Secker; New York: Thomas Seltzer, 1924.

Apocalypse. Florence: Orioli, 1931; London: Martin Secker; New York: The Viking Press, 1932.

The Symbolic Meaning. London: Centaur Press, 1962; New York: The Viking Press, 1964.

II. Biography

Aldington, Richard. *Life for Life's Sake.* New York: The Viking Press, 1941.

Brewster, Earl and Achsah. *Reminiscences and Correspondence.* London: Martin Secker, 1934.

Carswell, Catherine. *The Savage Pilgrimage.* London: Martin Secker; New York: Harcourt, 1932.

Carter, Frederick. *D. H. Lawrence and the Body Mystical.* London: Denis Archer, 1932.

Chambers, Jessie. *D. H. Lawrence: A Personal Record.* London: Jonathan Cape, 1935; New York: Knight, 1936.

Corke, Helen. *Neutral Ground.* London: Arthur Barker, 1933.

———. *D. H. Lawrence: The Croydon Years.* Austin: University of Texas Press, 1957.

Damon, S. Foster. *Amy Lowell.* Boston, New York: Houghton Mifflin, 1935.

Lawrence, Frieda. *"Not I, But the Wind . . ."* Santa Fe: The Rydal Press; New York: The Viking Press, 1934.
————. *The Memoirs and Correspondence.* London: Heinemann, 1961; New York: Alfred A. Knopf, 1964.
Luhan, Mabel Dodge. *Lorenzo in Taos.* New York: Alfred A. Knopf, 1932; London: Martin Secker, 1933.
Marsh, Edward. *A Number of People.* London: Heinemann, 1939.
Merrild, Knud. *A Poet and Two Painters.* London: George Routledge and Sons, 1938; New York: The Viking Press, 1939.
Moore, Harry T. *The Life and Works of D. H. Lawrence.* London: George Allen and Unwin; New York: Twayne Publishers, 1951).
————. *The Intelligent Heart.* New York: Farrar, Straus and Young, 1954; London: Heinemann, 1955.
Murry, John Middleton. *Between Two Worlds.* London: Jonathan Cape, 1935.
Nehls, Edward. *D. H. Lawrence: A Composite Biography.* Madison: University of Wisconsin Press, 1957–1959.

III. Critical Works on Lawrence's Poems

(a) *Books*

Kenmare, Dallas. *Fire-Bird.* London: James Barrie; New York: Philosophical Library, 1951.

(b) *Articles, Reviews, Pamphlets and Sections of Books*
Affable Hawk (Desmond MacCarthy). "Books in General." *The New Statesman,* XXXII (1928), p. 51.
Aiken, Conrad. "The Melodic Line." *The Dial,* LXVII (1919), pp. 97–100.
————. Review of *Birds, Beasts and Flowers. A Reviewer's abc.* New York: Meridian Books, 1958; London: L. A. Wallrich Books, 1961, pp. 256–61.
Aldington, Richard. "Note" to *Last Poems. Complete Poems,* pp. 591–98.
Alvarez, Alfred. "D. H. Lawrence: The Single State of Man." *The Shaping Spirit.* London: Chatto and Windus; New York: Charles Scribner's Sons, 1958. See also Bloom, Hassall, and Shapiro, *A D. H. Lawrence Miscellany.*
Corke, Helen. "Beyond the Gentility Principle." *The New Poetry.* Harmondsworth, Middlesex; Baltimore: Penguin Books, 1962.
Anonymous. "Recent Verse." *The New Statesman,* X (1918), pp. 406–407.

————. "Some Books of the Week." *The Spectator*, September 29, 1928, p. 403.

————. Review of *Look! We Have Come Through! The Times Literary Supplement*, November 22, 1917, p. 571.

————. Review of *Birds, Beasts and Flowers. The Times Literary Supplement*, December 13, 1923, p. 864.

————. Review of *Collected Poems. The Times Literary Supplement*, November 15, 1928, p. 852.

————. Review of *Pansies. The Times Literary Supplement*, July 4, 1929, p. 532.

————. Review of *Collected Poems. The Times Literary Supplement*, September 29, 1932, pp. 673–74.

————. "Lawrence the Poet: Achievement and Irrelevance." *The Times Literary Supplement*, August 26, 1965, pp. 725–27.

Auden, W. H. "Some Notes on D. H. Lawrence." *The Nation*, April 26, 1947, pp. 482–84.

————. "D. H. Lawrence." *The Dyer's Hand and Other Essays*. New York: Random House; London: Faber and Faber, 1948.

E. B. "What are those golden builders doing?" *The Nation and Athenaeum*, XLIV (1928), p. 216.

Bartlett, Phyllis. "Lawrence's *Collected Poems:* The Demon Takes Over." *Publications of the Modern Language Association of America*, LXVI (1951), pp. 583–93.

Beal, Anthony. *D. H. Lawrence*. London: Oliver and Boyd; New York: Grove Press, 1961.

Blackmur, R. P. "D. H. Lawrence and Expressive Form." *The Double Agent*. New York: Arrow Editions, 1935. Cf. *Language as Gesture* (New York: Harcourt Brace, 1952).

Bloom, Harold. "Lawrence, Blackmur, Eliot and the Tortoise." *A D. H. Lawrence Miscellany*. Edited by Harry T. Moore. Carbondale: Southern Illinois University Press; London: Heinemann, 1961.

Bogan, Louise. Review of *Selected Poems. The New Yorker*, March 20, 1948, pp. 102–106.

Bynner, Witter. *Journey with Genius*. New York: John Day, 1951; London: Peter Nevill, 1953.

Cecil, Lord David. "Lawrence in His Poems." *The Spectator*, August 4, 1933, p. 163.

Charques, R. D. *Contemporary Literature and Social Revolution*. London: Martin Secker, 1933.

Church, Richard. "Three Established Poets." *The Spectator*, August 3, 1929, pp. 164–65.

Clark, L. D. *Dark Night of the Body*. Austin: University of Texas Press, 1964.

Daiches, David. *Poetry and the Modern World.* Chicago: University of Chicago Press, 1940.

Draper, Ronald P. *D.H.Lawrence.* New York: Twayne Publishers, 1964.

Dupee, F. W. Review of *Selected Poems. The New York Times Book Review,* March 7, 1948, p. 4.

Eliot, T. S. "Introduction." *Revelation.* Edited by John Baillie and Hugh Martin. London: Faber and Faber, 1937.

Ellmann, Richard. "Barbed Wire and Coming Through." *The Achievement of D.H.Lawrence.* Edited by Frederick J. Hoffman and Harry T. Moore. Norman: University of Oklahoma Press, 1953.

Enright, D. J. "A Haste for Wisdom: The Poetry of D. H. Lawrence." *Conspirators and Poets.* London: Chatto and Windus, 1966.

ffrench, Yvonne. Review of *Last Poems. The London Mercury,* XXVIII (1933), pp. 262–64.

Fletcher, John Gould. "A Modern Evangelist." *Poetry,* XII (1918), pp. 269–74.

———. "Night-Haunted Lover." *The New York Herald Tribune Books,* July 14, 1929, pp. 1, 6.

Gregory, Horace. *D.H. Lawrence: Pilgrim of the Apocalypse.* London: Martin Secker; New York: The Viking Press, 1933.

Grigson, Geoffrey. "The Poet in D. H. Lawrence." *The London Magazine,* May 1958, pp. 66–69.

Hassall, Christopher. "Black Flowers: A New Light on the Poetics of D. H. Lawrence." *A D.H.Lawrence Miscellany.* Edited by Harry T. Moore. Carbondale: Southern Illinois University Press, 1959; London: Heinemann, 1961.

Hawkins, Desmond. "Introduction." *Stories, Essays and Poems.* London: J. M. Dent, 1939.

Hough, Graham. *The Dark Sun.* London: Duckworth, 1956; New York: Macmillan, 1957.

Hughes, Glenn. *Imagism and the Imagists.* Stanford: Stanford University Press; London: Oxford University Press, 1931.

Hughes, Richard. Review of *Birds, Beasts and Flowers. The Nation and Athenaeum,* XXXIV (1924), pp. 519–20.

Jeffers, Robinson. "Foreword." *Fire and Other Poems.* San Francisco: Grabhorn Press, 1940.

Leavis, F. R. *D.H.Lawrence.* Cambridge: The Minority Press, 1930.

Lerner, Laurence. "Two Views of D. H. Lawrence's Poetry." *The Critical Survey,* I (1963), pp. 87–89. Cf. *The Truthtellers:*

Jane Austen, George Eliot, D. H. Lawrence. London: Chatto and Windus; New York: Schocken Books, 1967.

Levy, Raphael. "Item 44." *The Explicator*, February 1964.

Lowell, Amy. "A New English Poet." *The New York Times Review of Books*, April 20, 1919, pp. 205, 210–11, 215, 217.

Lucas, F. L. "Sense and Sensibility." *The New Statesman*, XXII (1924), pp. 634–35.

Megroz, R. L. *Five Novelist Poets of Today*. London: Joiner and Steele, 1933.

Miller, James E.; Slote, Bernice; Shapiro, Karl. *Start with the Sun*. Lincoln: University of Nebraska Press, 1960.

Murry, John Middleton. Review of *Collected Poems*. *The New Adelphi*, II (1928–1929), pp. 165–67.

———. *Love, Freedom and Society*. London: Jonathan Cape, 1957.

Nin, Anais. *D. H. Lawrence: An Unprofessional Study*. Paris: Edward M. Titus, 1932; Denver: Alan Swallow, 1964.

R. P. "Dragging in Mr. Pound." *The Christian Science Monitor*, March 25, 1933, p. 8.

Panichas, George A. *Adventures in Consciousness*. The Hague, London, Paris: Mouton and Co., 1964.

Pinto, Vivian de Sola. *D. H. Lawrence: Prophet of the Midlands*. University of Nottingham, 1951.

———. "D. H. Lawrence: Letter-Writer and Craftsman in Verse." *Renaissance and Modern Studies*, I (1957), pp. 5–34.

———. "Introduction: D. H. Lawrence: Poet without a Mask." *Complete Poems*, pp. 1–21.

Pound, Ezra. Review of *Love Poems and Others*. *Poetry*, II (1913), pp. 149–51

Powell, Dilys. *Descent from Parnassus*. London: The Cresset Press, 1934; New York: Macmillan, 1935.

Powell, S. W. "D. H. Lawrence as Poet." *The Poetry Review*, September–October 1934, pp. 347–50.

Pritchett, V. S. Review of *Collected Poems*. *The Fortnightly Review*, October 1, 1932, pp. 534–35.

Pryce-Jones, Alan. Review of *Collected Poems*. *The London Mercury*, XXVI (1932), pp. 454–56.

Reeves, James. "Introduction." *Selected Poems*. London: Heinemann, 1951.

Rexroth, Kenneth. "Introduction." *Selected Poems*. New York: New Directions, 1947.

Richards, I. A. *Science and Poetry*. London: Kegan Paul, Trench, Trubner and Co.; New York: Norton, 1926.

————. *Practical Criticism*. London: Kegan Paul, Trench, Trubner and Co., 1929, pp. 105–17, 206, 269–70.

Sagar, Keith. *The Art of D. H. Lawrence*. Cambridge: Cambridge University Press, 1966.

Salgādo, R. G. N. Review of *Complete Poems*. *The Critical Quarterly*, Winter 1965, pp. 389–92.

Savage, D. S. "D. H. Lawrence: A Study in Dissolution." *The Personal Principle*. London: Routledge, 1944.

Seligmann, Herbert J. *D. H. Lawrence: An American Interpretation*. New York: Thomas Seltzer, 1924, pp. 19–28.

Shakespear, O. "The Poetry of D. H. Lawrence." *The Egoist*, May 1, 1915, p. 81.

Shapiro, Karl. "The Unemployed Magician." *A D. H. Lawrence Miscellany*. Edited by Harry T. Moore. Carbondale: Southern Illinois University Press, 1959; London: Heinemann, 1961.

Smith, L. E. W. "Two Views of D. H. Lawrence's Poetry." *The Critical Survey*, I (1963), pp. 81–86.

Spender, Stephen. *The Destructive Element*. London: Jonathan Cape, 1935; Boston: Houghton, 1936.

————. *The Creative Element*. London: Hamish Hamilton, 1953.

Squire, J. C. Review of *Birds, Beasts and Flowers*. *The London Mercury*, IX (1924), pp. 317–18.

————. Review of *Collected Poems*. *The Observer*, October 7, 1928, p. 6.

Stewart, J. I. M. "D. H. Lawrence." *Eight Modern Writers*. Oxford: Clarendon Press, 1963.

Tedlock, E. W. *D. H. Lawrence: Artist and Rebel*. Albuquerque: The University of New Mexico Press, 1963.

Thomas, Edward. "More Georgian Poetry." *The Bookman*, XLIV (April 1913), p. 47.

Tietjens, Eunice. Review of *Amores*. *Poetry*, IX (1917), pp. 264–66.

Trilling, Diana. "Introduction" and "Editor's Preface" to poems. *The Portable D. H. Lawrence*. New York: The Viking Press, 1947.

Untermeyer, Louis. "Strained Intensities." *The Bookman* (New York), LIX (1924), pp. 219–22.

————. "Hot Blood's Blindfold Art." *The Saturday Review of Literature*, VI (1929), pp. 17–18.

————. "Poet and Man." *The Saturday Review of Literature*, IX (1933), pp. 523–24.

Van Doren, Mark. Review of *Pansies*. *The New York Herald Tribune Books*, December 15, 1929, p. 15.

West, Anthony. *D. H. Lawrence*. London: Arthur Barker, 1951.

Wilbur, Richard. "Seven Poets." *The Sewanee Review*, LVIII (1950), pp. 130–43.
Wolfe, Humbert. Review of *Collected Poems. The Observer*, August 13, 1932, p. 6.
Young, Kenneth. *D. H. Lawrence*. London, New York: Longmans Green and Co., 1952.
(c) *Dissertations*
Salgādo, R. G. N. "The Poetry of D. H. Lawrence." University of Nottingham, 1955.

IV. OTHER WORKS CONSULTED

Auden, W. H. *Collected Shorter Poems 1930–1944*. London: Faber and Faber, 1950.
Blake, William. *The Complete Writings of Blake*. London, New York: Oxford University Press, 1966.
Brown, Norman O. *Life Against Death*. Middletown, Connecticut: Wesleyan University Press, 1959.
Browning, Robert. *The Poetical Works of Robert Browning*. London: John Murray, 1896.
Cassirer, Ernst. *Language and Myth*. New York: Harper and Brothers; Dover Publications, 1946.
Crane, Hart. *The Collected Poems of Hart Crane*. New York: Liveright, 1933; London: Boriswood, 1938.
Goldsmith, Elisabeth. *Ancient Pagan Symbols*. New York, London: G. P. Putnam's Sons, 1929.
Hardy, Thomas. *The Collected Poems of Thomas Hardy*. London, New York: Macmillan, 1960.
Hopkins, Gerard Manley. *Poems of Gerard Manley Hopkins*. London: Geoffrey Cumberlege, Oxford University Press, 1956.
Hughes, Ted. *Wodwo*. London: Faber and Faber, 1967.
Jung, C. G. *Memories, Dreams, Reflections*. London: Collins and Routledge and Kegan Paul; New York: Pantheon Books, 1963.
Lorenz, Konrad. *On Aggression*. New York: Harcourt, Brace, 1966; London: Methuen, 1967.
Lowell, Robert. *Life Studies*. London: Faber and Faber; New York: Farrar Strauss and Cudahy, 1959.
Matthiessen, F. O. *The Achievement of T. S. Eliot*. New York and London: Oxford University Press, 1947.
McLuhan, Marshall. *The Gutenberg Galaxy*. Toronto: University of Toronto Press; London: Routledge and Kegan Paul, 1962.
Meredith, George. *The Works of George Meredith*. Westminster: Constable, 1898.

Pound, Ezra. *The Letters of Ezra Pound 1907–1941*. Edited by D. D. Paige. New York: Harcourt, Brace, 1950; London: Faber and Faber, 1951.
Rilke, Rainer Maria. *Duino Elegies*. Translated by J. B. Leishman and Stephen Spender. London: The Hogarth Press; New York: W. W. Norton, 1939.
Swinburne, Algernon Charles. *The Poetical Works of Algernon Charles Swinburne*. New York: John D. Williams, 1884.
Thomas, Dylan. *Collected Poems*. London: J. M. Dent, 1952; New York: New Directions, 1953.
Vivante, Leone. *A Philosophy of Potentiality*. London: Routledge and Kegan Paul, 1955.
Whitman, Walt. *Leaves of Grass*. Philadelphia: David McKay, 1884.
Williams, William Carlos. *The Collected Earlier Poems of William Carlos Williams*. New York: New Directions; London: MacGibbon and Kee, 1951.
Wordsworth, William. *The Poetical Works of William Wordsworth*. Oxford: Clarendon Press, 1952.
Yeats, W. B. *Collected Poems*. London: Macmillan, 1950; New York: Macmillan, 1951.

Index